INDIAN TRIBES
THEN AND NOW

Dr. H.C. Upreti

Pointer Publishers
Jaipur 302 003 (Raj.) India

Distributed by
Prem C. Bakliwal
Aavishkar Publishers, Distributors
807, Vyas Building, Chaura Rasta
Jaipur 302 003 (Raj.) India
Phone : (0141) 2578159
e-mail : aavishkarbooks@hotmail.com

2019

ISBN 81-7132-482-7

Published by
Mrs. Shashi Jain for
Pointer Publishers
807, Vyas Building, Chaura Rasta
Jaipur 302 003 (Raj.) India
Phones : (0141) 2578159, 2708286
e-mail : pointerpub@hotmail.com
Visit us at : www:pointerpublishers.com

Price : ₹ 1400.00

Printed at
Sheetal Printers
Jaipur (Raj.)

Preface

India has a large concentration of tribal population. Though scattered all over the country their concentration is mainly in the Northern and Central region. Originally they lived at unapproachable places where the land was infertile with limited means of living resources. They were simple, poor and backward. Their economic hardships and encounter with the non-tribals at times made them violent, criminal and rebellious.

After Independence several efforts have been made through Five year plans and reservation policy etc. for their social and economic emancipation yet after more than five decades they have not been able to come at par with the rest of the society.

At several places the tribal people were uprooted from their original habitations owing to availability of mineral resources in their area and government's declaration of forests as its property. However, after the cultural contact these people are now rapidly waking up from their centuries old slumber.

The book primarily deals with the tribal social structure and the changes occurring there in. Some other aspects of tribal society viz. India's nomadic tribes, vanishing tribes, residence system, reservation policy and development aspects have been discussed in the separate chapters. Separate chapters have been devoted on tribes of Rajasthan and Tribal Development programmes. At the end of the book (in the appendix) two chapters have been added. One on the "Nature and subject matter of Anthropology" and second on some "Anthropological Concepts" with a view to enrich the readers. The concepts have been derived from various sociological and anthropological literature.

Several persons extended their help and cooperation in the completion of this work. My wife Nandini Upreti provided me all the necessary help and facilities at home. My children Nidhi Pradeep and Sameera, Mani-Tarun and Jay, Aparna and Sameer showered their love, affection and inspiration. The real credit goes to my daughter Nidhi who went through the whole manuscript and made necessary and valuable suggestions.

Shri Vipin Jain was kind enough to publish the manuscript and give it a book shape.

Dr. H.C. Upreti
Retired Associate Professor in Sociology
University of Rajasthan, Jaipur

Contents

1

Tribes in India : General Introduction

India has the largest concentration of tribal population in Asia and it is the second largest in the world in terms of tribal population. Tribal people are considered to be the original inhabitants of this sub-continent having a very simple way of life. Social scientists and Anthropologists have used various terms to describe these people. Some scholars designated them as 'primitives' meaning thereby ancient. Gillin and Gillin in their famous book entitled, Cultural Anthropology, defined the tribals as a collectivity of local groups having a common area, who use similar language and have a common culture.

Herbert Risely, Lele, Grigson, Sobert, Tallents, Selznick, Martin and A.B. Thakkar used the term 'Aborigines' for these people. Sir Baines referred to them as 'Hill tribes'. Nadel designated them as a society which is complete by itself, which has its own rules and regulations and these rules and regulations control the behaviour of its members. Similar definitions were given by some other thinkers who tried to identify the socio-cultural and economic features of the tribal society. Most of the tribals are well known for their rules and regulations and their social organization. However, there are scholars who have attached greater significance to the cultural characteristics of the tribal groups. According to Rivers, a tribe is a social group whose members speak a common dialect and work collectively for common objectives like war and aggression. Rivers did not include common habitation in his definition because several tribal groups lead a nomadic life also. Although it is a well established fact that a tribal community has its particular dialect, culture, social and economic system and racial characteristics etc. Generally, a tribal group has a particular territory where its members reside. In many cases the tribal people, because of the fear of outsiders and also from a safety point of view, used to reside at unapproachable places, owing to which these people had to remain cut off from the outside world for a long time.

Some scholars consider tribals at a particular stage of development of human society. Various studies have proved the contention that the tribal economy was very undeveloped. They used primitive means of production. Their kinship network was very strong, covering almost all aspects of their life. However at present these characteristics have changed in a majority of the tribal groups.

Tribals have an important place in Indian society. They can be placed among the most backward people in Indian society. Verrier Elwin in his book on 'Aboriginals', stated that they are the original owners of the country. This moral claim of theirs is thousands of years old. They were the first humans to inhabit the country. Therefore, according to Elwin these people should be given first consideration. G.S. Ghurye used the term 'the so-called Aborigines' or 'Backward people' for the tribals. Later on, it was professor Ghurye who first of all used the term 'Tribe' for these people. R.K. Das and S.R. Das used the term 'Submerged Humanity' for them. According to L.M. Srikant, these tribal people have been called by different names in different periods of time, for example, *Aranyak, Rani Paraj, Adivasi,* etc.

During the Pre-independence period, the British Administration in India collected information about tribals for the first time. In the Census Report of 1891, J.A. Bains, the Commissioner of Census classified the castes according to their traditional occupations. Under the category of 'Agricultural and Pastoral castes', he formed a sub-heading called 'Forest Tribes'. Later on, in the Census report of 1921, they were specified as 'Hill and Forest Tribes'. The Census of 1931 described them as 'Primitive Tribes'. The Government of India Act, 1935 specified the Tribal population as 'Backward Tribes'. However, in the Census Report of 1941, they were classified as 'tribes' only.

Definition of 'Tribe'

Oxford Dictionary defines Tribe as a 'group of people in a primitive or barbarious stage of development acknowledging the authority of a chief and usually regarding themselves as having a common ancestor'. Lucy Mair defined a tribe as an independent political division of a population with a common culture. Huntingford maintained that a tribe is a group united by a common name in which members take pride, a common language, a common territory, and by a feeling that all who do not share that commonality are outsiders & foes.

T.B. Naik proposed the following seven criteria by which a tribe can be recognized :

1. A tribe has the least functional interdependence within the community;
2. It is economically backward;
3. It is geographically isolated from other peoples;
4. It speaks a common dialect which may however be subject to regional variations;
5. A tribe is politically a unit under a common tribal authority;
6. A tribe's members are averse to change; and
7. A tribe has its own traditional laws which differ from those of the majority communities. To be a 'tribe', a community must have all these attributes.

At present the term tribe, according to western writers, generally means an ethnic group, geographically isolated or semi-isolated, identified with one particular territory and having distinct social, economic and cultural traditions and practices. In the Indian context the term has undergone further change, particularly in the post-independence period.

Under the Constitution of India, certain tribes have been listed as the Scheduled Tribes and those listed, have been given certain facilities in terms of social and economic benefits and other benefits under the constitution. The President of the Indian Union, under article 342 of the Constitution specified a particular group of people as Scheduled tribe irrespective of its religion whereas only those groups are scheduled castes who follow the Hindu or Sikh religion.

Various criteria were adopted for specifying communities as scheduled tribes. Most important of these were :

(a) Traditional occupation of the people.
(b) Distinctive culture dealing with the tribal way of life.
(c) Primitive traits depicting occupational pattern, economy etc., and
(d) Lack of educational and techno-economic development.

Thus, initially 212 communities were listed as scheduled tribes under the Indian constitution. Since then there has been a continuous increase in the number of tribal groups listed as scheduled tribes. At present there are about 700 scheduled tribes.

The term 'scheduled tribe' can be better understood in contrast with the term, 'scheduled castes'. Whereas scheduled tribes have, for a long period remained in isolation with distinctive socio-economic and cultural mode of living, the scheduled castes, though at the bottom of the social hierarchy have always lived as part and parcel of the so-called civilized society. While tracing the historical background of the term Scheduled tribes, some members of India's Constituent Assembly favoured the term *'Adivasi'* in place of 'Scheduled Tribes'. However, the Committee Chairman, B.R. Ambedkar opposed the term 'Adivasi' and professed the word 'Scheduled Tribes', as widely supported by several distinguished scholars and other experts. To make the concept more clear, it seems necessary to mention Majumdar's contention who stated the following facts :

1. In India a tribe is definitely a territorial group i.e. a tribe has a traditional territory.
2. All members of a tribe may not be kin of each other, but within every Indian tribe, kinship operates as a strong, associative, regulative and integrating principle.
3. Members of an Indian tribe speak a common language of their own and that of their neighbours.
4. The other distinguishing features of Indian tribes are their dormitory institutions, absence of institutional schooling for boys and girls, distinctive customs, peculiarities of religious beliefs and rituals which may distinguish tribes men from low caste Hindus.

However, the concept of a tribe in modern times has undergone a change from being a political entity consisting of a group of people to being a group of people identified with poverty and backwardness.

The famous Indian scholar A.R. Desai has tried to highlight the general characteristics of those tribes which at one time had been opposing sanskritization and assimilation. According to him, these characteristics are generally found in almost all the tribal groups. These are as follows :

1. They live away from the civilized world, in mountains, hills and forests and at times in unapproachable places.

2. They are associated with any one of the Nigrito, Astroloid or Mongoloid racial group.
3. They speak a common tribal dialect.
4. They believe in a primitive religion which follows the principles of animism and which has a special place for evil and ancestral/soul worship.
5. They are engaged in tribal occupations e.g. collection of useful natural/forest produce, hunting etc.
6. Mostly they are non-vegetarians.
7. A few of these tribes are at the naked or semi-naked stage.
8. They have nomadic habits and take special interest in dancing and drinking.

According to Desai, at present in India, only one-fifth of the tribal population bears these characteristics. Usually the size of the tribal groups is limited. Their technological knowledge is quite unrefined, economic sytem is simple, backward and based on exchange of goods. These people can be identified on the basis of geographical separation. The kinship relationship is deep and full of significance.

Classification of Indian Tribes

Tribes of India can be classified on the basis of geographical region, language, race, religion and culture contact. Yet a multiplicity of factors leads complexity to the effort of classification of these tribal groups. These factors are inter-racial mingling, geographical mobility owing to several reasons and the development process which began prior to independence in some of the tribal regions and was accelerated by the keen interest taken in these tribal groups by the British Administrators in India in the pre-independence period.

Geographical Classifications

The Indian Anthropologist, B.C. Guha classified Indian tribes into 3 zones :

1. North and North-eastern zone
2. Central zone
3. Southern zone

1. North and North-eastern Zone : This zone consists of the sub-Himalayan region and mountains and hilly tracts of the eastern region. Thus, this region, includes the Himalayan region right from Kashmir, Himachal Pradesh, hills of Uttar Pradesh, and all the north-eastern states of former Assam.

2. The Central Zone : The largest concentration of tribal population is in this zone. The tribes of M.P., U.P., Bihar, Southern Rajasthan, Orissa, Southern Maharashtra fall in this category. In other words, the zone consists of the Plateau and mountaneous belt between the Indo-gangetic plain in the north and Krishna river in the south.

3. The Southern Zone : This zone falls to the south of the Krishna river. The tribes of Andhra Pradesh, Karnataka, Tamil Nadu and Kerala come under this zone.

The classification of B.C. Guha does not mention tribals residing in the islands of Andaman and Nicobar. The main tribes living in these islands are Zarava, Onge, North Sentilese, Andamanese and Nikobari.

(a) North and North-Eastern Region : This region consists of tribes of Uttar Pradesh, Himachal Pradesh, Eastern part of Kashmir, East Punjab, Assam (old province) and Sikkim. The important tribes of the region of North-east are LePcha, Dafla, Pirmi, Garo, Naga, Khasi, Chakura, Gurung, Kuki, Apatani, etc. As these tribals reside in border areas of India they have got special significance. For example, the Bhotias of Kumaon and Garhwal are known for being traders. Besides business and trade they are experts in handicrafts. The Tharus of Tarai region of Uttar Pradesh also have distinguishing characteristics of their own where women have a special place. The Khas tribe of Jonsar Bhaver was once well known for polyandry. Nagas of eastern region had a special significance in Indian politics. Also, these people were known for their famous custom of Head hunting and war dance. Kukis, Lusai, Lakher and Cheri etc. used Tibetan-Chinese dialects. The Khasis and Garos are tribes which still follow matriarchy. Most of the tribes of the eastern region practise axe or shifting cultivation and have terraced farming. Handicraft is another important occupation after agriculture.

(b) Western and North-western Region : This region consists of tribals residing in Gujrat, Maharashtra and Rajasthan. Major tribes of Rajasthan are Bhils, Meenas, Garasias, Banjaras etc. while the main tribes of Gujrat are Mahadev Koli, Katkari and Dabla.

(c) Central Region : Maximum number of tribes reside in this region. The main tribes of Bihar (which fall in this region) are Santhal, Munda, Oraon and Birhor. In Orissa the important tribes are Bondo, Khond, Soara and Juang. In Madhya Pradesh the major tribes are Gonds, Baigas, Marias and Murias. Guha stated that the tribals residing in this region are relatively better off than those from the southern region. They have adopted organized cultivation from the civilized Hindus and are much more influenced by the Hindu way of living. Almost all the tribals residing in this region follow patriarchy. Some of them are completely Hinduised and their tribal identity is present in name only. This shows how rapid has been the process of sanskritization. In some cases tribal identity has been maintained by these people only with a view to avail of the constitutional benefits on account of the Reservation policy.

(d) Southern Region : This region falls below the Krishna river. The tribes of Travancore-Cochin, Karnataka, Andhra Pradesh and Tamil Nadu come under this category. The important tribes of this region are : Toda and Kota of Nilagiri region, Chenchu and Kurovan of Andhra etc. Besides, Kadar, Eurula, Chelli, Kurumba, Keni etc. are some of the important tribes of this region. Todas are famous for their polyndrous system, Nayars are known for Matriarchy.

In addition to the above 4 types of classification of Indian tribals, the tribals residing in Andaman, Nikobar and Lakshyadeep also have special significance. Thus, we find that the geographical conditions of the various regions of the country have affected the tribal groups in terms of customs, culture, economy and way of living. The tribal groups residing in different parts of the country have been able to maintain their distinct social and cultural identity owing to geographical and climatic variations. Besides, their economic activities have been affected by geographical conditions.

Racial Composition

Much research is needed to come-up with a reliable racial history of India. There have been streams of migration to this country from time to time in the past but actual routes of immigration were not known. Moreover, there has been so much of racial intermingling that the racial identity of a particular group was difficult to ascertain. Yet anthropological evidence shows that in each cultural region, some distinct traits of a particular race do exist. In this context the attempt made by B.S. Guha given in the Census of India in 1931 is quite significant. However, Stephen Fuchs, on the basis of Guha's classification, tried to give a slightly revised version and classified tribes into following racial categories :

1. The Negritos : According to anthropologists, Negritos were the earliest race in India. Guha believed that Kadar, Palayans of South India had a Negrite strain, though he admitted that they were, however, not the pure Negritos. D.N. Majumdar and S.S. Sarkar, however, denied the contention of Guha. According to them, some of the Negrito racial elements are found in other races also. Hutton believes in their existence in the Assam Region and gives the example of Konyak Nagas.

S.S. Sarkar traced Negrito strains among the primitive males and among small vagrant tribal groups which depend on the collection (food gathering) economy.

2. The Proto-Australoids : They are the second oldest racial group. This category of tribal groups can be found in some of the tribes of Central and South India. Guha compared these tribes with Veddas of Sri Lanka and the aborigines of Australia and finds these groups essentially alike. Thus, Indian Tribes have to a great extent retained the characteristics of this race. Guha considered the term 'Proto-Austroloid' as most suitable for these Indian Tribes.

3. The Mongoloid Type : In the sub-Himalayan region, north, north-eastern belt, the instances of Mongoloid race can be traced. Examples of these could be Bhotias of Kumaon and Garhwal Himalayas. Ladakhis and Baltesi, Lahoulis, the Limalbus, the Lepchas and Rongpas who have the Mongoloid element. In Nepal such tribes are Gurung, Murmi and Gurkhas (having a Mongoloid element). Besides, In N.E. states the Bodo group comprising of the Garos, Kacharis, Tipperalis, Lalungs, Rabhas Mache 'Nagas' can be placed in this category.

Besides, B.S. Guha and E. Fischer talked of the Oriental type of race in north-East India. The Aryans and Orientals were followed in the subsequent centuries by various invaders on a smaller scale. Between 500 B.C. and the beginning of the Christian era, north India was first invaded by Persians and Greeks, and later on by Sakas and Kushans (from Central India). Again during the 5th century BC, another horde of nomads from central Asia—the Huns came to India and permanently settled in northern India. Then there were Muslim invasions in the 8th century A.D. Such invasions continued until the sixteenth century when the Mughals established their empire. Later on, small scale invasions took place on the west coast of India. Portuguese and later on the Dutch landed on India's western coast. Later, after the Britishers settled in India, a new clan of Anglo-Indians came into existence, who are considered as the progeny of British settlers and Indian women of various castes. There has been a lot of intermingling between various races in India. This was prevalent to such an extent that even isolated tribal groups have not been able to maintain their pure racial characteristics.

Linguistic Classification

The people of India may be divided into four speech families. These are :

(a) Indo-European (Aryans)

(b) Dravidian

(c) Austrian (Kolor Munda) and

(d) Tebetan Chinese (Sino-Tebetan).

Majumdar (1985) believed that Aryan speech came into existence only as a consequence of cultural contact. In the context of tribal people a majority of experts believe that the most important groups is that of the Gonds who speak the Dravidian language. These Gonds are scattered throughout Madhya Pradesh and Andhra Pradesh. Another important language of this group is Koi which is spoken by the Kandhs of Orissa, the Oraons of Chhota Nagpur and the Maltas of Rajmahal hills. The speeches of Toda, Paliyan, Chenchu, Erula and Kadar are also included in the Dravidian family. The Adivasis who speak these languages are far less advanced than their other linguistic kinsmen.

Austric : The Austric speech family is also known as the Munda speech family i.e. the language of the Kol or Munda group; the Santalis are found in Bihar, Orissa, Bengal and Assam; Mundari, Ho, Kharia, Bhumij and a few others which belong to Bihar. Besides, Austric speech family inludes Korku in Madhya Pradesh, Savara and Gadaba in Orissa, Khasi in Assam and the language of the Nikobarese.

Mongoloid : This language is confined to the tribals residing in southern slope of the Himalayas and its north Bengal, Tripura, Assam, Nepal, Sikkim and the Darjeeling district of West Bengal. This is divided into two branches (i) Tibetans – Burmese and (ii) Siamese-Chinese. The tribals in Assam, Meghalaya and in other north-eastern parts of India speak this language. In Assam the Bodo, Abors, Miris, Daflas, Mikirs fall in this speech group. Besides, Nagas, Meithei or Manipuris, the (LUSHAIS) belong to this speech family.

India has been a melting pot of races, therefore, it is difficult to put Indian tribes under any particular category. Yet the efforts made by Anthropologists and other scholars in this context are worth appreciating.

Economic Classification of Indian Tribes

The classification made by Adams Smith, Thurnwald and Herskovits to classify the tribal people on the basis of their economic life is well known all over the world. The scheme presented by Thurnwald is taken as the most acceptable in the Indian context and it is as follows :

1. Homogeneous communities of men as hunters and trappers, women as collectors e.g. Kadars, Chenchus, Kharia, and Korwa etc.
2. Homogeneous communities of hunters, trappers and agriculturists viz. Kamars, Baigas and Birhors are examples of this type from tribal India.
3. Graded society of hunters, trappers, agriculturists and artisans. Most of the Indian tribes fall under this category. The Cheros and the Agarias are some of the famous artisan tribes.
4. The herdsmen—the Todas and some sections of the Bhil tribe are its examples.
5. Homogeneous hunters and herdsmen. This category is not represented among Indian tribes.
6. Ethnically stratified cattle breeders and traders. The Bhotias of the sub-Himalayan region of U.P. hills i.e. Kumaon and Garhwal breed yaks and are itinerant traders.
7. Socially graded herdsmen with hunting, agricultural and artisan population.

D.N. Majumdar did not fully agree with the above classification.

Taking into consideration mainly the technological achievements, a more lucid classification of the economic life of the Indian tribes may be attempted as follows :

1. Tribes hunting in forests.
2. Tribes engaged in axe/shifting cultivation.
3. Tribes engaged in cultivation on levelled land.
4. Simple Artisan tribes.
5. Pastoral tribes.
6. Tribals living as folk artists.
7. Agricultural and non-agricultural labour oriented tribes.
8. Tribes engaged in service and trade.

Broadly speaking the tribals in India can be grouped as food gatherers and agriculturists. Among agriculturists there are primitive cultivators and the plough cultivators. Animal keeping, handicrafts etc. are by and large the subsidiary occupations of most of the tribes. However, a few of them are exclusively artisans or herdsmen.

Classification According to Culture Contact

To classify Indian tribes on the basis of their cultural development is a really difficult task. Owing to rapid means of transport and communication various tribals came into contact with out siders and there was the process of culture contact which resulted into acculturation, enculturation and assimilation. Verrier Elwin has tried to classify Indian tribes into four categories on the basis of culture contact :

(a) In the first category are those tribes who are tribes in the real sense of the term. These people are at the earliest stage of development. Numerically they are present in smaller numbers at present and live in unapproachable places.

(b) The second category of people consists of those who are partially attached to their tradition, culture and other modes of living, yet more used to outside life and generally less simple and honest than the first category.

(c) Third category consists of those tribes who are numerically maximum in number, whose tribal characteristics in terms of religion, culture, policies and social organization are on the way to decline.

(d) Examples of another category are tribals like Bhils and Nagas who are said to be representatives of the old aristocracy of the country, who retain much of their oriental tribal life and who have won the battle of cultural contact.

In the opinion of D.N. Majumdar, tribal culture may be placed into following three groups :

(i) Those who are culturally most distant from the rural-urban groups i.e. more or less away from outside contact. Some of the tribals living at isolated places can be placed in this category.

(ii) Those who are under the influence of the culture of rural-urban groups and have developed discomforts and problems consequently.

(iii) Those who in spite of their being in outside-rural-urban contact have not suffered the problems of the second group, or in other words, they are acculturated into rural or urban culture.

The Indian Conference of Social Work in the year 1952 appointed a Tribal Welfare Committee which suggested the below classifications:

(i) Tribal communities

(ii) Semi-tribal communities

(iii) Acculturated tribal communities

(iv) Totally assimilated tribal communities.

(i) These tribal communities are those who reside in hilly, mountaineous or dense forest regions—in places which are unapproachable and are even now maintaining their tribal way of life to a great extent.

(ii) Semi-tribal communities—These people have started living nearer to the village communities and have adopted agriculture and other related occupations.

(iii) Acculturated tribal communities—These people have started residing in or near rural or urban communities and have started living in villages and towns/cities. These people have also started adopting occupational and other socio-cultural traits of the outside world.

(iv) Fully assimilated tribal groups—These people have remained tribals only for name sake and have totally adopted socio-cultural and other traits of the so-called/civilized people.

Professor G.S. Ghurye has divided Indian Tribals into following three categories :

1. In the first category he placed those tribals who had succeeded in attaining a respectable position in Hindu society and have successfully faced their problems.
2. In the second category are those tribal communities who have partially become members of the Hindu community. These people by initating the Hindu culture and its way of living (after close contact) have tried to become like the Hindu community.
3. Ghurye put in the third category those tribal communities who lived in hilly and mountaineous regions and resisted

the invasion of cultural and other social practices of the outside world in their tribal life.

It was natural to have problems and resistance in the beginning but ultimately the tribals (after culture-contact) gradually gave up their traditional cultural practices. The process of sanskritization began rapidly. And no doubt, at present tribal identity has remained only for name sake. In fact had there been no provision for reservation the caste identity would have also disappeared. This would have been similar to the way in which British administrators (during pre-independence days) recruited some of the tribals or lower caste Hindus (who were fit for an army job) for the 'British-Indian army', only after changing their surname or after adding the Rajput sir name 'Singh' after their first name. It is important to mention here that Britishers in India during their initial period, ruled this country according to the prevailing practices. During that period only 'Rajputs' could be recruited for army jobs and the Britishers identified 'Rajputs' by their surname 'Singh'. In short, the contention here is that as the process of culture contact became faster, there was rapid loss of tribal cultural and social practices almost all over the country and the tribals had little to gain and much to loose in this process.

Classification of Indian Tribals on the Basis of Religion

The process of culture contact affected the sphere of religion also and the tribals tried to assimilate themselves with various religious communities or various religions of the civilized people in India. Because majority of the tribals came in contact with the Hindus, therefore, they adopted Hindu religion. In this connection some information was collected in the 1961 Census which classified the religion of the tribes who were residing in rural areas at that time. Here it is necessary to point out that in the year 1961 about 97 percent of the tribals were residing in rural areas and their percentage was as follows :

Classfication of Tribals on the Basis of Religious Affiliations

Religion	Percentage of total rural tribal population
Hindu	89.40
Christian	5.53
Buddhism	0.34
Muslim	0.20
Others	4.53

This makes it clear that by and large the tribals have adopted Hindu religion. Those who have accepted Christianity are also quite considerable in number, and in number are next to those who have adopted Hinduism. An important point to be kept in mind is that even those tribes who have embraced any of the major religions, have not necessarily shed their beliefs and rituals and many of them practice their faith along with their newly acquired faith.

Tribal Demography

As has been stated earlier, India has the second largest concentration of tribal population, after that of the African continent. In the year 1991 the tribal population in India as enumerated by the Census department was estimated to be about 6.78 crores, constituting about 8.08 percent of the country's total population. This excluded the population of the State of Jammu and Kashmir (where census could not be conducted owing to unavoidable reasons). About 87 percent of the total tribal population was concentrated in the central belt, covering 8 states viz. M.P., Bihar, Orissa, Maharashtra, Gujrat, Rajasthan, Andhra Pradesh and West Bengal. M.P. has the highest concentration of tribal population.

In the year 1951 the tribal population was about 1.91 crores which was about 5.36 percent of the total population of the country. In the year 1961 the tribal population increased to 2.98 crores. The rapid increase in tribal population during this decade was because of the inclusion of several new tribal groups in the list of scheduled tribes.

In the year 1971, the tribal population increased to 3.8 crores which was about 6.94 percent of the country's total population. Further, in the year 1981 the total tribal population was 5.38 crores which worked out to 7.58 percent of the country's total population.

The population of scheduled tribes increased to about 25.67 percent during the decade 1981-91, which was much more than the country's population growth rate of 23.79 percent during this decade.

In some of the eastern states viz. Mizoram the tribal population was about 94.85 percent of the state's total population. In Lakshadweep the percentage was 93.15. Similarly in Nagaland the tribal population was 87.70 percent, in Meghalaya it was 85.53 percent while in Arunachal Pradesh and Nagar Haveli this percentage was 63.66 and 79.99 percent respectively. Roughly, about 44 percent of the country's total tribal population resided in 3 states viz. Madhya Pradesh (22.73 percent), Maharashtra (10.80 percent) and Orissa (10.38 percent). The largest state of India—U.P. has the lowest percentage of tribal population which is 0.21 percent only. Similarly, among union territories Andaman and Nikobar island had the lowest percentage of tribal population i.e. 9.54 percent. No tribal population was recorded in Delhi, Chandigarh and Pondichery. Similarly in Punjab and Haryana also no tribal population was recorded.

Statewise Classification of Tribal Population according to 2001 Census

States	Population	Percentge of Tribal Population
1	2	3
Total Tribal Population	**8,43,26,240**	**8.2**
Jammu & Kashmir	11,05,979	10.9
Himanchal Pradesh	2,44,587	4.0
Punjab	—	0.0
Chandigarh	—	0.0
Uttaranchal	2,56,129	3.00
Haryana	—	0.0
Delhi	—	0.0
Rajasthan	70,97,706	12.6
Uttar Pradesh	1,07,963	0.1
Bihar	7,58,361	0.9
Sikkim	1,11,405	20.6
Arunachal Pradesh	7,05,158	64.2
Nagaland	17,74,026	89.1
Manipur	7,41,141	34.2
Note : Some districts of Manipur have not been included in cenrus figures.		
Mijoram	8,39,310	94.5
Tripura	9,93,426	31.1
Meghalaya	19,92,862	86.9
Assam	33,08,570	12.4
West Bengal	44,06,794	5.5
Jharkhand	70,87,068	26.3
Orissa	66,16,596	31.8
Madhya Pradesh	1,22,33,474	20.3
Gujrat	74,81,160	14.8
Daman and Dieu	13,997	8.8
Dadra & Nagar Haveli	1,37,225	62.2

Contd...

Contd...

1	2	3
Maharashtra	85,77,276	8.9
Andhra Pradesh	50,24,104	6.6
Karnatak	34,63,986	6.6
Goa	566	–
Laksha Dweep	57,321	94.5
Kerala	3,64,189	1.1
Tamil Nadu	6,66,321	1.0
Pandichery	–	–
Andman & Nikobar Island	29,469	8.3

The number of tribal population residing in urban centres is quite low. Only 7.39 percent of the tribal population was found in urban areas. Thus, 93 percent of the tribal population resided in villages. Only 3 states of Karnataka, Maharashtra and Tamil Nadu had more than 10 percent of the tribal population residing in cities (i.e. more than 10 percent of their respective states' total tribal population).

According to the 1991 census, the percentage wise concentration of tribal population in various states and union territories may be grouped into 5 categories. These categories are as follows :

Category	Tribal population percentage	Name of the States
1.	63-95%	Mizoram, Nagaland, Meghalaya, Lakshadweep, Arunachal Pradesh, Dadra and Nagar Haveli
2.	22-35%	Madhya Pradesh, Orissa, Manipur, Tripura, Sikkim
3.	10-15%	Gujrat, Rajasthan, Assam, Andaman and Nikobar Islands, Daman and Diu
4.	5-10%	Maharashtra, Bihar, Andhra Pradesh and West Bengal
5.	Less than 5%	Uttar Pradesh, Karnataka, Tamil Nadu, Himachal Pradesh, Kerala and Goa

Further, more than 80 percent of the total tribal population was concentrated in 8 states according to the 1991 census. These 8 states are : Madhya Pradesh, Orissa, Bihar, Maharashtra, Gujrat, Rajasthan, Andhra Pradesh and West Bengal. Numerically, Gonds and Bhils are the first and second largest tribes respectively. According to the 1991 Census the schedlued tribe population formed 12.15 per cent of the total tribal population in the country. The statewise population percentage of north-eastern region is given as below :

Scheduled Tribe Population in the States of North-eastern Region, 1981

S.No.	State	Percentage of tribal population
1.	Assam	12.62
2.	Arunachal Pradesh	63.66
3.	Manipur	34.41
4.	Meghalaya	85.53
5.	Mizoram	94.75
6.	Nagaland	87.70
7.	Sikkim	22.36
8.	Tripura	30.95

In northern and southern state the percentage of tribal population is very little. According to the 1991 census data, the western and southern states comprise only 5.23 percent of the total tribal population in the country. The following table would give an idea of the tribal population in northern and southern states according to the 1991 census :

Scheduled Tribe Population in Northern and Southern States

S.No.	State	Percentage of tribal population
1.	Himachal Pradesh	4.22
2.	Uttar Pradesh	0.21
3.	Karnataka	4.26
8.	Tamil Nadu	1.10

Besides, in Lakshadweep the percentage of tribal population was 93.15 and in Dadar and Nagar Haveli it was 78.99 percent. While in Andaman and Nikobar islands the tribal population was 9.54 percent and in Daman and Diu the percentage was 11.54.

After Gonds and Bhils the numerically most powerful tribes are Santhals, Meenas, Oraons, Mundas and Khonds, having a population more than 10 lakhs as each. Apart from these, there are about 45 tribes, each of which is having the populaion of more than one lakh.

References

1. Majumdar D.N., *Races and Cultures of India.*
2. Braines Sir, *Ethnography.*
3. Beteille Andre, 'A Definition of Tribe' in Romesh Thapar (Ed.), *Tribe, Caste and Religion,* MacMillan & Co., 1977.
4. Verrier Elwin, *The Aboriginals,* Oxford University Press, Bombay, 1943.
5. Das R.K. and Das S.R., 'India's Sub-merged Humanity', *Modern Review,* 1955.
6. Srikant L.M., 'Classification of Tribals', *Tribal Souvenir.*
7. Verma R.C., *Indian Tribes Through the Ages,* Publication Division, Government of India, New Delhi, 1975.
8. Naik T.B., 'What is a tribe some of conflicting Definitions' in L.P. Vidyarthi (ed.), *Applied Anthropology,* Allahabad, 1968.
9. Desai A.R., *Rural India in Transition,* 1961.
10. Fuchs Stephen, *The Aboriginal Tribes of India* (2nd edn.), MacMillan India Ltd., Delhi, 1992.
11. Adapted from Nadeem Husnain, *Tribal India Today,* Human Publications, New Delhi, 1933.
12. Verrier Elwin, *The Aboriginals,* Oxford University Press, 1943.

❑❑❑

2

India's Vanishing Tribes

One can observe a lot of diversity among the Indian tribes. The causes of this diversity are : social, cultural, geographic and economic. Some tribals, because of their peculiar nature (reserved and shy) kept themselves away from the outer world till recently. Outsiders also looked at these people with great suspicion. In this way, in the opinion of the out siders these people for long remained the subject of curiosity.

Some of the tribals developed the feeling of hatred and anger for the people out side their Tribal Community. The outside contact usually caused conflict, anger and violence. On occasions the people of outside world also left no stone unturned to exploit the innocent tribal people to the maximum extent. As a result of which the tribal people developed negative attitude toward the outsiders. Moreover, these tribal people could not organize themselves against the outsiders. Tribal people's own cultural practices and some of their customs were responsible for their own decline. For example, the polyandry was the cause of sex disease i.e. syphiles and gaenoria. The prevalence of bonded labour adversely affected their social institutions i.e. the institution of family and marriage. In some cases their institutions of marriage and family were controlled by their masters. The natural economy, which was based on forest and other natural resources could no longer remain as a successful means of livelihood. The survival of the tribals who did not change their occupation in changing circumstances became quite difficult because their traditional occupations had failed to provide two ends' meal.

Out of several hundred tribal groups in India, there are a few tribals whose number is constantly on the decline owing to one reason or the other. For example, 'Rajis' (Van Rawat) owing to their shy nature, remained cut off from the out side world for a long time. Till a few decades ago these people were cave dwellers. The 'Rajis' are found in the Himalayan region of District Pithoragarh in Kumaon. There have been several instances of deaths caused by hunger among these people owing to non-availability of any means of livelihood. Such instances have been reported by District Administration in the past.

The Lepchas of Sikkim became the victim of geographical conditions on one hand and Nepalis and Bhotias on the other. Both Nepalis and Bhotias exploited them to the maximum extent. Similarly, the tribals of Andaman and Nicobar Islands suffered natural calamities and external aggression which they could not face for a long time. As a consequence, there was decline in their number. Similarly, there are a few other tribes which could be placed in this category. Though the tribals after culture contact and owing to process of assimilation and integration, lost most aspects of their tribal cultural identity, yet these people maintained some of the tribal identities for the sake of own benefit. But the loss of tribal identity did not at all cause fear of survival. In this chapter, an attempt has been made to discuss some of the tribes whose number is constantly on the decline and only due to several external efforts, their existence (and identity to some extent) have been maintained.

The Rajis or Van Rawat

These people are found in District Pithoragarh of Kumaon region in Uttaranchal. They are also known as 'Vanraji', or 'Van Rawat'. Their places of abode were the dense forests and caves of the district, which were not easily accessible in the past. Another name used for them is 'Raj Kirat', but the 'Rajis often introduce themselves as 'Bankhaniya Rawat', possibly signifying their dependence on the forest and its produce. These people are wandering and nomadic and also inhabit the forest areas of Nepal, across Kali river and frequently cross the border in either direction. On Indian side their concentration is confined to Dharchula, Askot and Champawat region of Pithoragarh district.

According to a survey conducted in 1973 their total population was estimated as 337 with 78 families. However, during the year 1974 the district authorities contradicted this figure and treated 5 more Raji families in Champawat region of district Pithoragarh and with this their total population was estimated as 400. While on the other hand in 1970 a report estimated the 'Rajis' total number to be 252 individuals, belonging to 66 families. Rajis, perhaps, are the smallest tribal community and lead an isolated life. These people are also known as Cave dwellers, their places of residence were unknown to the out siders till recently. Thus, caves and rock shelters were their abodes.

Inspite of their backwardness the Rajis claim a royal ancestry by claiming the descendents of the elder branch of the erstwhile ruling family of Askot, the Rajbars. There is a saying that the ancestor of Raji (the elder brother of the Royal family) was so found of hunting that he left his throne to indulge his passion for hunting and wandering in the forest. Thus, the legend provides a rational explanation for present day Raji nomadism. Another significant factor which is curious to notice is 'Rajis' the discendents of the elder branch of Askot's ruling family, never salute any out sider whatever the social or official position the visitor might hold.

It is claimed that the 'Rajis' are one of the earliest inhabitants of this part of the country. They are found in Nepal also across the Kali river. In June 1967, these people were listed as 'Scheduled tribes'.

So far as the origin of 'Rajis' is concerned, an English scholar, William Cook said that these people resemble with 'Raj Kirat'. The British Commissioner of Kumaon Region called them Kshatriya descendents, belonging to Royal clans. Famous scholar and Administrator, Atkinson also supported this contention. Rahul Sanskritayan in his book *Kumaon*, called them as the descendants of Kirt.

Further, according to survey conducted in the year 1987, their total population was estimated 456, having a total of 102 families, residing in 9 unapproachable villages. Out of these 9 villages, there is only one village named Kimkhola in Dharchula region which is easily accessible. This is the largest village of the Rajis having 22 families with a total population of 105. Yet there are contradictory versions regarding the number of 'Rajis'. One Kumaoni scholar Bhagwan Singh who has worked on 'Rajis' gives a different estimate of 'Raji' population, indicating their declining trend.

Contrary to tribal male-female population ratio, we find that the situation among Rajis is quite typical. The number of women among these people is quite low. According to one recent survey the percentage of male population among Rajis is 57.67 whereas female population is 42.33 percent only. This unfavourable sex ratio is due to high rate of maternity deaths (mother and child deaths) on account of their being in isolation and non-acceptance/non-availability of timely medical and health care assistance. Because of high infant mortality rate, these people do not give name to the child immediately after the birth. Early naming ceremony of the child is considred as inauspicious for the family. In the past there was a custom among these people to leave that place for ever where some member of their family/community had died. Earlier these people used to burry the dead body. Now lately, they have adopted the Hindu custom of cremating the dead person.

'Raji' speak Tibet-Burman dialect with Austric sprinkling and exhibit some Mongoloid features, having some resemblances with the Tharus and Bokshas of U.P. terai region. Nomadic life style is the significant way of their living. It affects their social life as well. They always live in group. Rather the group cohensiveness is the significant aspect of their life which gives them social security. These people move from one place to another in small groups and these groups are linked by kinship ties. These people have small families which are generally nuclear in nature. After marriage a couple lives in a separate dwelling. Thus, by nature it is of neolocal type. Bride price is prevalent among 'Rajis', which was generally in the form of kind in the past.

So far as Raji economy is concerned it is one of the simplest in nature. Basically, these people for a long time were dependent on forest produce. Still partially these people depend on forests to some extent. Lately, some Raji' families have started land cultivation also. Government of Uttar Pradesh (now Uttaranchal) launched several schemes to ameliorate the economic lot of these people under special planning schemes and tried to rehabilitate these people. These people were given land for cultivation and some subsidy for house construction. These people had developed traditional skills for making wooden bowls like 'Theki', 'Pai' etc. In addition to this, these people make beautiful ropes out of the forest grass and baskets from the branches of the trees. They perform these activities throughout the year.

Silent Trade

As these people in the past had no knowledge of agriculture, they depended on forest produce for their survival. Moreover traditionally, these people had developed the custom of silent trade with the neighbouring villagers. In silent trade (e.g. invisible) the two trading partners neither meet each other in a face to face situation nor do they ever interact with each other directly or indirectly. As they used to prepare several wooden articles, ropes and collect forest produce, they wanted some market for its consumption. Because of their very shy nature, these people in the past never came in face to face contact with the people out side their community in the past. During night hours while neighbouring villagers were asleep and their doors were closed, the 'Rajis' used to visit the village and placed their articles in front of the door. It is necessary to point out here that the neighbouring villagers always found these articles very useful in their day to day life. The villager, at whose door these articles were placed, if accepted them, he in exchange would keep eatable items/ food grains at the same place on the next day evening before sleeping in lieu of the articles brought by 'Rajis'. In case the food items were not given by the villager or given in less quantity, the Rajis used to get annoyed and during the dark hours of the night put dirt and filth including human excreta at the front door of the house in the form of protest. This type of exchange of goods was also known as Invisible trade as the two parties did not see each other face to face.

The Rajis practise a sort of shifting cultivation and grow the crop 'ragi' which is locally known as 'mandua'. At present, these people are neither invisible traders nor do they practice shifting cultivation. As is well known, in hills the agriculture could never be a complete source of livelihood because of the uncertain natural conditions like excessive rainfall, hailstorms etc., therefore these people need to revise their traditional skill as an additional source of livelihood.

These people have now started adopting the life style of local Kumaonis. Though after independence, especially after 1967 when these people were declared as scheduled tribes, they were given land by the government under the rehabilitation programme. But the land holdings were quite small in size and moreover the barren land could not provide them sufficient food grains. According to one report the land allotted to them was 0.81 acre per person, which too was unirrigated and unlevelled, which could provide them food for 2-3 months only. In present time the male member of the Raji clan take up the task of labours, casual workers etc. These people are also employed as labourers by the forest contractors.

In April 1985, a Raji Development Project was started whose head quarter was at Jauljivi in Pithoragarh district. But due to unavoidable reasons the scheme was abandoned. Because it was felt quite unwise to invest rupees sixteen lakhs on a total population of 456 from the year 1977-78 to 1985-86. Minor efforts were made at the governmental level as well as by NGOs to ameliorate their socio-economic condition, but without much success. They were provided houses which they occupied for some time but later on left for their rock shelters.

In 1979 one voluntary organisation *'Seemantak Anusuchit Jati avam Janjati Sansthan'* after lot of difficulties started six primary schools in Raji villages, which met with great success. These institutions were started with the special assistance from the Central government. Had the efforts been made to motivate Raji children to send to school along with other village children there would have been little success because of the shy nature of Raji people, but incase of separate schools there was favourable response for children's education. The state government also showed farsightedness by providing books and clothings to the children of Rajis studying in these schools.

Thus, in spite of all efforts and Rajis taking up new occupations, their economic lot has not improved. So much so that there have been several instances of deaths on account of hunger. According to certain reliable estimate in the year 1970, 18 percent of the Raji population died on account of hunger. Thus, there is a need to help them favourably. Also the greater need is that of their socialization i.e. to motivate them to live with the outside people and abandon their habit of living in isolation.

There is also need to remove their traditional skill of making wooden utensils by providing financial subsidy. The exploitation of Rajis by Seths, Sahukars and contractors by engaging these people as labourers at a wage rate much below the prevailing rates, also needs to be checked. The health care, medical facilities and construction of roads in unapproachable Raji habitations would further help them a lot.

Lepcha Tribe of Sikkim

Lepcha are found in the state of Sikkim. They live in difficult and hostile geographical conditions where the economic conditions are also very miserable. It is believed that these people have migrated to this place from Tibet and Mongolia. Lepchas believe that their original habitation was Kanchan Changha valley. The terrain where they reside is not very suitable for agriculture. The better and fertile land in Sikkim state was under the possession of Nepali and Bhotia people. These Lepchas came in contact with the above two communities who (Nepal and Bhotias) treated these people (Lepchas) like slaves. These people (Nepalis and Bhotias) exploited Lepchas for a long time, extracted maximum labour from them for minimum amount of payment. Thus, Lepchas are very poor people. They do some agricultural work also but the land they possess is very infertile. That is the reason that these people never became economically self-sufficient. Cardamom, which they cultivate, has an important place in their economy. The cultivation of cardamom had started from Nepal.

These people are simple, honest and hard working. But at the same time they are completely devoid of economic resources. Their poverty reflects from their dwellings as they live in small cottage, with thatched roof. These people are very hospitable and entertaining their guests and relatives is considered as pious duty by them. The head of the tribal clan is known as 'Mandal'. He decides the marriages and settles disputes within the community. He represents the community for every matter.

The religion of Lepcha is known as mun. In several respects the mun (religion) resembles Buddhism. The mun priest performs animal sacrifices and thereby protects the Lepcha people from diseases and supernatural fears. The Lepcha priests put on robes like Lamas and also perform duties and rituals. Even these mun priests take alcohol at the time of religious prayers. They go door to door along with sacred religious books and give their blessings to the people. In modern times, lots of changes have taken place in their customs and practices.

The polyandrous system which was traditionally prevalent among these people, is no longer in existence now. Now these people practise monogamy.

At present besides agriculture, these people are actively engaged as labourers in tea gardens of the region. Some Lepchas, after attaining some education, have taken up work in the government and the private sectors. In the past these people were exploited by the more powerful groups of Nepalis and Bhotias. Their entry into shrines (religious) was banned. These people are very suspicious. Besides agriculture and labourers they resort to hunting also.

'Knife' is an important and only weapon which these people used to possess. It was considered as a manly ornament which every male possessed and which was used for various activities. These people are orthodox and suspicious. Their belief is that if a particular type of snake enters the house, it will cause death in the family. Similarly, it is inauspicious to call a woman by name after marriage.

There is ample amount of cooperation among the members of a clan or a village. Members of one family give their fullest cooperation to the members of another family in construction of house and all other activities. Such cooperation continues without any personal interest. The family is partiarchal and father is head of the family. After father's death the eldest son automatically becomes the family head. In case of division, the land, animals and other property is equally distributed among brothers. There are instances of joint families also. Only male members enjoy ownership of the land, while women members are devoid of this right.

As we have stated earlier, these people were exploited by Bhotias, Nepalis and other neighbouring seths and sahukars who gave money to these people as loan and later extracted huge amount of interest. The rate of interest realized was more than double as one time fixed by Sikkim state. Even the attitude of Sikkim royal family was never favourable toward these people. In the past there was a custom to send the Lepcha boys to the service of royal family. As these Lepchas were expert in carpentry, whenever their services were required, these people had to leave their native village and go to the service of royal family. Thus, their being skillful in carpentary work also became the curse for their exploitation.

The institution of marriage among Lepchas reflects the bond of solidarity. Usually the boy and girl do not even know each other before marriage. But marital ties bind the groups/families together. The girl after marriage is considered as the property of the group/ community of which her husband is a member. Even if her husband dies, she continues to be treated as the property of her deceased husband's clan and she can even be married to any other member of the group without consulting her parents.

By nature these people are very shy like 'Rajis' and do not like to mix up with the outsiders. Among these people there is a custom of giving 'gifts' to the close and acquainted persons. Whenever they visit some one's home, they do not go without gift. The gift is accepted by both the hands and children are taught this behaviour right from the early age. The exchange of gift takes place on reciprocal visit.

By and large Lepcha community is crime free. The only crime committed at times is that of 'suicide'. Though poor, yet people are devoid of theft and other deviant habits.

Like women, Lepcha men also keep long hair. At times, it becomes difficult to distinguish between a boy and a girl because of common dress and long hair of both.

In marital matters, the decision is taken by clan relatives. The parents do not decide about their children's marriage. This is because of the superstition among these people that the marriages decided by parents are temporary in character. Therefore, the marital proposal is put forth by mukhia (mandal) and close relatives like grand parents, or uncle-aunt etc. help in giving it a final shape.

Tribes of Andaman Islands

The total number of Andaman islands is 204. The main island is located at a distance of about 590 kilometers from the delta of Hubli river whereas from Burma's Cape Negris its distance is only 120 kilometers. Among these islands, three most important islands are northern, middle and southern Andaman. These islands are separated from each other by a narrow strait.

The total number of Nicobar islands is 19 out of which 12 have human population. Out of these 12 islands, two important islands are : Great Nicobar and Carnicobar. The total area of Carnicobar island is only 49 sq. miles. Here the land is very fertile. The whole island is covered with coconut trees.

For a long time it was presumed that the Andaman islanders were the descendents of African slaves. But several Anthropologists who have been studying the characteristics of these people, believed them to be as Negritos. Basically, these people were nomadic by nature and used to move from one place to another in search of food. Not more than 30 persons used to reside in one particular region.

First of all British administrators discovered this island. That time these tribals were divided into 12 groups which could be broadly divided into 3 parts :

(a) Tribes of North Andaman group

(b) Tribes of Southern Andaman group

(c) Tribes of Onge group

The tribes of Andaman islands are quite backward. Till a few decades ago, they used to move naked. But they always used to keep fire burning at their house for the protection from cold. Among these tribes there was no restriction on pre-marital sex relations. But after marriage rules of incest taboo were strictly followed. Unaware about divorce and dissertion, these people used to practise monogamy.

Andamani people used to give name to their children before birth. After the birth of the child they added this name after the new name of the newly born child – boy or girl. This is because the name signifies a particular gender. The marriage ceremony is very simple and without any sort of religious ceremony. The moment the elders of the community knew that a particular boy is interested in marrying a girl, they make a separate hut for the boy. The girl is taken to the newly built hut and made to sit there. Later on the boy is brought and also made to sit on the lap of the girl and the marriage ritual is considered as complete. Marital ties are considered as life long and broken only by death. Remarriage takes place only after the death of either of the marital partner. The right of remarriage is equally common both in case of man or woman.

The people of South Andaman keep their heads clean shaved while the people of other tribal groups of Great Andaman keep long hair. They tatoo their body to look beautiful.

These tribals have great interest in hunting. Besides, fisheries is another important occupation. In the past these people were unaware of making fire. Therefore, they used to preserve the fire. At times, the fire was not available in the whole village. In such a situation, the people used to go to the neighbouring village for the same.

These people had special interest for dance and music. They had very little faith in religion. They were ignorant regarding the notion of hell or heaven. The outsiders had once/upon a time, fake notion about these tribals being as cannibals because whenever they saw any outsider these people tried to kill him with their bow and arrows. But this was a mere illusion. Whenever they killed any person, they immediately burnt the dead body, a tradition of burning the dead was prevalent in their community. Even if the dead person was an enemy, they used to dance around the dead body while cremating the same.

Onge

These people reside in little Andaman island which is located in the remote south of all the islands. The area of this island is 448 square miles. Traditionally food collection and hunting was their source of livelihood. Until a few decades ago the Onge were the only inhabitants of this island but during the period 1967 and 1974 three thousand people, who were originally the inhabitants of India and Car-Nicobar came to this island and settled there permanently. These people (the outsiders) took up work in governmental and non-governmental undertakings.

The tribals of the island had least knowledge about the health and hygiene. In their society there was no custom of daily bath. As we have said earlier, their idea about religion was very vague, though they believed in soul and they believed the souls were sacred. But these people did not correlate it with any religious idea. These people used to bury the dead person inside his cottage (residence) itself.

The family among the tribals was an important institution. The family was of monogamous. Polygamy was unknown to them. Similar was the case with regard to divorce of which also they had never heard of. The consent of parents was always sought before marriage. Before marriage the bride and groom used white clay on their body and after the blessings of elders the marriage was considered as complete. In actual marriage ceremony, like Andaman Islands, the elderly persons put the hands of bride and groom on each other's shoulders and after that they made groom to sit on bride's lap. An interesting thing was that in the traditional greeting practices also there was the custom of sitting on the lap. Famous anthropologist Rad-Cliffe-Brown in his book *'Andaman Islands, a Social Study'* (1922) gave a detailed account of the customs of these people.

These people were expert in canoe making. They decorated those boats like their own body. Like the Andaman tribes, dance had great significance in the social life of these people. It was also one of the most important means of recreation. Men, women and children also participated in the dance programme.

Owing to external contact the traditional economy of Onge has almost changed. Use of several goods, e.g. metal tools etc. have increased. Moreover, after the settlement of outsiders in this island, the culture contact has widened in various non-material spheres too. It is important to note here that before 1887 these tribals got the feeling of confidence among these people after using their tools. Prior to that they used wooden tools and weapons. They used metal tools only after coming in contact with outsiders. The use of metal not only facilitated them in hunting, it also changed their attitude toward the outsiders. At present, the population of outsiders have multiplied on the island, compared to the tribal population. As a consequence of which these people had to change their hunting places. Also there was change in the seasonal migration as they were displaced from several places. The external interferences are increasing day by day in all walks of their life. There was decline of forests and forest product, construction of road and building took place and there was expansion of agriculture. Consequently, these people have taken up governmental and other vocations.

Tribes of Nicobar Islands

Col. Henry Maine in 1867 first of all captured these islands and put them under British control. Car Nicobar, which resembles Australia in appearance, is most important among all the islands. It seems these people are not the original inhabitants of this island and had migrated from outside. These people closely resemble the tribes of Malaya. The prevalence of couvade relationship among the two tribes clearly confirms this contention. According to the custom of couvade relationship, in every village, there is a special hut near the residence of a married couple where the husband and wife go to reside at least a few days before the birth of a child. After the birth of the first child, both husband and wife have to observe certain rituals. For one month both husband and wife are considered as impure. The duration of this impurity decreases after the birth of second or the third child which is confined to one or two days only.

The naming ceremony of the child takes place immediately after the birth of the child. The father of the child gives the name. Afterwards, a family friend gives additional name to the child.

By and large people follow monogamy but instances of polygamy are also there and confined to chiefs and rich among the tribals. Girls have complete freedom to select their marital partner. Marriage takes place after attaining the youth (puberty). These people do not put much control on premarital sex relations. But after marriage, sex relations are strictly regulated. Marriage ceremony is quite simple. In case of dissolution of marriage (divorce) the consent of both husband and wife is considered as final.

Their huts are of circular type. They keep their houses quite neat and clean. These people are very superstitious, orthodox and suspicious. For every misfortunate they blame the evil soul. These people have full faith in animism. According to John Richerdson, Nicobarese have no faith in religion. They only have faith in evil spirit and try to please evil spirits by sacrificing cock and pig. Usually this is done at the time of misfortune. Community feast is their main attraction. Coconut is the main property which is used in several ways. Fishing is their another main occupation.

These tribals are expert in making cannoes. These boats are beautifully decorated. Some times boat race is also organized as a means of entertainment.

There is prevalence of joint family system. Coconut trees are the main family property which they assess by counting these plants.

Among the Car-Nicobar Islands, great Nikobar Island is the largest one but still its population is very small. But now migrants have started settling in this island. Here a tribe named Shompens, who reside in the forests, are very shy in nature. A few decades ago they were in a naked stage but now these people have started using some clothes. Coconut and other forest products are their means of livelihood.

People of Jarawa Tribe are very small in number. Hunting and collection have been their main source of livelihood till recently. For a long period these people vehemently opposed the outside contact. Even these people did not have any faith on the other tribals of Andaman Islands. Morgan while describing a Jarawa village, stated that in a Jarawa village there were 10 to 12 huts (houses), where 20 to 30 Jarawa people used to reside. The village was situated in the midst of dense forest. They always preferred to live in isolation and did not have faith in other tribals of the island. They always avoided contact with outsiders. That is the reason even the Jarawas have been reduced to very small number.

References

1. Negi R.S., M.K. Raha and J.C. Das, "The Rajis and their economy" in Singh K.S. (Ed.), *Economies of the Tribes and their Transformation*, 1982.
2. Mathur K.S., *Nikobar Islands*, 1937.
3. Spittal R.S., *Vanished Tribes*, 1950.
4. Thurston, *Castes & Tribes of South India*, 1909.
5. RadCliffe-Brown, *Andaman Island : A Social Study*, 1922.

❑❑❑

3

India's Nomadic Tribes

Nomadic tribes are those tribal groups which do not live permanently at a fixed place (on a permanent basis) by constructing their houses, rather they move from one place to another place throughout the year with their tents or other make shift arrangements. Their movement is based (living) on resources available to them at a particular place on a particular period of the year. Thus, instead of living at one place on a permanent basis they live at different places in a year. And instead of permanent houses, they make their temporary dwellings out of cheap material. Mostly, these dwelling are of mobile nature in the form of tents and other such material which can be easily taken from one place to another place. The nomadism has become part and parcel of some of the tribals life or even of caste Hindu/Muslim communities in India and inspite of all efforts to rehabilitate them at a particular place, there has not been much success. The Governments' efforts and incentives have failed in this regard and these people could not be motivated to settledown at one place on a permanent basis.

It seems that the nature and type of economy of these tribal and non-tribal nomadic groups and communities have made them to move from one place to another. In due course of time this become part of their habit and life style. In appears that initially some of these tribal groups moved from one place to another in search of food and other economic (living) resources, their economy must have been that of collecting nature. Thus, initially these people moved from one place to another for the sake of hunting and collection of living resources.

Gradually, they started catering to the needs of people (else where) by exchange of goods and services. Their stay at one place varied from few days to a month or so-depending on the availability of work or (living) resources. Here it is important to point out that in certain stage of economy (i.e. consumption economy) people moved from one place to another in search of food and this ultimately became part and parcel of their habit and life style and this eventually debarred them from permanent ownership of property at a fixed place. Their movement was confined to the places where living resources were available to them.

As we have stated above, besides tribal groups there are certain Hindu and Muslim communities in India, who, till date, have been following nomadic life style. But these people move from one place to another in search of work or owing to their specialized occupational skills, cater to the needs of those people in whose area they move. For example, musicians, drummers and even iron smiths etc move from place to place and cater to the needs of the people. Such people have fixed clientage in a particular place/locality and they cater to their needs.

It seems that the tribal or non-tribal groups who resorted to collecting economy from different places, adopted this mode of living. later on, when the food resources were not easily available or the resources started dwindling (exhausting), the people engaged in these activities started developing deviant tendencies into form of stealing and robbery. The stealing was sometimes of the small nature. For example, stealing of agricultural products from the fields for the fulfillment of one's basic needs etc. Thus, economic hardships at times compelled them to do so.

One assumption as to why some people adopted the nomadic life is that a section of people drifted (separted) from their original group and thus adopted this sort of living. These people lost touch with the traditional occupation also. For example, BAWARIA or BORIS who lived in W. Bengal, Orissa and Rajasthan, were once agriculturists and used to live at a fixed place later on started leading nomadic life. Another nomadic tribe AHERIAS used to reside in Rajasthan and in the neighbourhood of Delhi and still live into outskirts of the villages. These people are very timid, they prepare mats and move from place to place to sell them off. They also collect forest produce.

Bahelias are mainly found in UP, Bihar and West Bengal. In Bihar, they are known as 'Mula', their main occupation is hunting and bird catching. Now these people have adopted Hindu religion. They are more or less Hinduised, started calling Brahmin priest at their house on various religious and social functions. Some of the Bahelias have adopted Islam also. These people live outside the village and also work as agricultural labourers. Yet to some extent they follow nomadic life even today.

Saharias who lived at Bundelhand and in the nearby area, were another nomadic tribe. They used to collect forest produce and committed minor thefts. But now these people have resorted to settled living.

Lodhas are found in West Bengal and Bihar. These people trace their origin from Savara. Originally lodhas used to collect food from the forests of midanapur. Besides, these people worked as agricultural labourers. Once these people had earned the notoriety as a criminal tribe. Another nomadic tribe 'TURI' who are found in Bihar and West Bengal, trace their origin from Munda and speak Mundari dialect. They prepare mats and live in the outskirts of the Hindu villages. Dharkars are known as Forest tribes but now these people have adopted to settled living and reside in Hindu villages and do all sorts of agricultural tasks.

The Musahars and Rajwars of Bihar work as agricultural labourers. After the abolition of Jagirdari some people have started cultivating their own land and have started living at one place on a permanent basis. But owing to economic hardships these people are at times forced to leave their places, in search of work.

'Musahars' are rat eaters, that is why they ore known by this name. They observe tribal behaviour to a large extent and have their own tribal priest. However, they have started calling Brahmin priests at their house on specific occasions.

The 'Bhars' of Uttar Pradesh used to consider themselves as land lords in the past, but now they are no more in possession of land and work as labourers on other's land. According to them the Rajputs, after defeating them, took away their land. Later on, the remaining land was taken away by the Muslims thus making them totally landless.

These people, later on, cleared the forest land and started cultivating it. The 'Bhars of West Bengal enjoy superior status and position than Bhars of Bihar and Uttar Pradesh. The Bhars of West Bengal are more Hinduised and they call Brahmins at their house on important festive occasions, where as to Bhars of Uttar Pradesh and Bihar do not call the Brahmin priests.

The Bagadis of west Bengal and Madhya Pradesh are the nomadic tribe whose traditional occupation was agriculture. Besides, these people do labourers work e.g. wood cutting and labourers in the construction work of various types. Bedia is another tribe of this region who are nomadic by nature and are at present listed in the category of scheduled castes. Yet one section of Bedia is known as scheduled tribe. They prepare nets for fishing. In addition these people prepeare ropes, wooden articles etc. The savarna Hindus considered them as untouchables in the past.

Pardhis are the nomadic tribes of Maharashtra. In addition, these pople are also found in Madhya Pradesh. Pardhis are further sub divided into several types on the basis of their profession (work). For example, Phansi pardhis catch birds and other forest animals. Takankar or Takia pardhis prepare grinding stones and repair them. Similarly, longoli pardhis and shikari Pardhis are known for their specalised activities. These people also commit theft and are engaged in other deviant activities. Sometimes these people resort to violent means also.

Like Pardhi, mang garudi is another tribe found in Karnataka state of South India. Besides, these people are also found in Gujrat. They move along with their belongings including animals. The poor 'Mang Garudis make their living by begging also. Their women are also engaged in the collection of forest produce. Sometimes, women are also engaged in immoral trafficking.

Kaikadis are nomadic tribes of south India. These people are known as Korwa in Andhra Pradesh. These Korwas are further divided into various Gotras and each of these have their own customs, dress, occupation and way of living. These people resemble to a great extent Mirasis of north India. In their community the chief (male member) has very high respectable position and all people obey his orders. Besides, these people commit theft and highway robbery. These people worship female deity.

Some other Professional Nomadic Castes

In our country their number is so large that to trace their origin and classification is a difficult task. Majority of these are associated with the Hindus who are at the bottom of the caste Hierarchy. For example, the Drummers are engaged in sharpening of knives, selling grinding stones etc. These people may have tribal origin, yet most of these are associated with lower caste Hindus and because of economic hardships, they resorted to nomadic life.

Bhagats are nomadic castes of Kashmir, and resort to begging by singing songs. A section of Bhagats, is the follower of Islam. They act as musician on specific occasions like marriage and other important festivals. Their songs and musical instruments are quite popular.

The Bahurupias of Panjab very much resemble with Bhagat caste of Kashmir. These people also make their living by entertaining the people.

The Kalanders are a muslim caste of Uttar Pradesh, who entertain the people by showing the acrobats. They also train animals like Bear and monkey for entertaining the people and there by make their living. The Bhaios caste of Gujarat, entertain the rural people by their jokes and play on the occasion of marriage and important festive occasions and on the occasion of fairs. The Gondhalis of Maharashtra also entertain people by their music and dance.

The Dafli and Nagarchis castes are followers of Islam and make their livelihood by art and music. Similarly, the Dholi of Rajasthan, the Banjara and Turhia caste of Uttar Pradesh are well known for their art and music.

The Nats and Bajigars are other important nomadic castes. The maximum number of nuts are found in Madhya Pradesh, followed by Uttar Pradesh and Bihar. Bajigars are mostly found in Punjab. The nuts and Bajigars move from one place to another and make their living by entertaining the people. Besides, sometimes, their women are found involved in flesh trade also. Nut women are known for tattooing their body. Nut males are known to have good knowledge of herbs. In Punjab and in many other parts of Northern India the Mirasi caste is known for their music and dance.

Kanjars are specially found in Rajasthan and Uttar Pradesh. Till recently they were living in hunting stage. They are experts in birds catching. Besides, they remove the hides of dead animals and sell the same. They themselves also make use of these hides in several ways. Their women are also engaged in flesh trade.

Thoris of Gujart are found near Rajkot region and are very small in number. These people prepare mats while moving from one place to another, they make use of donkeys for carrying goods and other belongings, and make use of tents for making the temporary dwelling.

The Bardundas in the past, used to reside near Ratlam in Madhya Pradesh and like thoris, these people also used to prepare mats. In their dialects, they use several Tamil words, therefore, there is one assumption that there people had their origin in south India and from there they migrated to the North.

They are non-vegetarian. They even kill snake and reptiles and after removing their poison eat these away. These people also worship the spirits and deities of Lower Caste Hindus. They have immense faith in evil spirits and are scared of the same.

Travelling Castes

In this category we can put Saiqlgars and sikligars. Both are Muslim castes. They move from one place to another and perform the task of sharpening knives etc and polish the utensils and thereby make their livelihood. Similarly, the Ghisara, a caste is also engaged in similar activities. Ghisaras are found in several parts of south India.

Khumars, a muslim caste of North India make grinding stones, 'silpatta etc' and sell them in the villages. They move from one place to another and make use of animals for carrying their luggage and other articles.

The nomadic Lohar castes (iron smiths) are found in various parts of the country. The Gadolia lohars of western Rajasthan are well known in this respect. They move in group along with their animals. They prepare and repair agricultural tools and sell animals. Usually they move in bullock carts. Their women and children are also found busy in the preparation of agricultural implements. Thus, the whole Gadolia family acts as a working unit.

In the past there were several criminal castes who were nomadic by nature and who used to trace their origin from upper castes, such as Rajputs etc. According to them they were defeated in the battle by Rajputs and later on by muslims. To protect themselves from atrocities of Rajputs and muslims, they left their original places and moved to else where. Economic hardships forced them to adopt deviant traits. During British period, people and the administration both were scared of their organized criminal activities. Initially, they were listed in the category of criminal tribes and castes. Later on, after independence, they were designated as denotified communities, instead of criminal castes.

Sansi is another scheduled tribe who trace their origin from Rajputs. According to them their land was taken away by Rajputs in 13th century. Later on, the remaining land was taken away by Muslim invaders and these people were reduced to landless and were forced to move from one place to another in search of livelihood. Initially, they worked as labourers as a means of livelihood. Later on, they started committing thefts. Thus, these people were known for stealing animals, agricultural produce and the articles of day today needs of the local villagers. During British period these people were declared as criminal tribes and were placed under strict control on several occasions and at seversal places.

Sansis are found in several parts of north India and presently some of them have started cultivation work and resorted to settled living. Yet one section of these people is leading a nomadic life. Among sansis, the women enjoy relatively better position in their community. Women can attend and express their ideas in the community panchayats. Customarily, women also have right to the family property. They can inherit property, a women can divorce her husband and remarry another person. Polygamy is disapproved among Sansis. Levirate and sororate are quite common. Besides, they follow the practice of 'Bride price'. The Sansis are sub divided into various Gotras and Sub gotras.

Haburas, were once a nomadic criminal caste of north India who traced their origin from chauhan Rajputs. They resemble sansis to a large extent. Women enjoy respectable position in their society. The unmarried girls enjoy ample amount of liberty. These people also commit theft and robbery.

The 'Fakir; caste of Punjab, at present live mostly in Bijapur district on a permanent basis. Similarly, the Miyana caste of Kathia Barh and Kutch, who are both Hindus and Muslims are well known for their criminal activities. Miyans consider themselves as descendents of Rajputs.

Bhantu was another famous criminal caste of north India. They used to commit organised theft and robbery. These people also trace their origin from Rajputs and consider Chittorgarh as the original abode. According to them when Chittorgarh came under muslim control, these people were forced to leave that place and take shelter elsewhere and were compelled to move to the forest in search of food and shelter. These people resemble Haburas, Kanjars and Karwal castes, to a large extent. In 1926, a group of Bhantu caste was sent to Andaman Island for rehabilitation, where these people started agricultural work and left the criminal activities.

Sanaurhia and Chandravedis are the nomadic castes, who associate themselves with sanad Brahmins. They commit theft in disguise and their main centre is Bundelkhand.

Waghris of central India, closely resemble with the Bagadi group. Also they associate their kinship relationship with the Sansi caste of Panjab. Baghris are known for committing theft and other criminal activities. The local police keeps strict vigil on their movements.

Thus, the nomadic castes and tribal groups can be placed into following categories

(1) First group consists of those pople who live on food collection and hunting stage of culture.

(2) Second group consists of those who are culturally a step ahead than the people of first category. They used to reside in or near forest areas and performed axe cultivation (shifting cultivation) as a means of livelihood.

(3) The third group consisted of those migrant nomadic tribals who came to India from central Asia.

In the absence of adequate anthropological evidence, it is difficult to ascertain the caste and the tribal origin of these nomadic people. But one thing can be said with certainty that in the social organisation of these tribal people, stages of food collection and hunting are clearly evident. Though, mostly these people marry outside the kinshipfold yet usually sex relationships are in a loose form and there is no rigid control over pre-martial sexual relationships. Among several tribal and caste groups there are instances of flesh trade and immoral trafficking. The institution of marriage is not very strong and well organised. The nomadic people usually move in groups of families. There is strong feeling of cooperation among the members of the group. Economic hardship have made them to resort to begging. The instances of violence are rare.

Occasionally, the violence is used, that too in self-defence or it is used to escape from the clutches of police and law.

The nomadic tribes have been primarily associated with Hindu religion though later on, some of them adopted muslim religion also.

The Nomadic groups have their own moral patterns and code of conduct, which they strictly follow within their own group. For example, they help the members of the group at the time of need, like their own family members, obey the orders of the group leader. But these people look to the outsiders with suspicion.

Whatever might been the reasons in past, in modern times the main reason for any caste and tribal group for leading nomadic life is, economic. Gradually, the movement from one place to another, has become important part of their life. Crime and other deviant tendencies were also primarily associated with their economic existences.

This was the reason that most of the nomadic people used to steal the food products. Even in modern times, these were several caste and tribal groups in seversal parts of the country, have permant places of habitation, yet they partly lead nomadic living. Gadaolia Lohars and similar other artisan castes are its best examples. For the sale of the tools and implements prepared by them and for selling the forest produce etc. they move from one place to another. By and large these people have not been able to move upward and still are at a subsistance level.

Thus, now a days no particular tribal or caste groups is leading fully nomadic life, rather many of them lead a semi nomadic life.

References

1. Bhargava B.A., *Criminal Tribes* (1949).
2. Hutton J.H., *Caste in India* (1951).
3. Rouhela Satpal, *The Godulia Lohars of Rajasthan* (1968).
4. Katiyar, T.S., *Social Life in Rajasthan* (1964).
5. Shah, P.G., *Denotified Communities of Western India* (1967).
6. Singh Sher, *Sansis of Punjab* (1965).
7. Singh Sher, *Shilpkars of Panjab* (1965).
8. Mishra S.C., *Muslim Communities in Gujrat* (1964).
9. Bhonmick, P.K. *The Lodhas of West Bengal* (1963).
10. Das A. K., et al, *Handbook of Scheduled Castes and Scheduled tribes of West Bengal (1986).*

❑❑❑

4

Tribal Social Structure : Family

The structure of anything consists of the stable relationships among its parts: moreover, the term *part* itself implies a certain degree of stability. Since a social system is composed of the interrelated acts of the people, its structure must be sought in some degree of regularity or recurrence in these acts. The term *social structure* has often been used interchangeably with *social organization* in social anthropology and has been used particularly in the analysis of kinship and of political and legal institutions of primitive societies. R. Firth explicity distinguishes between two terms. According to him, 'a social organization is concerned with the choices and decisions included in the actual social relations (the working arrangement of society) while social structure refers to the more fundamental social relations which give a society its basic form and which set limits to the courses of action organizationally possible. Fortes believes that the term can be applied to any ordered arrangement of distinguishable wholes *i.e.* to institutions, groups, situations, processes, social positions: but Evans Pritchard restricts the term to the relationships between groups.

Social phenomena constitute a distinct class of natural phenomena. They are all, in one way or another, connected with the existence of social structures, either being implied in or resulting from them. Social structures are just as real as are individual organisms. A complex organism is a collection of living cells and interstitial fluids arranged in certain structures, and a living cell is similarly a structural arrangement of complex molecules.

The social phenomena which we observe in any human society

are not the immediate result of the nature of individual human beings, but are the result of the social structure by which they are united.

Radcliffe-Brown considers all the social relations of a person with others as a part of a social structure; and he includes in the social structures the differentiations of individuals and of classes by their social roles. He says: "In the study of the social structure, the concrete reality with which we are concerned is the set of actually existing relations, at a given moment of time, which links together certain human beings." Lucy Mair says that the word *structure* is now the central concept in a large part of the work being done in social anthropology. She adds: We think of the society, not the culture, as an orderly arrangement of parts, and that our business is to detect and explain this order. It consists in relationships between persons which are regulated by a common body of recognized rights and obligations.

Beteille states: there is some advantage in viewing the social structure as a set of relations between groups of persons having a high degree of consistency and constancy. One can then identify these groups, define their boundaries and specify their mutual positions.

Here we have defined *social structure* as an ordered arrangement of relationships between members of a given social group. We have tried to examine the nature of relationships obtaining in the various spheres of the life of a tribal group. These spheres include family, marriage, kinship, religion and political relations.

Family is one of the most important primary social institutions. It is one of the oldest institutions of the human society. Although sociologists are convinced that the family is the basic unit of social organization, the term itself remains one of the most loosely defined in their vocabulary. The family is an organized group. Its members occupy a definite set of mutual statuses, interact according to definite behaviour patterns, and are motivated by reciprocal attitudes and sentiments. Without this institutional organization, the family's performance of the four main functions, mentioned above, could not be accomplished.

It is an institution which fulfills basic human needs of its members. Man has several fundamental needs which are to be fulfilled if he has to survive. Food, clothing and shelter are the most important primary needs to be fulfilled. Along with these, he needs mental and physical security which are provided to him by the family. Therefore, without family, the very existence of man, though not imposible, but certainly is very difficult.

In different stages of civilization, family has been the most important and inseparable institution of the society. It has existed in all the stages of the development of culture.

Man is born, brought up and socialized in the family. Family usually consists of husband and wife and their children or parents and their children. It is a group of closely knit individuals, related to each other by the bond of blood relationship or marriage.

Thus, universality has been claimed for the institution of family and this has been located either in the biologically created mother child dyad or in the socially constructed mother-father-child triad.

Traditionally, family has been viewed as a unit with several functions, notably legitimate sexual outlet for the partners, procreation, socialization of children, and in some cases production.

There are many different family forms: nuclear, joint and extended etc. Each family goes through a life cycle. People are born into the family of their origin, after marriage start of their own family of procreation, become parents and then grand parents, when their own children start their own family of procreation. Family roles change as the individual moves through the life cycles of the family.

Nuclear family consists of parents and their children (unmarried). A joint family is a group of people who have members of at least three or more generations, who generally live under one roof, have common purse and common hearth, who hold property in common and who participate in common worship and are related to each other as some particular kind of kindered.

According to I.P. Desai, we call that household a joint family which has greater generation depth (i.e. three or more) than the nuclear family and the members of which are related to one another by property, income etc, to mutual rights and obligations.

Tribal India exhibits a colourful diversity of families because of varied rules and customs among different tribes. Different forms of family came into existence at different stage of cultural and social development viz matriarchal family, patriarchal family, polygamous family and monogamous family, joint family and nuclear family. Though it is quite difficult to ascertain as to which form of family came into existence first or which was the earliest form of family.

In different forms of family, certain common characteristics are observed viz marital tie, a system of descent, common habitation and an economic system. Different scholars have emphasised different characteristics of family. For example, according to Kings Ley Davis, family is a group of those persons who are related to each other by blood. But, some other scholars consider this definition as incomplete but blood relationship is only one characteristics of the family. According to Mac Iver and Page the other main characteristics are: universality, emotional basis of family, constructive influence and nucleus position of family in the social structure, limited size, responsibility of the members, social regulation and permanent or temporary form of the family.

The above definition includes several characteristics of the family and these are applicable to the family system among Indian tribes. Among Indian tribes, there exist different forms of family organization. There is reciprocal cooperation among its members. Family members by means of cooperation and division of labour, fulfill their basic needs. For example, kadars, till recently were in a collecting stage of economy. They used to collect forest and other produce and then distributed it equally among themselves without any discrimination. Thus, in some of the tribes, who were very backward from the point of view of development, we found instances of equality and maximum cooperation.

In different societies, an important function of the family is regulation of sexual relationship between husband and wife. Usually family solidarity is based on sexual direction between husband and wife and their affection towards children. In tribal societies sex education was given due importance. For example, dormitories (a sort of night club) were found among some of the tribes in our country. These dormitories were known by various names. The Ghotuls among Maria and Muria were quite popular till recently. These 'dormitories' regulated the 'sex behaviour' of young unmarried boy and girls and imparted sex-education also.

On to contrary, in our so called civilized traditional Indian society, the knowledge of sex-education among unmarried boys and girls is considered as undesirable. Rather it is a sort of taboo. But the tribal people were more liberal so far as sex relationships were concerned.

Another important task of family is to provide primary security to its members, looking after and caré of children, make them aware of customs and culture of the society. It is first socializing agency for the child.

In tribal families, the member even at a tender age are attracted toward economic activities eg. grazing of animals, knowledge of forest produce, agricultural activities and tribal indigeneous handicraft. From the early childhood, these people try to develop know how of the above traits.

Family transmits the culture, customs and tradition of the tribal group from one generation to another. As the tribals have no scripts of their own, these things pass from one generation to another, orally. But as here tribal people come in contact with the people, outside their society, their socialization process is affected. Because, the internal socialization, process tries to maintain and preserve their tribal cultural heritage, where as the outside contact tries to bring changes in the same. Inspite of all these changes, the family plays very significant role in maintaining the tribal culture.

Tribal family also provides education to its members. As a social cultural agency it fulfills its role. Excepting a few tribal groups viz Nagas, Gonds, Bhotias, Munda, Oraon, Maria-Murias etc. where boys and girls are imparted education through the institution of 'ghotuls'. In all other tribal societies family plays role of providing education to its members. Besides the socialization, mental and cultural development of the members take place in the family.

Characteristics of Tribal Families

The characteristics of the tribal families can be viewed on the following basis:

(1) membership of the family and nature of family members.

(2) Form of marriage.

(3) Family authority and descent.

On the basis of membership or number of members, the tribal families can be classified into the following-

(a) Nuclear family.

(b) Family of procreation, and

(c) Joint family.

(a) Nuclear family

This type of family consists of parents (husband and wife) and their unmarried children. This is the smallest and most probably the earliest family unit. Compared to joint family its composition is easy and this small units is responsible for looking after the needs of its members. Among the 'Ho' tribe the family and the clan (kabila) were dependent on each other, but there is clear cut division of work between family and clan. For example, clan or 'kili' was collectively responsible for the collection of forest produce and leter on, it distributed the same (equally) among the families. Similarly, they collectively workship the village deites, but each family cooperated in a separate way. Yet for the personal needs of its members, the family was deemed responsible. If a person fells sick, all the family membes took care of sick person. Now a days because of dowry and high bride price, the girls among 'Ho' tribe remain unmarried for a longer period and unmarried girls remain with the parents.

(b) Family of Procreation

Though the basis of formation of this type of family is marriage, but some other relatives also stay with the family. In India, among kharia tribe, this type of family is specially found.

(c) Joint Family

This type of family has been basically the characteristics of traditional Hindu society and many tribal groups in India also seem to have adopted this form of family. Where as in the nuclear family there is network of primary kins, in the joint family, besides primary kins, there is presence of secondary kin members, thus there is a wider network of kinship members.

On the basis of family authority, descent and residence, family system among Indian tribes can be divided into 2 categories.

(a) Matrilineal Family

Such type of family is also termed as matriarchal family as authority in such family rests with the mother. These are also known as mother centred family. This is perhaps the oldest form of family, in which children are known through mother and descent is traced from mother's side. In this family five relationships are found: mother-son, mother, daughter, brother-brother, sister-sister, brother-sister. In such type of family women have exclusive rights over family property and on all sorts of economic activities and social matters. Husband, after marriage, leaves his parental place and goes to his wife's home to live on a permanent basis and his wife's home is the basis of his family. Mother plays more important role in looking after the children. In other important tasks, the role played by mother's brother (maternal uncle) is more important than that of the husband (father). Even on religious matters women play key role. Matrilineal type of families in India are fond in the following three areas:

1. Khasi and Garo tribes residing at the southern coast of Bhramaputra.

2. Nayars of kerala and
3. Kadar, Eurula and Pulayan tribes of south India.

Khasi

Khasi are matriarchal and matrilineal. These people are matrilocal also. Among these pople, having no daughter into family is considered as inauspicious. If a girl is not born in the family, there is a custom of adopting her as customarily she is the only legal heir to the family property. Thus, property is inherited by daughter from the mother. The youngest daughter usually performs family's religious activities and she gets major share is family property. Daughters automatically inherit mother's property. A man, before marriage gives his earning to his mother and after marriage, to his wife. Thus, women enjoy control over property.

Garo

Garo tribe is another interesting example of matriarchal family. women enjoy rights over family property. Yet all women do not have equal rights over property matters. Though wife (mother) is the owner of family, yet she gets this ownership through her husband. Women enjoy property rights so long as her husband is alive. As one could find among Garo Nokroms where the mother-in-law married son-in-law (after her daughter's death) so that the property remains intact and no other person could inherit the family property. Among these Garos if a woman becomes widow, her property rights are in danger. Therefore, she marries her own-son-in-law within a specified period, after which the property could easily be inherited by the daughter in the family. Thus, a widow is devoid of property rights if she does not marry again within a specific period. This second marriage at times used to take place irrespective of her age specially with a view to retain the property. The Nayars of south India, were once practicing matriarchal system. The girl after marriage did not accompany her husband to the new home. Rather, she stayed back into the family of orientation and her husband used to visit her from time to time. The maternal uncle (mama) had more important position in the family than the father. The children in the family were more responsible to the maternal uncle than the father. He (mama) looked after the children. All property matters were dicided by the mother. Thus, in matriarchal societies, all property rights, descent and inheritance etc were from mother to the daughter. But after coming in contact with the outside world their traditional family system is on a decline and these people have also started adopting the patriarchal model.

Patriarchal Family

Patriarchal family is also patrilineal and patriclocal. This means in such type of family all the authority and economic rights pass from the husband or father to the son. The descent is traced from male line. After marriage the girl leaves her present's house and stays with her husband. After marriage, the husbands home is considered as her own home. In Patriarchal family, the head of the household is usually a man. His decision on family matters is supreme and all the family members are expected to follow his decision. There are a few tribal societies which have matriarchal system, while in all the remaining societies, there is patriarchal system. In the following pages, some important tribes, from various regions of the country, having patriarchal system, have been briefly discussed.

Kharia Tribe

Reside into hilly region of Orissa. These people strictly follow patriarchal system. The male head of the family enjoys highest authority. The descent is reckoned through him. The girls after marriage, leave the parental home and stay with the husband. Usually these people follow monogamy.

Bhils

Bhils are important patriarchal tribe. Father has extraordinary powers in the family but he does not misuse his powers arbitrarily. These people have a sort of joint family system which varies from Hindu Joint family system. After marriage, all the sons (married ones) instead of staying with the father, make their own house, near to father's house and live there. Father gives his each married son, some land and a few domestic animals. The son, later on does not economically depend on his father. Though they live and eat separately, yet father keeps a watch on all the activities and conduct of his sons. The sons perform all the tasks under their father's guidance and he is a highly respected person in the family. On various festive and ceremonial occasions, father's house is the centre of all the activities. At the time of son's marriage, bride-price is paid by the father. The patriarchal family system is very strong among the Bhils of Rajasthan & Gujrat.

Naga

Among Naga tribe also there is patrilineal system. Like Bhils, these people also make separate dwelling after marriage. Thus, there is system of neo-local residence. Father gives some part of his property to his sons after their marriage. But if he does not like any son, he can debar him from his property (the property which he has earned or inherited. If, there is no male child in the family or if a father dies before the son is born in the family, in such a case, the property goes to his father and after his death, the property is inherited by the youngest son. Now it is purely up to the youngest brother whether he keeps his deceased brother's property himself or distributes among other brothers also. Thus, in Patriarchal family the property is inherited through male line. Women are debarred from the property rights. In husband's house the property is inherited by her sons and in father's house by her brother. Thus, in Patriarchal system, usually the condition of woman has been by and large unfavourable.

Yet in India there are certain tribal groups where inspite of patriarchal system, women play important role in family's economic activities. At times, they seem to play more important role than their men fack. Women among Bhotias are the best example in this regard. The Bhotias are the transhumane residing in the northern parts of Kumaon and Garhwal into Himalayan region. The whole Bhotia economy centres around their women folk. She is expert in making garments and in the preparation of carpet, weaving of shawls, wollen rugs and several wollen garments at home. The men are traders, who usually move from one place to another. Women are the custodians of the family purse and take decision on important economic matters. Thus, by their skill and hard work, these women have been able to attain a respectable position in the Bhotia society. After their coming in contact with the Hindu society, we can observe changes in the position of women. In family and other matters, the outside contact has adversely affected their position. The Bhotia women now, no more enjoy extra-ordinary freedom and economic independence. The introduction of dowry and early marriages have also adversely affected the position of Bhotia women in the family.

On the basis of marriage tribal families can be classified into the following categories.

(a) Monogamous family and

(b) Polygamous family

 (i) Polygneous family

 (ii) Polyandrous family

Monogamous Family

The monogamous family is the most popular form among tribal groups also. In this system a man marries only one woman. This type of family generally consists of husband, wife and children. Among tribals, Kharia Ho, Santhals and Kadars etc are monagamous. Some of the tribals seem to have adopted monogamy owing to economic hardships. 'Ho' tribe follows monogamy because of high bride price, due to which it becomes very difficiult for a man to marry more than one woman. The Gonds of Madhya Pradesh are monogamous but some of the rich Gonds keep second wife also in the family. Among Tangsa tribe, there is a custom of marrying one woman. However, these people marry again, if the first wife dies or if she is barren or ill and is unable to perform agricultural work and other economic activities. This is important to point out that in monogamy, the opportunity of alternative marriage (second marriage) is available to man only.

Polygamous Family

In this type of family system man and woman, (husband and wife) both by custom, have more than one life partner. This type is further subdivided into two i.e. polyandrous family and polygenous family.

Polyandrous Family

In this type of family, a woman has two or more than two husbands. Its earliest instance could be taken from the famous epic Mahabharata where Panchali or Draupadi had five pandavas as her husbands. Among Toda tribe in south India, several brothers have (one) common wife in the family. There are several other Indian tribes, following this customs. Some of these are Khas tribe (Jaunsaris) of Jaunsar Bhavar, Kota, Tiyan and Ladaki Botas etc. In this type of family the biological father of a child may be any one of the husbands, but the legal father is one who performs a special ritual at the time of child's birth, when the first child is born, then the eldest brother among the husbands performs the ritual. Like wise the other brothers perform the ritual in subsequent births. Among some of these tribes, there was custom of female infanticide in the past. The main reason behind was economic hardships and fear of abduction of young girl by neighboring tribes. The prevalence of the practice of female infanticide was seen till nineteenth century when the British government in India banned this practice by law. However, banning of this practice altered the sex ratio in tribal areas, but the custom of polyandry was in existence till recently.

In due course of time changes occur in the form of polyandrous marriage. Because, several brothers, combined together, marry many women instead of one. Thus, instead of polyandrus marriage it could be termed as group marriage. The group marriage came into existence because of wide range of age gap between the brothers. When the eldest brother becomes of marriageable age and marries a woman, the youngest brother sometime is of very tender age or even sometimes he is born after the eldest brother has already married. The woman (eldest brother's wife) at times looked after to new born child (her husband's youngest brother) and treated him as her husband when he became young. The other younger brothers bring new wife to the family when they become young and she automatically becomes wife of all the brothers. Thus, many brothers share many wives, depending on the economic status of the family.

Polyandrous family consists of 2 types:

(a) Fraternal Polyandrous family

(b) Non-fraternal polyandrous family

In fraternal polyandrous family type all the husbands in the family, are siblings (real brothers), where as in the later type (non fraternal polyandrous family), a husband may be a person other than the real brother viz a cousin or a near or a distant relative. Extreme poverty and high bride price system seem to be one of the important factors for this type of marriage. Among Eravans (south India), the economically backward persons and artisan tibes of Malawar followed this practice. There has been a feeling that polyandry brings harmony and unity in the family. It also protected agricultural land from becoming uneconomic. The tribals such as Toda, Badaga and Kurumba who are traditional artisans, prepare iron tools, and wooden utensils and also earthen pots. These people also do some agriculture along with their artisan activities. These people have this feeling that all these activities in the family bring better coordination among the brothers having fraternal polyandrous family. These factors have been responsible for the existance of this type of family in the past. However, outside contact has encouraged them to adopt monogamous family, which has become universal in character.

References

1. Johnson M. Harry, *Sociology: A Systematic Introduction* (1962).
2. Meyer Fortes, *Time and Social Structure and Other Essays* (1970).
3. Duncan Mitchel (ed.) *A Dictionary of Sociology* (1968)
4. *American Anthologists*, Vol IV, No 1 (1953).
5. Lucy Mair, *An Introduction to Social Anthropology* (1972).
6. Radcliffe A.R., Brown, *Structure and Function in Primitive Society* (1971).

❑❑❑

5

Marriage

Like family, marriage is one of the most important primary social institution in human society. Family and marriage, both are the oldest primary institutions. It is difficult to say that between marriage and family which one is the earlier one i.e. which came into existence first. It is assumed that both came into existence simultaneously.

The institution of marriage is usually associated with the sexual gratification and regulation of sexual behaviour. But marriage does not mean only sexual gratification. No doubt, sexual satisfaction is one of the important functions of the family. The fulfillment of sex need is partly biological and partly social and cultural. The marriage in human society is much more than the fulfillment of sexual need. Because sexual need could be fulfilled outside the marital fold also. There are instances of pre-marital and extra-marital sexual relationships in human society. But this did not have general approval and most of the tribal societies also adhered to regulation of sexual behaviour or sexual norms.

The gratification of physical need is essential also from psychological point of view. The desire to become father or mother is always there in the mind of the couple after marriage. The couple wants a child with a view of inherit their property.

Definition of the Term Marriage

According to Lucy Mair, marriage is a union between a man and a woman and children born to the woman are recognized offsprings of both the parents.

In his famous book on History of Human Marriage, Westermarck defined marriage as a relation of one or more men and women which is recognized by custom or law and involves certain rights and duties both in the case of the parties entering the union and in case of children born out of it.

Murdock who studied around 250 societies, considers the basis of marriage as (a) sex (b) economic cooperation and (c) looking after the children.

According to D. N. Majumdar and T. N. Madan, marriage ensures a biological satisfaction (that of sex) and a psychological satisfaction (that of having children) on the individual plane. On the wider collective plane, it ensures a two fold survival, viz, that of the group and its members.

In the words of Gillin and Gillin, marriage is an accepted way of establishing the family of procreation.

W.H.R. Rivers considers marriage as regulating sex relationships in human society.

According to Bogardus marriage is an institution by which men and women enter into family life.

Purpose of Marriage: In short the purpose of marriage can be enumerated into following:

1. Sexual satisfaction.
2. Procreation or having children in the family.
3. Sentimental or psychological or emotional. The desire to become father and mother is inherent among the couple after marriage.
4. Economic purpose : Along with the above functions man in association with other human beings could fulfill his economic needs in a much better way than he could have done alone.
5. Transmission of culture and
6. Religious purpose : Every type of marriage involves at least some kind of religious activity or function. Whether a marriage is a contract or a sacrament, religion is associated in one way or the other.

Besides above purposes there is social purpose also as man becomes a responsible being after marriage. Thus, marriage includes legal, religious and social acceptance.

Thus, in human society, the institution of marriage is associated as a means of fulfillment of multidimensional and different needs.

Even the primitive man had in mind the idea of having a child for reckoning the descent in addition to economic corporation, procreation, looking after children and sexual satisfaction. The institution of marriage in tribal society is as important as in any other civilized society though may be seen at times in a loose form.

In some of the tribal societies marriage is considered important from economic point of view also. They (tribal people) believe that economic life is based on cooperation and division of labour between the two heterogenous sexes. To make economic life smooth they enter into social bond of marriage. The Kadars used to collect the forest produce which was their means of livelihood. This activity was performed by both man and woman in cooperation with each other. The same thing could be found among Andaman islanders, the Bhotias of Himalayas and the Gonds of Central India. Among tribals the contribution of women in family economic activities is always considered very important.

Among the tribals the rituals or the religion has little significance in marriage. It is more of a contract based on corporation and reciprocal needs.

Various forms of marriages are fond among Indian tribes. In several tribal societies marriage is full of simplicity-without any pomp and show.

The like and dislike of the marital partners is given due consideration, though the marriages are usually arranged by the parents. Some of the tribals seems to be very much concerned regarding the adjustment of the marital partners. Its instances could be found among Darlung and Kuki tribes of Assam and other parts of north eastern region. They follow the custom of probationary marriage. In this custom a marital male partner is given permission to go the girls house and live there, provided both of them love each other and wish to enter into marital alliance. Sometimes they (boy and girl) live together for months and if they like each other then they marry, otherwise the boy or his father pays some compensation to the girl or the family and returns back to his home. On the other hand, some tribes have started adopting Hindu customs and practices of marriage, and thereby have started adopting more rigid attitude in this regard. The parental control on the institution is becoming stronger and the freedom given to marital partners has been curtailed to a great extent.

Age at Marriage among Tribes: Among tribal people, generally marriage takes place at a late age, compared to age of marriage prevalent among Hindu castes in rural India. Among Hindus, the marriage takes place at an early age. The instances of child marriage are also found even today in certain parts of northern India. However, there is no uniformity in the age at marriage among these tribal people. There are certain tribal groups adopting the practice of early marriage. The following table indicates the age at marriage among some of the tribes.

Tribes	Age At Marriage	
	Girl	Boy
Garasia	14-18 years	18-24 years
Bhotia	Above 15 yrs	Above 20 years
Tangsa	15-20	25-30
Tharu	10-12	12-14
Bhil	15-20yrs	Above 20 years
Santhal, Munda	9-10	12-13
Naga, Kuki	15-20	18-25 yrs

Thus, by and large the age at marriage among the tribal people has been more, compared to the other civilized Hindu caste groups. This has been more so in case of those groups who live at a little distance from to so called civilized communities, and have to some extent retained their tribal cultural values and practices.

Prohibitions Regarding Marriage

The main purpose of marriage is to regulate and control the sex-relationship. In this context most of the tribal groups follow certain norms as to who one could marry. There are certain relatives, groups or subgroups whom people do not marry. In other words, marriage does not take place among those persons between whom sexual relationship is prohibited or tabooed by custom or law. For example, marriage is prohibited between siblings, within certain relations, members of kinship groups, within a gotra, moiety or fratry etc. such rules are followed not only by the tribal groups, even high caste Hindus and other religious communities follow such rules. A tribal group identifies certain groups or subgroups for marital purposes, within which marriage is considered as an ideal one. More over, among certain tribal groups there are certain relatives among whom marriage is given top priority. For example, in cross cousin or parallel cousin marriages, priority is given by custom to a fixed relationship.

In ancient times, the marriages used to take place even among primary kins (between brothers and sisters) in the royal families of Egypt, Persia, Peru and Hawai islands. This practice was followed with a view to maintain purity of blood. But these are exceptions. By and large the rules of incest taboo (prohibition of sex relationship between near relatives) were strictly followed. Some scholars believe that if incest taboo is not checked then neither there would be culture nor society itself. Philosophers consider violation of incest toboo as a sinful act. According to them such a person should be punished in the society.

In the opinion of sociologists if there is violation of sexual taboo, there will be confusion in human relationship. The confusion in relationship would create confusion in roles. There will be confusion in family authority and relationship. The atmosphere of family would be full of conflict and tension. And it will affect the process of socialization.

Thus, incest taboo is essential for social unity, social organization and social progress. The psychological fear regarding incest is that it would cause insanity and physical deformity. It is believed that some of the tribal groups are decreasing in number because they do not follow the rules of incest. Toda tribe is an example in this regard whose number is constantly on decline.

According to Malinovaski, incest taboo and exogamy are complimentary to each other.

Forten believed that the marriage between brother and sister is not performed because people want to establish relationship with other groups. Actually speaking exogamy takes place simply with a view to check incest taboo.

Endogamy : Opposite to exogamy is endogamy, according to which a person marries within his or her own group or within certain prescribed groups or subgroups for example, in Hindu society caste is an endogamous group and a person marries within his own caste. Likewise, Toda tribe is divided into two groups (fratry) and each group marries within his own fratry. The Bhils of Rajasthan are divided into 2 groups and both are endogamous. Thus, as Rivers stated in an endogamy, a person marries within his own group.

There are certain reasons associated with the emergence of endogamy. These are:

(a) Fear of the new. In one's own group people had large

number of acquaintances and reciprocal relationships that removed their all doubts.

(b) The groups used to have one language, culture, customs and rituals.

(c) Due to illiteracy, myths and superstitions, people avoid marriage outside group or groups. As in Hindu society, there is the system of caste endogamy and even today the orthodox Hindus consider it as inappropriate to marry outside the caste.

(d) Lastly, the religious orthodoxy further supported the notion of endogamy.

Exogamy : To check incest taboo, exogamy came into existence. Exogamy means marrying outside one's own group e.g. Gotra, totem group, village, fratry and moiety etc. the practice of marrying outside these groups is common among most of the tribal groups. Maclenen was the first scholar who first used the term 'exogamy' in Anthropology.

Causes of Exogamy

The following are the reasons responsible for the prevalence of exogamy.

(1) Female infanticide: Due to female infanticide, there was scarcity of girls in the groups that led to the practice of marrying outside the group.

(2) The custom of marriage by capture. According to Spencer exogamy is the gift of warrior tribes. These people used to capture women and later married them. Among the Neurs of Africa there is a saying that they marry among those with whom they fight.

(3) Principle of reciprocity: for social existence tribal groups considered exogamy as essential.

(4) Westermarck in his famous book, *History of Human Marriage* stated that to avoid incest taboo, exogamy came into existence.

(5) Desire for new also led to the prevalence of the practice of exogamy.

Some of the tribal groups seem to adhere strictly the rules regarding exogamy. For example, among Khasi tribe of Assam, marrying within gotra is not only prohibited, rather it is punished.

The Mundas of Chota Nagpur follow the norms of village exogamy. Similarly, the Nagas of Nagaland & Eurulas of southern India, are divided into various groups, subgroups and each of which follow the norms of exogamy. The Santhals are divided into 12 descent groups, known as PATIS. Each descent group is further subdivided into various sub groups which are known as KHUNT. A santhal not only marries outside his descent group, he also marries outside the subgroup (Khunt) to which his mother belongs.

Preferential Marriages

The following are some of the preferential forms of marriages prevalent among some of the tribal group in India—

(1) Parallel cousin marriage: In this type marriage takes place between the children of two brothers or two sisters. This has been the practice among muslims also. Bedouin the nomadic tribe of Arab follow this practice.

(2) Cross cousin marriage: In cross cousin marriage, the marriage between to children of real brother and sister, takes place. This can be further divided into two-

(a) Maternal cross cousin marriage

(b) Paternal cross cousin marriage

When a person marries the daughter of mother's brother i.e. of maternal uncle it is known as maternal cross cousin marriage while the paternal cross cousin marriage takes place with father's sister's daughter. Most of the people among Gond tribe follow this custom of marriage. The Purum kukis of Manipur, the Kharia, Oraon, Kadars, Bhils and Mikirs of Assam and several other tribes follow the custom of cross cousin marriage. Cross-cousin marriage was once very much common among some of the Hindu castes of south India.

(3) Levirate: In levirate a widow used to marry her deceased husband's younger brother or in other words, in levirate a person marries his deceased brother's wife. Levirate is of two types.

(a) Senior levirate and

(b) Junior levirate

In Junior levirate the marriage takes place with deceased younger brother's wife, while in senior levirate marriage takes place with the deceased elder brother's wife.

Reasons for the Prevalence of Levirate

(1) Security after husband's death. The widow gets protection in the family itself.

(2) Looking after the children—Sometimes a widow has children from the previous husband and she cannot move outside the family to marry someone else. In such a situation it is considered ideal to marry someone from within the family itself.

(3) Inheritance of property and for reckoning descent.

(4) In many traditional and tribal societies marriage is an alliance between the two families which does not end even after the death of a marital partner.

The other reasons are-

(5) The dependence of women in the society.

(6) The resemblance of husband (physical) with his brother.

(7) Levirate checks the division of family and avoids tension.

(8) Among some tribal societies and even among lower caste Hindus there is custom of bride price. In levirate there is no problem of bride price.

(9) Better understanding among family members as they live together for a long time.

(10) Tylor believed levirate as the outcome of the obligation between the two families.

Sororate

In sororate a person usually marries his sister-in-law (wife's younger sister)—Sororate may be further divided into two-

(a) Restricted sororate and

(b) Simultaneous sororate

In Restricted sororate, a person after the death of his wife, marries her younger sister and in simultaneous sororate, he marries his sister-in-law even if the wife is alive.

Some Other Forms of Marriage

The following are some of the forms of marriage, which was confined to a few tribal groups in the past. Such a marriage used to take place in rare cases. These forms are no more in existence now. These were-

(a) Marriage between mother-in-law and son-in-law : Such a marriage takes place among Garos, following matriarchy. In such a marriage the mother marries her son-in-law (after her daughter's death) just with a view to retain the family property.

(b) Grandfather-grandaughter marriage: This type was once prevalent among Gonds of central India.

(c) Marriage between widow and widower : The Santhals of Santhal Pargana used to follow this practice.

(d) Marriage between a son and his step mother: This practice was prevalent among Lakher tribe of Lusai hills and among the Sema Nagas of Naga Hills. The purpose was simply to give protection and care to step mother after the father's death.

Ways of Acquiring Mate

Selection of marital partner is very important in marriage. In this context we find that various tribes follow different methods in mate selection. Scholars have described various methods of selecting a marital partner. Indian tribes follow the following methods of mate selection :

(a) Probationary marriage: In this type of marriage the marital partners i.e. the eligible boy and girl who wish to marry each other, are given an opportunity to know and understand each other, know and understand each others' liking and dis likings. If they develop liking for each other and wish to enter into marital alliance then only the marriage takes place. Sometimes the boy who loves a particular girl, is allowed to live in the girl's house. The girl's parents grant the permission. They try to understand nature of each other. The boy lives at girl's house temporarily for sometime. If the boy and girl wish to marry each other, then only the marriage takes place otherwise the boy returns back to his parents house after paying some money, in the form of compensation to the girl's parents. The Kukis of Assam used to follow this practice. It is important to note that inspite of the fact that the girl has lived with the boy for some period, she has right to say 'no; if she does not like the boy, she can refuse for marriage.

(b) Marriage by purchase: This has been a popular practice not only among some of the tribal groups, even several lower caste Hindus also adopted this method. Under this type of marriage a person had to pay some amount (in the form of cash or kind) to the girl's parents for securing a wife. This is usually known as bride price. There are certain economic questions associated with bride-price. It is assumed that the girl's parents avail the price at the time of marriage, for upbringing of their daughter. It is also assumed that the girl is an economic asset to her parents who get some economic compensation in lieu of her marriage. This form of marriage is found among several tribes, outside India also. For example, the 'Kirgis' of central Asia, follow this practice. To avoid the higher amount of bride price they marry their children at an early age because as the age increases, the amount of bride price also increases. Sometimes, part of the bride-price amount is paid to the girl's parents, but she continues to stay with her parents till the whole amount is paid, after which only she is sent to her husband's house. Sometimes, the amount of bride price was so high that the divorce was not at all possible. If the girl left her husband's house and returned back to her parents or runs away with someone, in such a situation also bride price had to be returned back as per custom. The amount of bride price has exorbitantly increased in last few decades. For example, among Bhils of Rajasthan the amount of bride price has increased from few hundred to thousands of rupees.

In India, this practice is followed by Santhals, Ho, Oraon, Kharia, Gond, Khas and Bhils etc. Almost in all the regions of the country we find tribes following the practice of bride price. But at the same time these tribal groups have the custom of "Ghar Jawai' i.e. keeping son-in-law at home. This practice is followed when there is no male child in the family. As there has to be someone to look after the girl's parents during old age and also to look after the family property, the socially accepted practice of 'Ghar Jawai' has been quite common among these tribal groups. The non-tribal societies in India also have the practice of 'Ghar Jawai'. In case of Ghar Jawai, no bride-price is taken at the time of marriage.

Various scholars have criticised this form of marriage (marriage by purchase) . According to them the custom of marriage by purchase adversely affects the position of women in the society. They are treated as commodity which can be purchased and sold. According to Beals and Hoiser the custom of marriage by purchase treats women as chattels which can be purchased and sold. Thus, this custom is opposite to 'dowry system' in Hindu society in which cash and kind is given to boy and his family for securing a husband. Those tribal groups who have come closer to Hindu society, have abandoned bride price and adopted dowry system. The dowry system has further deteriorated the status and position of women in the society. The excessive of dowry has made marriage of girls much more difficult and problematic in certain sections of the Hindu society and the 'dowry' which was unknown to tribal society in India, has come into existence only after culture contact. As a result of which the girl has become unwelcome in the family.

(c) Marriage by capture: In human society this is one of the oldest form of marriage which is based on physical strength. In ancient times, a tribal group used to attack another tribal group and after capturing their women, married them with the youths of its own community. The Bahima tribe of Africa followed this custom of marriage. In India this custom was once popular among Naga, Ho, Bhils, Gonds and several other tribes of Madhya Pradesh, Bihar and Assam regions. 'Ho' tribe followed this practice because of excessive bride price in their society. Because among 'Ho' tribe, high bride price sometimes delays the marriage of girls, therefore (in consultation with parents) the marriage by capture is dramatized. Among Gonds also, the silent consent of the girl's parents is inevitable (in marriage by capture). The same situation exists among Bhotias of Kumaon and Garhwal Himalayas. The marriage by capture takes a dramatic shape. The boy and his friends after capturing the girl take her to 'Rangkuri' (Dormitory) while her parents are already in knowledge of this event well in advance. Among Kharia, Santhal and Birhor tribe when capture was not smooth and easy then in that case, the boy used to put vermilian on the forehead of the girl whom she visited at any public place i.e. any village ceremony, fair etc. By putting vermilian on her forehead, it was customarily presumed that he has authorized to marry her. Ultimately the parents of both the parties i.e. the boy and the girl agreed for the marriage. The following are the factors responsible for marriage by capture.

(a) Unfavourable sex ratio i.e. scarcity of females in the society
(b) High bride price
(c) Inter-tribal rivalry
(d) Difficulty in marriage of girls till late age, owing to one reason or the other.

(d) Marriage by trial : Practically speaking trial marriage is show of boy's (eligible groom) strength (physical powers) and skill in which the most powerful or the winner is eligible to marry the girl. The life of the tribal people is full of hardships. Under such a situation a girl would prefer to marry a boy who is most skilful / powerful and would provide adequate protection and safety to his wife during times of crisis. The most interesting example of trial marriage is found among Bhil tribe of Rajasthan and Gujrat which is known as "gol gadhero'. In 'gol gadhero', the girls of marital age form a ring by tightly clubbing each other's, hand. At the center of the ring a bamboo pole is fixed on the ground containing a coconut, (jaggry) gur and some other eatable items on the top of it. Inside the ring also a few girls stand having sticks in their hands. Now the trial of strength begins. The boys try their luck and strength one by one. One boy enters inside the ring and tries to climb on the pole. He is first of all prevented by the girls who have made the ring. If he breaks the ring enters inside and tries to climb on the pole, he is further prevented by the girls standing inside and is beaten by the sticks, of course, below the belt, on the back. He is forecefully prevented by the girls from climbing on the pole. The boy, as a rule, should not retalitate (not even touch the girls), rather concentrate on climbing the pole. While climbing the pole, the girls further prevent him by pulling his legs. Inspite of all these hurdles, if a boy succeeds in climbing the top of the pole and brings down the packet of eatable items tied on the top of the pole, he is given the choice of selecting any one of the girls present there as his marital partner. Outside, the ring of the girl, the boys also form the ring. Both boys and girls sing songs and dance in the circle and people watch closely from a distance so that the rules of the game are not violated. Thus, in this process the basis of marriage is the attainment of success in the trial. Similarly, among Naga tribe, there was the custom of 'head hunting'. In several other tribes good hunters and warriers were considered as suitable marital partners. Among the 'Aravak' tribe of British Gayna the boy while standing on a running boat had to aim at a fixed target. If he succeeded at aiming the target he was considered as successful marital partner.

(e) Marriage by exchange: In some of the tribal societies, getting a girl for marriage was not an easy task. The condition of exchange marriage is that in both boy and girl (in each family) should be eligible for marriage. Thus, wife is brought from a family where sister is given in marriage this reduces economic burden on both the families. This form is found among reversal tribal groups and among some of the non-tribals also. But among 'Khasi' tribe such a marriage is prohibited. According to Lowie, in exchange marriage, both the sides are free from any sort of economic burden.

(f) Marriage by service: As we have stated above in some of the tribal communities there is a custom of bride price and the boys of poor families find it difficult to pay the amount. Therefore, the poor boys have one alternative left before them. The boy instead of paying money to the girl's father, provides his services to the girls family if permitted he goes to the girls family and lives and works as a servant for a fixed period, he does all sorts of agricultural work and looks after animals etc. This service is in lieu of the bride price (which he was unable to pay). Consequently, the parents of the girl agree to give their daughter to him in marriage. Among Gonds and Baiga tribes, the boys of poor families adhere to this practice. In Gond tribe, such a boy (who serves at girl's family) is known as 'lamnaio' while Baigas call him 'lamsena'. Among Birhors the parents of the girl lend some money to their would be son-in-law who serves at his in law's house for a certain period in lieu of the money untill he returns back the amount. The Khas tribe of Uttaranchal and gujars of Himanchal Pradesh also once upon a time followed this practice.

(g) Marriage by intrusion: In this type of marriage the girl seems to play the leading role. The initiative for marriage is also taken by the girl herself. If a girl develops liking for a particular boy and decides to marry him, she goes to the boy's house along with some eatable items and starts living there. The parents of the boy, may not initially accept the girl and would abuse, tease or taunt her and ask her to go back. She is an unwelcome guest to the family, but she enters the boys house and starts living there. If she bears all the humiliation given to her then ultimately, the members of the boys family accept her for marriage. It is necessary to point out here that the girl faces humiliation but no physical punishment is given to her as per tribal community norms. All efforts, except physical force, are made by the boy's family to turn her out of the house and when she succeeds and continues to sit inside the house, she is finally accepted as wife after performing the marriage rituals.

Santhals call this type of marriage as "nirbolok bapla'. Among Santhals the girl carries with her some eatable items and enters the house of the boy whom she decides to marry. The family members, if do not approve of the proposal, use all sorts of means to turn her out of the house. If all means fail, then they burn some chilly on the fire and all family members come out of the house and close the door. If the girl passes this test and continues to sit inside, then she is ultimately accepted for marriage. The 'kamars' of Madhya Pradesh call this type of marriage as 'paithu'. If a boy and girl are in love with each other and have pre-marital sex relationship resulting into pregnancy, then in such a case 'paithu marriage' takes place. This is particularly so when the boy's parents do not accept to girl as their daughter-in-law. Among Kamars, if an unmarried girl adopts this practice (intrusion), it is not considered bad but the problem arises when a married woman adopts this practice.

(h) Marriage by mutual consent and elopement: Usually, among tribal people marriage takes place at a late age i.e. after attaining the maturity. In marriage the consent of the boy and girl is given significance. In tribal societies having 'dormitories' or ghotuls, the boys and girls meet at the dormitory and decide about the marital partner and later on, inform their parents. The parents, then perform their children's marriage ceremony as per their tribal custom. This is done once the parents of both boy and girl had agreed to the marriage. But at times, the parents do not agree to the wishes of their children or refuse for marriage. In that case the boy and girl run away from home and marry each other. Usually there is silent consent of both the partners in marriage and it takes place after the boy and girl had run away from home, therefore, such a marriage is known as 'marriage by elopement and mutual consent'. This practice is popular among 'Kamars' of Madhya Pradesh, 'Ho' tribe of Bihar and Bhils of Rajasthan. Once the boy and girl had run away from home and got married, the parents under social pressure were bound to give their consent later on. In such a marriage no ritual takes place. However, after culture contact and with the introduction of concept of early marriage and modern legislation has also prevented this type of marriage.

(i) Marriage by adoption: In such type of marriage, a person (usually) who has no male child in the family, first of all adopts a person and later on, marries his daughter to him.

Types of Marriage

There are two types of marriage

(a) Monogamy and

(b) Polygamy

Polygamy is further divided into two types

(a) Polygyny and

(b) Polyandry

Polyandry can be further divided into

(a) Fraternal Polyandry and

(b) Non-fraternal polyandry

Monogamy: Monogamy is a form of marriage in which a man marries one woman at a time i.e. there is one man and one woman as a marital partner. Monogamy is considered to be as the highest and most civilized form of marriage. Yet it existed among the primitive and most backward primitive people. The reasons of its prevalence might have been economic, high bride price and the similar other factors. It appears, that the primitive people accepted monogamy under compulsion becaue basically these people were free to keep more than one woman but at times were forced by natural circumstances and economic hardships to have one woman only. It seems that at a later stage after these peoples contact with the so called more civilized communities, they adopted monogamy as a custom. In India, some of the lower Hindu castes had followed the practice of bride price. Some of the primitive communities who had come in contact with such castes, adopted this practice, thus were forced by circumstances, not to keep more than one wife. In Indian the 'Ho' tribe of central India, has become strictly monogamous. The economic hardships had made them monogamous.

Recently, after India's independence, the strict enforcement of one man and one woman rule, had forced even the affluent tribal groups like Shaukas of Dharchula and Munnshayri, the rich Oraon, the Bhil sardar and Gond raja to go in for monogamy. Reservation policy opened doors for tribal people in the public sector. This policy had made as a condition to enforce monogamy. After India's independence, the customary law for the enforcement of monogamy, gave some relaxation for second marriage (keeping a second wife) to those who did not have male child from the first wife but later on, Hindu personal law was changed and a person, under law, could not have a second wife if the first wife was living. Only, after the death of his first wife, a man could remarry under law.

Polygyny : Under this custom a person keeps more than one wife at a time. Mostly the economically well off people used to keep more than one wife, which was considered to be a status symbol. The traditional agricultural practices (which required multiplicity of hands) also encouraged polygyny. In India polygyny prevailed among Nagas, Gonds, Baigas, Todas, Bhotia, Bhils and other tribals of central India. Contact with the civilized world, spread of education and legislation made tribal people abandon this practice. It is important to point out that during the middle Period even afterwards till the feudal regime was there the polygyny was practised and it was considered as a status symbol among the well off sections of the so called civilized society in India and else where also. In India, one could notice during such regimes the greater the affluence or higher the status and position in the society, more was the number of wifes. A Raja or maharaja used to have several wifes.

Polyandry : Mythological stories and ancient texts in India depict revesal instances of polyandry system. In this system a woman has at least two or more husbands at a time i.e two or more brothers in the family marry a woman. There are reversal instances of polyandry system prevailing among Indian tribes. Some of the tribes who were having this custom of marriage were Tiyan, Toda, Kota, Khas and Ladaki Bota. The polyandry system existed outside India also. This custom was prevalent among American Indians, Eskimos and the tribes of alaskan coast of North America. Besides, polyandry system existed among people of Madagaskar, Malaya strait and Bahuna region of East Africa. The prevalence of the custom of polyandry can be found traditionally among of section of Tibetan community even today.

Type of polyandry- There are two types of polyandry

(a) Fraternal polyandry and

(b) Non-fraternal polyandry

(a) Fraternal polyandry: In fraternal polyandry, only the real brothers have a common wife. If the eldest brother or any of the brothers, brings a wife in the family, she automatically becomes wife of all the brothers. Like Princess Draupadi who was wedded to Arjuna and became wife of all the pandavas.

(b) Non-fraternal polyandry: In non-fraternal polyandry system, a person (a relative or a kinsman) other than the brothers, acts as a husband and is thus included to the marital fold.

Thus, among Khas of Jaunsar Bhavar, and Todas of Nilgiri hills, there was custom of fraternal polyandry. But some times, a person from the same gotra was also included in this fold. As Rivers once stated that at one time the Todas did not fully obey the rules of fraternal polyandry. The tribal people had also laid down their own rules for kinship relationship. As in polyandry, the mother is clearly identified but who is the father of the child, is difficult to ascertain in polyandry. But the tribals had laid down rules and regulations to overcome this problem. For example, among the Todas of Nilgiri hills in south India, when a wife (under polyandry system) became pregnant, a ritual was performed by one of her husbands. The ritual was named as 'Parsurpimi'. Who so ever among the husband performed this ritual, is deemed to be father of the would be child. However, there is no problem or the confusion among the husbands as to who will perform the ritual. The general practice is when the first child is to born, the eldest brother-among the husbands performs the ritual and similarly the age order seniority is followed into subsequent births. The joint aspect of the family remains intact so long as the brothers (husbands) live together. If some brother leaves the joint family and lives else where he no more remains a husband or a father i.e rights of a husband or father of a child are customarily withdrawn. Thus, jointness of family remains intact.

Among Khasas of Jaunsar Bhavar, if any brother brings a wife to the family, she automatically becomes wife of all the brothers. All brothers have joint ownership of women (wives) in the family. Yet the eldest brother, as per custom, has more right on the wives. All the children born in the family consider all male members as their father. Yet for certain identification purposes the children call their father by the occupation he performs. For example, if a person in polyandrous family is engaged in looking after animals, he is known as 'Dangar baba' ('Baba; word is used for father while dangar is used for cattles). Similarly, father who looks after goats and sheep is known as 'Bheri baba'. Among these people no person by custom, is allowed to keep a separate wife. He is at liberty to marry a woman but the woman is considered as a common wife of all the brothers. As, we have stated above, the eldest brother enjoys more rights and privileges compared to other brothers. A woman who denies to cohabit with eldest brother (husband), can be deserted from the family fold. If any woman, having a child, is brought to the family as wife, the eldest brother is considered as a father of that child. Family property is inherited equally by all the male members into family. Though, all children call all father (baba) yet, the eldest child is considered a son of eldest brother, while the second child belongs to the second brother and like wise the sequence order takes place.

Changes in Tribal Marriage

After culture contact and owing to the spread of education, there has occurred several changes in the institution of marriage of the tribal people. Some of these changes are as follow:

(1) Change in age at marriage : After culture contact, the immediate impact was declining trend in the age of marriage. However with the spread of education among tribals increasing dowry demand etc. have further increased the marital age.

(2) The freedom of girl and boy in selecting the marital partner has been curtailed such freedom which tribal society had enjoyed in the past, is now looked down upon. Specially in the rural areas it is treated as an usual affair.

(3) Increasing role of parents. At the lower rungs of the tribal society it is purely a parental affair. They decide the marriage of their son or daughter without consulting them.

(4) There is decrease in the bride prize system in the tribal society now. This is also the impact of Hindu society and other than non-tribal groups. However, it still exists among certain poorest sections of the tribal society.

(5) Increasing dowry system. Dowry system, an evil which exists among non-tribal societies, has not spared tribal people also, even several tribal people marry their daughters at a late age because they are unable to make dowry arrangement because of poverty. Unfortunate aspect of this evil custom is that the dowry has increased with the increase in education and attainment of a status position in the occupational field. In many tribal communities the dowry amount is predetermined on the education and status position of the boy.

(6) Couples living as husband and wife before marriage: In some tribal areas (especially in Rajasthan) couples live out of wedlock for several years. It has nothing to do with liberal thinking and has everything to do with rigid customs that make weddings unaffordable. A national weekly magazine, INDIA TODAY (dated 13th sept 2004, pp. 63-63) reported such instances.

"Last March 28 couples in Berrali village in Kotra tehsil of Udaipur distt solemnized their marriage. It was an unusual ceremony. Most of the couples had children. One had six while one bride was visibly pregnant. All the couples had been living as husband and wife with out being legally or socially married. One couple had been cohabiting for 20 years but had not been able to get married. In tribal Rajasthan, especially in the districts of Sirohi and Udaipur this is a fairly common practice. The reason is everything to do with social customs that make weddings too expensive for most people to afford.

In this society the groom spends an average of Rs. 30,000 which is more than his annual income, on his wedding Rs. 10,000 is the normal bride price given to the bride's family who in turn spends about Rs. 7000/- on various ceremonies. The actual cost depends on the number of guests at what is also a community affair. It is mandatory for the groom to invite about 60 of the bride's relatives for feasts that include a meat dish. An additional Rs. 3500 has to be shelled out for gifts for the bride's family apart from paying for the conveyance of a few hundred baratis. The pre marriage ritual is no less expensive. The fixed amount in the form of cash and kind goes to girl's family.

Since most people from the region just about survive on meagre produce from their land, the concept of living in and postponing marriage till the groom could afford it has become prevalent. In fact there have been cases where the marriage of parents are held just a day before their children. Socially such couples are despised and the bride refuses to touch the feet of elders in the groom's family. Legally too it is beset with problems. Where caste panchayats are rigid, lack of certification of live in relationship creates problems in inheritance of land after death. Besides, grooms always live in fear of paying heavy compensation that may run into a lakh if the bride dies before becoming a legal wife".

Thus, the above social evil is the re-emergence of a type of marriage which has been termed as marriage by service, which existed among poorer sections of several tribal communities.

References

1. MacIver and Page, *Society* (1961).
2. *Adivasi*, Publication Divison, Government of India.
3. Kapadia, *Marriage and Family in India* (1962).
4. Sharma Shiv Kumar, Sharma Kamal, *Madhya Pradesh kee Janjatiyan* (1997).
5. Majumdar D.N., *Races and Cultures of India* (1961).
6. Yogesh Atal, *Adivasi Bharat* (1965).
7. Ghurye G.S., *The Scheduled Tribes* (1957).
8. Hasnain Nadeem, *Tribal India Today*.
9. Verma R.C., *Indian Tribes through Ages* (1925).

❑❑❑

6

Kinship

Man is a social creature. He cannot live in isolation. The moment he lives in isolation i.e. away from other human beings, he ceases to be a social being. Man is different from other living creatures. This difference is because of the culture which he has originated for himself. The culture separates him from other living beings. In the absence of culture he would have been just like a beast.

Man lives in proximity with other human beings, most of whom are related to him in one way or the other. The closest to him are those whom we refer as kins. It is said that kinship system refers to a set of persons recognized as relatives either by virtue of blood or by marriage relationship.

In sociology, all blood relationships are known by a technical term, consanguinity. Similarly, all relationships through marriage are called by the term affinity. For example, the relationship between mother and son/ daughter, sister and brother/ Sister, Father and son/ daughter are consanguinal, while relationship between father/ mother-in-law and daughter/son-in-law are affinal. Mostly, it is the social recognition of these relationships that is more important than the actual biological ties.

Thus, kinship refers to a set of persons recognized as relatives either by virtue of a blood relationship or by virtue of a marriage relationship. CHARLES WINICK in dictionary of Anthropology, defined kinship as a system which includes socially recognized relationship based on supposed as well as actual geonological ties.

According to Rivers kinship is social recognition of biological ties.

In different societies, ties of kinship give people claims to land for cultivation, to other kinds of property, to mutual assistance in the pursuit of common interests, to authority over others. Kinship is one of the universals in human society. The organization of kinship is based on the recognition and implementation of relationship derived from descent and marriage. The relationships are constructed and cemented between relatives or kins in an orderly manner. Every individual in every society is a kin and has kin. Kinship is both voluntary and involuntary. It plays an important role in the social and cultural life of the people by defining kin through its nomenclature or terminology by regulating inter relationship or behaviour.

Basic Concepts of Kinship

The basic concepts of kinship are descent and inheritance.

The Principles of Descent

Under this principle a person is socially affiliated with the group of his or her parents. In some societies he is regarded as descendant of both the parents, though usually titles and surnames are passed down from the male line. Such a system is termed bilateral or cognate. The individual belongs simultaneously to several descent groups- those of the two parents, four grand parents and eight great grand parents and so on. This link is limited only by memory or by some conventionally determined cut off points at, say, four or five degrees. There are some cognatic systems where the individual has the right by descent to membership of several cognitically recruited groups, but this right is actualized if the person is able to reside in a particular group's territory.

Types of Descent

A person is usually associated either with the group of father, i.e. patrilineal descent or with the group of mother, i.e,. matrilineal descent. In some societies one finds that child is affiliated to the group of either parent, depending on choice, or to one parent for some purposes (for instance inheritance of property) and to the other parent for other purposes (for instance inheritance of ritual or ceremonial roles). This is called double unilineal descent.

The principle of unilineal descent provides the individual a clear cut identification with a founded social group that existed before he or she was born and has continuity before he or she dies. Members of a descent group have a shared identity. They are known as brothers and sisters, even when no genealogical relationship can be traced.

Descent groups are usually characterized by exogamy i.e. marriage must be with the persons outside the group.

Functions of Descent Groups

(a) Exogamous-all marriages take place usually outside the group.

(b) Unilineal descent groups tends to cooperate in several other senses. The members may often come together for ritual and ceremonial functions, for instance, for collective workship of lineage Gods, Iotems or ancestors.

(c) The descent group has a built-in authority structure, with power normally exercised by senior males, and it may well own corporate property.

(d) An individual's economic rights and responsibilities will be defined by his or her position into descent group.

(e) In many societies, unilineal descent groups are also jural units, internally deciding their own disputes, and externally acting as a unified group in relation to other similar groups in the case of feud etc.

Rules of Inheritance

The rules of inheritance tend to coordinate with reckoning of descent in most societies, but not necessarily in a one to one manner. For example, certain types of property passes from father to son and other types from mother to daughter. In most parts of India, in the past, immovable property such as land and House, was inherited only by sons. In case there is no son, the property would go to the nearest male relative on fathers side. On the other hand, movable property in the form of cash and ornaments was given to the daughter at the time of her marriage, with a certain amount of jewellary also passing from the mother-in-law to daughter-in-law.

In addition to property of various kinds, rights and obligations, estoric knowledge , crafts and skills etc. pass in accordance with kinship rules, succession to office of chieftainship, kinship, etc and to other social roles and statuses, is also determined by kinship criteria. In such cases, the individual's status is said to be 'ascribed' not achieved. Generally, it is presumed that ascriptive status is a characteristic of primitive, tribal and traditional societies where as 'achieved status' is a characteristic of modern industrial societies. It does not mean that the kinship has become less effective/ significant.

Rules of Residence: This means place of residence after one's marriage. It has great significance in a kinship system. If a husband and wife set up their own separate residence after marriage, it is known as neolocal residence. This is the case of modern, western society. If a wife goes to live with the husband in his parent's home, this type of residence is known as verilocal, patrilocal or patrivirilocal. On the contrary, if the husband moves to live with the wife at her parent's residence, it is termed as matrilocal. If a person lives with mother's brother (mama), such type of residence is known as Avunculocal. However, rules of residence may not harmonize with the rules of 'descent'. Thus, basic kinship concepts like inheritance, descent and residence are important in all societies.

Thus, fundamental relationship between human beings is based on kinship. It has already been stated earlier that kinship relationships arise out of different kinds of bonds that cement people together. They are consanguinal and affinal. While consanguinal originates from birth, the affinal develops through sex and marriage. The relationships based on the consanguinal bond of birth are called 'descent' and relationship between affinal bond of sex and marriage are called alliance. The mutually conditioned interplay between descent and alliance constitutes kinship.

Kinship Categories

Kin or relatives are of several kinds. They may be identified and differentiated on the basis of three major aspects as follows:

1. Primary, Secondary and Tertiary Kins

(a) Primary kins are directly related to each other. They belong to the same nuclear family. There are 8 primary kins including father, mother, brother and sister in the family of orientation and husband, wife, son and daughter in the family of procreation. The relationships are between father-son, father-daugther, mother-son, mother-daughter, husband-wife, brother-brother, brother-sister and sister-sister.

(b) Secondary Kins: Secondary kins are those who are primary kins of other primary kins. But it does not include all primary kins. For example, it excludes those with whom we are directly related, as in the case of primary kins. Our secondary kins are of 33 types. Some of these are father's father (grandfather), father's brother (uncle), mother's mother (name) mother's brother (maternal uncle-mama), brothers wife (sister-in-law), husbànd' father (father-in-law etc). Husband's wife (i.e. co-spouse) would also fall is this category.

(c) Tertiary kins: A tertiary kin is the primary kin of a secondary kin. For example, uncle is secondary kin and uncle's wife (aunt who is uncle's primary kin) is our tertiary kin. Similarly, maternal uncle's wife (maternal aunt-mami) is tertiary kin. There are 151 possible tertiary kins, for example eight great grandparents, eight first cousins, the spouses of all uncles, aunty, nephews, nieces, and many others.

2. Consanguinal and affinal kins

A consanguinal kins is a person who is related through blood, such as father, mother, brother, sister, son and daughter. An affinal kin is one who is related through marriage such as wife, wife's parents etc.

3. Lineal kin and collateral kin

Lineal kin is a person who is related by a direct line of descent such as father, father's father, son and son's son. A collateral kin is a person who is related indirectly through the mediation of another relative such as father's brother, mother's sister, father's sister, mother's brother, father's brother's children, father's sister, mother's sisters' children and so on.

Kinship Terminology

Kinship relations consist of interacting roles that are customarily ascribed to the different statuses of relationship by the people. Every culture includes a set of words, or levels that symbolizes each of its kinship statuses. These levels are called kinship terms, and the whole is called system of kinship (or relationship) terminology of the culture. (Hoebel, EA, *Man in the primitive world,* 1949). According to Leslie white, kinship terminology consists of terms which designate in the first instance, social relationship or persons occupying such relationship sestablished by marriage and parenthood, and which are subsequently extended to relationships formed in other ways.

Kinship terms are used for designating kin of various types.

L.H. Morgan was the pioneer of kinship studies. He called the study of kinship terminology the royal road to the understanding of kinship systems. Being an evolutionist, he was interested in the study of kinship system and for this he utilized kinship terminology as a basis for establishing the past state of the system.

Categories of Kinship Terms

The subject of kinship terminologies has for long played a dominant part in the study of kinship. Morgan coined the following nomenclature for the two broad categories of kinship terms.

(a) Classificatory kinship terminology

(b) Descriptive kinship terminology

(1) Classificatory Kinship Terminology

In classificatory kinship the same kinship term is used for a number of relatives. It is basically through the liberal use of classificatory terms that all societies reduce the number of kinship terms from the thousands that are theoretically distinguishable to a very modest number. Krober has estimated that it is generally practicable in actual usage to employ, on an approximate average, only twenty five kinship terms. According to Murdock a classificatory term can arise only by ignoring one or more fundamental distinctions between relatives which, if given full linguistic recognition, would result in designating them by different denotative terms.

Thus, all systems equate, lump or merge some relatives of different genealogical positions into one single category which is identified by a specific term. There are numerous instances of classificatory terminology among primitive societies, almost in all the parts of the world. For example, komanche Indians equate the father, father's brother, and mother's sister's husband : all under one term 'ap'. similarly, a komanche calls his sons, his brothers son, his wife's sister son and his sister's daughter's husband, all by to same term 'tua'.

The Sema Nagas of Nagaland use 'aja' for mother, father's brother's wife and mother's sister. These people use the term "ami" for father's sister, wife's mother, husbands' mother and husband's brother's wife.

Among Angami Nagas, the term 'she' is used for elder brother, wife's elder sister, husband's elder brother, elder sister's husband elder brother's wife, mother's brother's wife, father's brother's wife. In this system we find that the same term being used for members of opposite sex.

Similarly, among kuki tribe, the term 'Hepu' is used for father's father, mother's father, mother's brother, wife's father, mother's brother's son, wife's brother, brother's son. Thus, the people of three generations, belonging to various age groupings are called by the same term.

The Hindi terms 'samdhi' is used as a classificatory term for father of son in law and daughter in law. Similarly 'samdhin' is used for two relatives i.e. mother of son-in-law and 'daughter-in-law'. Similarly, the English word uncle and cousin are used for a number of relatives.

(2) Particularising or Descriptive Terminology

In this type a kinship term is used for one (singh) individual. Hoebel has called it a 'particularising system' of kinship terms in which each relationship term applies to a particular geneological status and no other. These terms of reference are very specific. For example, the term 'father', mother refer to one person only.

Thus, where as a classificatory terminology groups together two or more kins and assigns each category a single kin term, a descriptive terminology provides a specific kin term for each person.

Thus, almost in all the societies of the world, both classificatory and descriptive system of nomenclature is used and no society can boast of having purely participating (descriptive) system of kinship terminology.

Kin Behaviour

Kin behaviour refers to the kind of relationships that are existing and/ or stipulated between relatives. The family forms the basis of certain primary relationships. The relationships established in the family group are affected by generation, relative age, and by similarities or differences of sex. Those members of the parental generation who are in a position of authority, are entitled to obedience and respect; others may share an intimacy without super or sub-ordination, mutual affection, loyalty and support are expected of brothers and sisters, although often there are restrictions on certain behaviour between brother and sister after marriage.

The patterns of behaviour that prevail between relatives define their relationships and as such are an integral part of the kinship system. With the set of relatives outside the family, there is often a greater variety of behaviour patterns, some seemingly based on the model of intra-family relationships, but others of a diverse nature such as 'Joking' on the one hand and 'avoidance' on the other.

Kin behaviour consists of not merely the show of culturally determined patterns of relation but more importantly the show of socially imperative rights and obligations between kinsmen. This may include certain culture/specific practices such as the giving of gifts, say be a maternal uncle of his nephew or more particularly his niece during the latter's wedding, or mandatory participation in certain functions and rituals such as during the death ceremony of a relative and so on.

Kinship is thus a broad socio-cultural field which comprishes residential patterns, descent principle, marriage practices, kin relations in the forms of terminological specificity, behavioural aspects, compulsory rights and obligations. In all societies and cultures of the world, kinship thus plays a crucial role.

Joking Relationship

Radcliffe-Brown stated joking relationship as a relation between two persons in which one is by custom permitted, and in some instances required to tease or make fun of the other, who in turn is required to take no offence. It is important to distinguish two main varieties. In one the relation is symmetrical, each of the two persons teases or makes fun of the other. In the other variety the relation is asymmetrical, A joke at the expense of B and B accepts the teasing good humourdly but without retaliating; or A teases B as much as he pleases but B in return teases A only a little.

The joking relationship is a peculiar combination of friendliness and antagonism. The behaviour is such that in any other social context it would express and arouse hostility, but it is not meant seriously and must not be taken seriously. Joking relationship is generally between the relatives who come into existence after the martial tie. Examples of joking relationships between relatives by marriage are commonly found among tribal people in Africa, Asia and other parts of the world. Examples of joking relationship between a person and his wife's brother and sister are quite common. But the distinction is made between wife's younger and elder sister. In case of a letter at times the custom of avoidance is observed.

By and large joking relatives are those of a person's own generation, yet a distinction of senerioty within the generation is made. As we have stated above, a persons wife's elder brother or elder sister is treated with respect while the younger ones come in the category of joking relationship. Yet in certain societies this relationship cuts across generation gap and age category. There are instances of joking relationship inspite of large age gaps. For example, among 'Gond' tribe in India there is joking relationship between grand father and grand daughter. Similarly, the grand mother and grand son also tease each other.

Among societies practicing cross-cousin marriages, joking relationship exists between a man and the sons and daughters of his mother's brothers. For example, Ojibwa Indians of North America, the Chinga of Uganda, the tribals of Fiji and new Calendonia etc follow this practice. Thus, the joking relationship is established before marriage and is continued, after marriage, with the brothers and sisters in law.

In some parts of Africa there are joking relationships that have nothing to do with marriage. Instead, there is a joking relationship between two distinct tribes, though such instances are very rare. The two such clans are not connected by inter-marriage. The relationship between them is an alliance involving real friendliness and mutual aid combined with an appearance of hostility.

In the south-eastern Bantu tribes there is assimilation of two kinds of joking relatives the grand father and mother's brother. The grand father and brother-in-law are similarly grouped together.

It is also significant to mention about the one sidedness of the joking relationship. For example, the Cherokee Indians of Northern America have such type of relationship in which a man teases his father's sister's husband. The same custom is found among the mota tribe of the Bank Islands. Both these tribal groups are matrilineal in which mother's brother is respected.

There is a form of alliance of great importance in many societies, in which two persons or groups are connected by exchanging gifts or services. Joking relationship is a special form of alliance. It is at times combined with the custom of avoidance. Thus, in Andaman islands the parents of a man and parents of his wife avoid all contact with each other and do not speak. At the same time it is a custom that they should frequently exchange presents through the medium of the younger married couple. But the exchange of gifts may also exist without either joking or avoidance. At the same time in an alliance by blood-brotherhood there may be joking relationship and mutual teasing.

But the joking relationship is in some ways the exact opposite of a contractual relation. Instead of specific duties to be filled there is privileged disrespect and freedom or even licence, and the only obligation is not to take offence at the disrespect so long as it is kept within certain bonds defined by custom, and not to go beyond those bonds. Any default in the relationship is like a breach of the rules of etiquette.

Thus, teasing and making fun of other persons is of course a common mode of behaviour in any human society.

Avoidance

It is a custom fond in tribal societies, almost all over the world. Besides, the custom is prevalent in traditional societies also. According to this customs, two persons who are related to each other, are supposed to respect each other by following certain prescribed norms. For example, the custom of avoidance is prevalent among Hindus in India. Under this custom there is avoidance between a person's wife and his elder brother, a person's wife and his father, a person and his wife's elder sister. These two persons are not supposed to touch each other (i.e. maintain some distance), the woman partly covers her face, does not call that person by name as a mark of respect, avoid meeting each other when alone, etc.

Similarly, it has been found among many tribes that many sets of kins avoid each other. The avoidance between daughter-in-law and parents-in-law is quite common. Likewise, though less universally and less rigorously, a son-in-law's relations with his parents-in-law are found to be cramped by certain restrictions. Among the tribes of Andaman and Nicobar Islands, the elder brother does not talk to his younger brother's wife. According to Radcliffe-Brown, avoidance is a social fact, and must, therefore, have a social explanation. He says that whenever people come in contact with each other the possibilities of cooperation and conflict are always equally present. But there are certain kin relatives where hostility is regarded as against social norms. The best way to prevent such hostility from becoming manifest is to put restrictions on the growth of intimacy; and hence the kinship usages of avoidance. Freud's psycho-analytical explanation is based on sexual attraction and the need to prevent sexual intimacy between various kinds of relatives.

Avoidance may continue throughout the life of a person as in the case of parent-in-law avoidance, or may be reduced or even erased, say after the birth of a child, or sometimes, after the exchange of gifts.

Another form of avoidance may exist between those related by blood ties also, such as that between father and daughter and that between brother and sister. In such cases, quite obviously the practice of avoidance is an attempt to reduce any form of initimacy that is prohibited due to incest taboo. In other cases, the avoidance serves to repress or suppress any conflict or hostility that is likely to arise between people. The degree of avoidance varies from the practise of not sitting but standing in the presence of an elder person towards whom the avoidance is directed, keeping one's head bent or not meeting the other person eye to eye or even vacating (immediately) the room, immediately or place, where the person to be avoided comes or stays. Individuals who stand in an avoidance relationship do not dine together or smoke from the same pipe. An extreme form of avoidance may also take the form of prohibition to enter the very village where the person to be avoided lives.

'Joking' and 'avoidance' are extreme forms of behaviour which when placed in the opposite ends of a continuum reveal the presence of several tempered forms of behaviour in between them.

Murdock divides the continuum into five segments, as follows-

1. From complete avoidance to marked restrains
2. From respect to moderate reserve
3. From informality to intimacy
4. From formality to privileged joking
5. From obligatory joking to extreme license.

Couvade

It is a custom, especially found among tribals which indicates close relationship, love and mutual respect between husband and wife. Through this custom a husband tries to understand the pains and sufferings to his wife.

Herodotus, the Greek philosopher, was the first to report about the prevalence of couvade (a custom in which the husband observes labour pains and other taboos which are to be imposed on his wife).

According to krober the couvade is a custom under which on the birth of a child the mother got up and resumed her Household duties, while the father went to bed in state and lay in. This piquant habit attracted even more interest when it was found that a good many primitive and backward peoples did more or less the samething in south America, Africa and in India and china. These all believed that child would suffer if they did not observe the custom. However, most of them did not go quite as far as the Basques are said to have done; the father lay in, but so did the mother. Cessation from labour by both parents was demanded for the child's health. In still other tribes, both parents refrained from work and certain foods. But mother refrained more strictly and longer than the father. Among others, the mother alone was under restrictions. Among southern Ute, where the mother lies still on a bed of Hot ashes for thirty days, the father lies with her only for four, and then, after a good meal, must run and hunt as actively as possible for one or several days (Kroeher, *Anthropology*).

Tylor called couvade as a custom where by a husband is required to imitate the processes of pregnancy and parturition and all the behaviour that is enjoined upon his wife for the sake of her child's welfare. Tylor was of the opinion that a society has passed through matriarchal to patriarchal. He collected data from 282 societies. He concluded that matrilineality and matrilocality had preceded Patrilineatity and patrilocality. In this connection he cited the example of couvade, which is not at all practised in matriarchal society, for in women's position was dominant. Nearly 20 societies in the intermediate patri-matrilineality stage adopted the custom of couvade, as men needed to establish their authority over women thus, imitated their habits, but in the patriarchal societies it were only 8 societies which practised couvade and others had already dropped this custom, because it had lost its function and utility.

Among several Indian tribes, there is prevalence of the practice of couvade. Notable among these are 'khas' tribe of Jaunsar Bhavar and Todas of Nilgiri hills. Among khas a husband is supposed to strictly observe certain rules and practices during his wife's pregnancy. He is supposed to avoid certain tasks which his pregnant wife is also not supposed to under take. For example, like wife a husband will not cross river, he will not carry heavy load on his head or cut a tree and act like his wife when she undergoes labour pains. A khas husband observes these restrictions until a child is born. Anthropologists feel that this practice brought love, affection and closeness between husband and wife among tribal people. Famous anthropologist Malinowski, supported this contention.

Teknonymy- According to this custom a person does not call his kin relative directly by name, instead he or she calls him indirectly. There are societies, both primitive as well as civilized which follow this custom. Thus, instead of calling a kin member directly by name, he or she is called through another kin member wHo is generally a child (a person of younger grouping). For example, in traditional Indian society where a woman is forbidden by custom to call her husband by name, she calls him (husband) through her child i.e. if the name of her son is X. then she would call her husband as X's father.

The word teknonymy has been derived from the Greek language and Tylor was first to use this in Anthropological literature. Tylor, on the basis of his work on primitive societies concluded that this custom is related to matriarchal society. In such societies, women enjoyed superior status while the husband was considered as an outsider, having inferior status in the family. Therefore, instead of treating as a primary kin he was treated as a secondary kin. He helped in the procreation and therefore, he was called through the medium of child. Later on, along with the extension of this custom the mother was also called through the child.

Tylor's study included 30 tribes; Among which tribes from south Africa, Western Canada (kro) and India (khas) had special significance. Frazer also found this practice among tribals of Australia, New Guinea, Malaya, China, North, Siberia, Bantu tribes of Africa, and tribes of northern British Columbia etc.

Lowie stated that this custom of teknonymy is used for women also and he disagreed with Tylor's views that the custom originated first in matriarchal society. According to him in different societies different reasons have been responsible for its origin. In certain societies lower social position of women is responsible for its origin (e.g. tribes of Gold coast), where as in certain other societies lower position of men has given rise to this practices. In few other societies lack of terminology (words) have been its cause.

Avunculate : This indicates toward matriarchal societies, pointing out the relationship between maternal uncle and nephew or niece. Maternal uncle has very significant and powerful position in matriarchal society. He controls most of the family affairs. He has greater respect, power and authority and control in the family than the father. Among all the male members in the family, the maternal uncle enjoys maximum respect as well as importance.

Among in khasis, Garos, Nagas and a couple of other societies the maternal uncle enjoys preeminent place in the life and affection of his nephews and nieces as a matter of convention. He has special obligations towards them which exceeds those of their father. The maternal uncle's property is inherited by his nephew.

Among the Haida tribe of North western America there was a custom that a child, after attaining 10 years of age, leaves his father's Home and goes to live with his maternal uncle. He starts living there and after attaining maturity, starts looking after maternal uncle's property. The maternal uncle takes nephew's full responsibility. The nephew automatically has right over the clan (gotra), magic, religion and property of the maternal uncle which he inherits. Among Tribriand Islanders, the similar practice is followed. Among 'Hopi' and 'Juni' tribes, a son stays at his father's House till he is unmarried or he is of marriageable age. After that he leaves for his maternal uncle's place. The maternal uncle performs his marriage and then accepts him as member of his family.

However, the custom of avunculate is not accepted peacefully in all the societies. For example, among Trobiand Islanders, there is often clash between the prevailing practice of avunculate and affection of a father towards his son. At times, he loves his son so much that he would like to give his property/magic etc to his son and thus may cause tension in the relationship between a father and maternal uncle.

It is true that avunculate is the characteristics of matriarchal societies. However, it does not mean that patriarchal societies are completely devoid of this custom. For example, Thonga Tribe of South Africa is patriarchal. A wife (after marriage) goes to her husband's place and live there. The father also has full right over his children. Even then for children, maternal uncle's Home is considered as secondary heaven. Similarly 'komache tribe' which is patriarchal, follows the practice of avunculate.

Amitate

In Amitate, the father's sister plays similar role as in the case of avunculate in matriarchal society. Amitate is the characteristics of patriarchal society. In this custom, special importance is given to father's sister. Rivers has made mention of the prevalence of this custom among several tribal societies. According to him in this custom a person gives more respect to his father's sister than his own mother. All the rituals for a child are performed by father, sister. She performs naming ceremony, selects bride for him and at times performs the death rites. A person has full right over his father's sister's property. Some tribes of south Africa also follow this practice of 'amitate'. They pay very high regards to father's sister.

Among Toda tribe of Nilgiri hills in south India, naming ceremony is performed by father's sister. Thus, a special role, similar to that outlined in case of maternal uncle, for one's father's sister is designated as amitate. This is applicable in patrilineal tribes.

References

1. Redcliffe-Brown, *Structure and Function in Primitive Society* (1952).
2. Lucy Mair, *Introduction to Social Anthropology* (1972).
3. Makhan Jha, *An Introduction to Anthropological Thought* (1983).
4. John Veter, *The Other Cultures* (1964).
5. Fortes M., *Kinship and Social Order* (1970).
6. Iravati Karve, *Kinship Organisation in India* (1953).
7. Nelson Grabner, *Readings in Kinship* (1971).
8. Adrin C. Mayer, *Caste and Kinship in Central India* (1960).
9. Barber B., *Social Stratification* (1957).
10. Bott E., *Family and Social Network* (1957).

❑❑❑

7

Descent, Inheritance and Succession

Human beings have tendency to live in close proximity with each other. The tendency, especially among the people in simple societies, has been to live in close proximity of those with whom they are either related by blood or marriage. Or more specifically, with whom they share property, from whom they inherit property, rights and other obligations etc.

The structural principle of genealogical connection by which attachment to a particular ancestral group is attained, can be designated as descent. Descent rules specify relative importance of maternal or paternal filiation for special purposes, such as inheritances of property or status or kinship rights and obligations.

Kinship is important not merely as a way of defining a range of relatives but as providing a system of exclusive groups or overlapping groups within and between which many significant aspects of social life are organised. These may include not only transmission of property, rank and office but also arrangement of dealing with marriage, defence, offence, religious action and so on. Descent group is one of them. A rule of descent affiliates an individual at birth with particular group of relatives with whom he is especially intimate and from whom he can expect certain kinds of services.

People claim that different physical and personal qualities are derived from descent. Some say blood is derived from the mother, bane from the father. Others state that body is derived from the mother, the spirit or personality from the father. Most cultures link many non-biological phenomena to descent. Nearly all cultures link some legal rights into actual or putative descent.

Descent has been defined by many social scientists as a biological phenomena where as some Anthropologists like Radcliffe-Brown consider it as a jural concept. Rivers pointed out that it refers only to social allocation and has nothing to do with genealogical relationship.

According to Ralph Piddington, the rules of descent are those which regulate the birth right membership of a social group, though such membership might also be acquired in special cases, by adoption.

According to Bohanan, when a child is born to a mated pair, it is related to both of the type of relationship called descent. In the words of Fortes "A descent group is an arrangement of persons that serves to attainment of legitimate social and personal ends". Murdock stated that a descent group refers solely to a cultural principle where by an individual is socially allocated to a specific group of consanguineal kinsmen. Rivers emphasised that the membership of a descent group is inborn.

Thus, descent has several meanings. Biological descent commonly forms a cultural image on which jural descent is based. Jural descent comprehends both inheritance of property and succession to social positions.

Jural descent is a mechanism by means of which property is handed over from one generation to the next. The system of jural descent selects some criteria of biological descent in determining suitability for inheritance and succession.

Corporate groups i.e. continuing property holding groups-based on kinship are recruited by descent and a clear principle of descent is established by the rule that is generally traceable in one line only either through males or through females. This is called the principle of unlineal descent.

Rules of Descent

All societies follow certain rules of descent. The fundamental rules of descent are as follows.

(a) Patrilineal descent : In this type a person is affiliated with a group of kinsmen who are related to him through males only. More specifically when it is based through father, it is known as patrilineal descent. In this type of descent the child adopts the surname of his father.

(b) Matrilineal Descent : In this type a person is affiliated to a group consisting exclusively of relatives through females. In other words, descent is treated through mother and a child takes surname from her.

(c) Bilateral Descent : Bilateral descent associates a person with a group of very close relatives, irrespective of particular geneological connection to him. A few societies trace descent in the male line for some purposes and the female for others. Some Anthropologists have taken a critical view about bilateral descent. For example Leach pointed out that it is meaningless to talk of dsecent unless you are talking of a relationship that follows the consistent direction which we picture as a line, and a line must be traced through parents of one sex only; if people trace their ancestry by quoting, a father in one generation and mother in another, there is no such line.

Rivers made this point clear long ago. In his first published book on *Social Organization* (1924) he remarked that the use of the term 'descent' has little sense and consequently little value in case of the bilateral grouping.

(d) Double Descent : This continues both patrilineal and matrilineal descent by assigning the individual to a group of each type. Sometimes descent may be traced either through the father or through the mother. This is known as double unilineal descent. In such cases two sets of groups-patrilineal and matrilineal coexist in the same society.

According to Lucy Mair in double unilineal descent a society traces descent in the male line for some purposes and female for others. Usually the distinction is that people inherit fixed property in the male and movable property in the female line.

The Andamanese, Pygmies, the paiute of Great Basin and the yaghan of Tierradel fuego, the Lapps of Sweeden and Norway are bilateral in descent. The vedda of Ceylon, the Ramkokamekara of East Central Brazil, Bantu of Central Africa and the Kutchin of Northern Canada, Garo, Khasi and Nayars of India are matrilineal and wito to (WITOTO) of Amazonia, the Gilyak of Siberia, the Miwok of California and many Indian tribes are patrilineal, while several native Australian tribes are characteristicsed by double descent. Evolutionists believe that the matrilineate is primitive, to partilineate intermediate, and bilateral descent is associated with higher civilization. But the ethnographic evidence does not support this contention.

Anthropologists are not entirely unaminuous about the application of the term descent and descent group. Fortes has made a distinction between descent and filiation. According to him the relation of a person with his own parents is filiation and only his relation with his ancestors should be called descent. According to him nearest ancestor is a grand parent.

Leach pointed out that it is meaningless to talk of descent unless one talks of a relationship that follows the consistent direction which is known as a line and a line must be traced through parents of one sex only.

Rivers states that a descent group is a distinct group which recruits its members by birth on a recognized principle, and the only principle that can be recognized is unilineal principle.

The members of a lineage who actually do live in close, every day contact, have been called by Leach the local descent group.

In societies where patrilineal descent is most important structural principle, the unity of lineage is usually a deeply cherished ideal. People remember their lineal ancestry for several generations.

Significance of Descent

The significance of descent is as follows—

(a) The descent group can fulfill political, economic, financial and various other functions.

(b) The rules of descent regulate jural descent, control marriage and help in forming mutual aid societies.

(c) Further, the rules of descent can be of great importance in political activities, supplying groups within which political offices must be transmitted. They may even take over all the functions of government creating a viable polity in the absence of a state.

(d) When a person dies, his status is kept alive by being taken up by an heir and this is selected on the basis of descent rules. Thus, descent group performs the functions of selecting individuals for social positions and roles.

(e) Descent is a connecting link between the external i.e. political and legal aspects and internal or domestic aspects. It is a source of title to membership of the group or to specific jural status, this means in rights over and towards persons and property.

(f) It is the social relations among the persons who are identified with one another in the corporate group. Descent forms the basis of corporate group.

(e) It is most closely connected with the fact that rights over reproductive powers of women are easily regulated by a descent group system. In modern era descent still takes primacy over all the criterion of association and classification of persons in the regulation of social life.

Inheritance : It is a mechanism by which the material wealth of an individual, family or community is passed from one generation to the next. According to Rivers inheritance is the transmission of property. In the words of Piggington, "The rules of inheritance are true which regulate the transmission of property from one generation to the next.

The rules of inheritance are sometimes simplified by the custom of burrying the belongings of dead person. For example, a man, in an Australian tribe, possesses a few weapons, tools, utensils and personal ornaments, things of little value or no permanence. On his death some of them may be destroyed, others may be distributed among his relatives and friends. The pima of Arizona not only kill and eat the livestock and burn personal belongings, but also burn down the householder's hut.

In many tribes, property is distributed on the basis of sex. Since in primitive societies, the generalized form of wealth is lacking and things like money and material possessions belong to different sexes. Division of society on the basis of sex also plays an important part in inheritance. For example, an Aranda woman's tjrunga (a kind of sacred object) is inherited by her brother. A woman's articles of dress or artifacts made and used by woman, such as earthware vessels are transmitted to her daughter and man's weapons to his sons. In many societies widows are not allowed to inherit the husband's property. The reasons may be the low status of women. The Ostyak widow is not given her husband's reindeer but the herds go to man's nearest relatives. In Hopies, houses belong to women and consequently descent is from mother to daughter. In Hidatsa, gardens are transmitted matrilineally and sacred bundles partilineally.

Anthropologists believe that such a mixed type of inheritance is a sign of change in the rules of descent either from maternal to paternal or vice-versa.

Property is also transmitted on the lines of matrilineal and partrilineal. In patrilineal type of inheritance a man's property passes to his son. If property passes to his sister's son, it is matrilineal. Yet among many matrilineal tribes, property is not transmitted to man's sister's son but to the sisters or to his daughters.

In many tribal societies marriage is considered to be a contract between two distinct kin groups. Husband and wife are considered as allies and their property is inherited by the groups of their respective origin.

In Kai, man's heirs are his brothers and maternal uncles. The valuables of woman are given to her brothers and mother's brothers. Among Hopi tribe the property is passed to nearest sib-relatives.

The Rules of Primogeniture and Utimogeniture

The rules of primogeniture i.e. senior right and utimogeniture (junior right) are also observed in the transmission of property. When the property is transmitted to the eldest son or to the eldest daughter it is know or primogeniture and when it is passed to the youngest son or daughter, it is called utimogeniture. Primogeniture rarely occurs in tribal societies. Among vedas property is distributed to all children and daughter's property goes to her husband. Among Kandh of Orissa land is distributed equally among all the sons but headmanship is descended to the eldest son. In Ifugao and maritine chukchi, the eldest child gets the best share of the property. Among Masai, the eldest son of Principal wife inherits the largest share of his father's property. A dying Kikuyu may allot his herds to his sons larger and smaller according to his affection.

Among Baganda, the youngest son remains with the parents and supports them in their old age and after their death automatically becomes the heir of their home and other property. Among Todas of Nilgiri hills buffaloes are divided equally among the brothers but additional animals are shared among eldest and youngest brothers. The youngest daughter among Khasi tribe performs the family rituals and inherits family house and jwellery etc. Among Kirgiz of central Asia, a father seeks to establish his sons as independent stock-breeders and the youngest sons remains heir of the paternal pastures and other possessions.

In many societies heirs are selected by the owners of the property or after the death by the kinsmen or disposed off by the testament at the death of the owner.

Complexity of inheritance rules : Sometimes there is a great complexity of inheritance rules. They are far from rigid. The usual tendency is to emphasize the rules of property distribution between males and females, elder and younger children but such rules are subject to modification on the basis of particular consideration such as the wishes of the owner, availability of an heir of appropriate age, sex and character.

Succession

Many times, inheritance and succession are used as synonyms. Anthroplogists have made distinction between inheritance and succession. According to them inheritance is related to property and wealth, whereas succession is transmission of title or rights. For example, the transmission of kingship from a dead king to his eldest son is succession.

The term succession is usually referred to as transmission of rights in general. A right exists in, and is definable in terms of, recognized social usage. R. Brown defined right as a measure of social control that a person or a collection of persons, has, over the acts of some person or persons, said to be thereby made liable to the performance of a duty. Brown classified rights into three categories.

(a) Rights over a person imposing some duty or duties upon that person. For example, a father may exercise such rights over his sons or a nation over its citizens.

(b) Rights over a person as against the world', is imposing duties on all other persons in respect of that particular person.

(c) Rights over a thing i.e. some object other than a person as against the world, imposing duties on other persons in relation to that thing.

The rights classified under (b) and (c) are fundamentally of the same kind, distinguished only as they relate to persons or to things and are of a different kind from those classified under (a).

For example, among people in simple society, a man has certain rights over his wife. Accordingly, he may require from her to perform certain duties. Among several Australian tribes and else where there is custom of levirate where by a wife after husband's death, marries (his) husband's younger brother. Thus, after the death of a person all his rights over his wife are transferred to his younger brother, or failing such, to an agnate cousin. This is a simple instance of fraternal succession.

In patrilineal succession of the Australian horde the most considerable part of the body of rights of a male person, his status, his personal estate etc are derived by him through his father to the exclusion of his mother and are transferred in turn to his sons to the exclusion of his daughters. Yet there are instances where some rights are transferred through the mother also. For example, in the Kariera tribe a man has certain rights over his mother's horde, over the individual members and over its territory.

In matrilineal succession the greatest part of the body of rights of an individual, over things, over persons, or as member of a corporation, are derived by him through his mother and can not be transmitted to his children but devolve upon his sister's children. For example, among Nayars of Malabar (India), a taravad is an incorporated matrilineal lineage. It includes all living descendents in the female line of an original ancestress. It has therefore, both male and female members, all of whom are children of female members of the group, i.e. a joint family, possessing house and land and right over (the persons of) its members. Oldest male member was incharge. It denies legal rights to a male parent. The lineage group (among Nayars) maintains as continuity and does not admit any outside person to any share in its estate. It retains possession of its own women and claims exclusive rights over the children born to them.

Every where in human society the status of an individual is very largely determined by birth as child of particular father and particular mother. Behind the question of succession, therefore lies the question of what elements of status i.e. what duties and rights are transmitted to the child by father on one hand and mother on the other.

The system of patrilineal or matrilineal succession centres largely around the system of marriage. In an extreme matrilineal society a man has no rights over his own children. The rights remain with mother and her relatives.

Thus, thè power and status of man and woman in society brings us to the rules of succession. Piddington says, "the rules of succession are those regulating the transmission of office or rank." Rivers also defined succession as transmission of rank like inheritance. It may be patrilineal or matrilineal.

In primitive societies women do not generally play any important role in political affairs, the actual administration is carried out by men. It is evident from Iroquois matrilined society. In fact matrilineal succession means that tittle or office is transmitted from males to males through females. Generally, in both patrilineal and matrilineal system, succession to rank or office may pass first to a man's younger brothers and then to sons of brothers according to seniority in the descent. In both the cases, there is sufficient amount of flexibility regarding actual succession. If the successor is incompetent, immature or unpopular, the office or title may be passed over to suitable one. thus, it can be stated that the rules of inheritance or succession are not very rigid. Sometimes the chief himself nominates his successors before he dies, and occasionally it is elected among alternatives.

References

1. A.R. Radcliffe, Brown, *Structure and Functions in Primitive Society* (1971).
2. Ralph Piggington, *An Introduction to Social Anthropology.*
3. Lowie, *Primitive Society* (1920).
4. Bohanan P., *Social Anthropology.*
5. Murdock G.P., *Social Structure* (1949).
6. Goody J., *Kinship.*
7. Lucy Mair, *An Introduction to Social Anthropology* (1972).
8. Fortes M., *Kinship and the Social Order* (1970).
9. Evans-Pritchand, *Social Anthropology* (1951).
10. Firth R.W., (ed.) *Man and Culture* (1957).
11. Rivers, *Social Organization* (1924).
12. Fox Robin, *Kinship and Marriage* (1950).
13. Firth, Hubert and Forge, *Families and their Relatives* (1970).
14. Line Hardt R.G., *Social Anthropology.*

8

Tribal Culture

Culture came into existence along with the origin and growth of the human society. Or in other words it is as old as the human society itself. Man is a unique creature. Among all the living beings, it is only he who has culture. Anthropologist Tylor, long back defined culture as 'that complex whole which includes knowledge, belief, art, morale, law, custom and any other capabilities and habits acquired by man as a member of society". Culture then consists of commonly accepted or expected ideas, attitudes, values and habits of individuals which they learn in connection with social living. The culture is the product of social learning rather than of biological heredity.

Malinowski, the famous British Anthropologist defined culture as an instrumental reality and apparatus for the satisfaction of biological and derived needs.

Culture may be briefly defined as shared learned behaviour. Culture could not exist were man not a social animal. Salir talked about material and non-material aspects of culture. According to Bidney culture is an attribute of human behaviour, not as if it were a dynamic entity capable of acting and developing apart from the organisms who express themselves through it.

In the words of Ralph Piddington "the culture of a people may be defined as the sum total of the material and intellectual equipment whereby they satisfy their biological and social needs and adopt themselves to their environment. Murdock presented the list of such universally accepted facts which are found in every human group of the world.

Hoebel states that culture is the sum total of integrated learned behaviour patterns.which are characteristics of the members of a society and which are therefore not the result of biological inheritance.

Man is the originator of culture and nature has given him this capacity. By birth man has certain mental and physical qualities which makes him capable of constructing the culture. Leslie Whyte has made mention of five such qualities-

(a) Man has the capacity to stand erect.

(b) Capacity to move hands independently. Because of this capacity he has been able to do several important tasks.

(c) Coordination between fingers (specially index figure) and thumb.

(d) Developed mind, and

(e) Language and symbols.

According to Bidney four facts i.e. artifacts, sociofacts, agrofacts and mentifacts could be considered as the characteristics of culture.

The most elaborate attempt to account for the universality of certain aspects of culture is seen in the works of Malinowski. He set forth the cultural response for the fulfillment of the basic needs. His scheme is as follows:

Basic needs	Cultural Responses
1. Metabolism	1. Commissariat
2. Reproduction	2. Kinship
3. Bodily comforts	3. Shelter
4. Safety	4. Protection
5. Movement	5. Activities
6. Growth	6 Training
7. Health	7. Hygiene

Basic human needs, manifest in the cultural activities of men, in turn set up a series of derived needs which means that culture supplies man with derived potentialities, abilities and powers. From derived needs come a series of cultural imperatives, which give form to the institution of a culture. Malinoswki indicates how these are built up.

Imperatives

1. Economics: The cultural apparatus of implements and consumer's goods must be produced, used, maintained and replaced by new production.

2. Social control : Human behaviour, as regards its technical, customary, legal or moral prescription must be codified, regulated in action and sanction.

3. Education : The human material by which every institution is maintained must be renewed, formed, drilled and provided with full knowledge of tribal tradition.

4. Political organisation : Authority with each institution must be defined, equipped with powers and endowed with means of forceful execution of its orders.

Thus, the word culture has been defined in various ways by several scholars. Krober and Kluckhohn made collection of the definitions of culture. Elliot considered life itself as a part of culture. Philosophers like Hegel and Kant correlate culture with morality.

Characteristics of culture: The characteristics of culture may be enumerated as under:

(1) Culture is man made. Herskovits defined culture as man made part of the environment.

(2) Culture is a learned behaviour.

(3) Culture is transmitted from one generation to another.

(4) Culture of every society/human group has its peculiarities. Geographical and social conditions determine the peculiarities. Though certain characteristics are universal in nature, yet there is peculiarity in each one which is unique. For example, cloth making is common every where, yet every place has its own particular characteristics.

(5) Every society has its own culture.

(6) Culture has social qualities.

(7) Culture fulfills man's needs. It has utilitarian value. The element of culture which has lost its utilitarian value, ceases to exist. For example, any habit or custom which was once popular, ceases to exist or abolished in due course of time if it looses its significance or not considered appropriate in changing situations.

(8) Culture has the quality of adaptation, equilibrium and organisation. Culture is not static rather it is dynamic in character. It has quality to adapt with nature/ environment.

(9) Culture is ideal for human group. Every person in the society is expected to behave in accordance with the cultural norms.

(10) Culture is super-individual and super-organic. Culture is superior to man. No individual can claim to have knowledge of all aspects of culture even during his life time. Though man has made culture but no single individual alone can claim to have this credit. Several individuals in cooperation with each other form/ construct culture. Thus, culture is a very broad term and is superior to individual. Man is creator of culture and culture creates several aspects of man's personality. As a matter of fact man and culture, both affect each other. Culture moulds a person in a particular shape.

Thus, as Herskovits said that man is the only culture building animal.

Paradoxes in Culture

Herskovits said that for understanding the basic nature of culture it is essential to understand some of the paradoxes in it. These are as follows:

(1) Culture is universal in man's experience, yet each local or regional manifestation of it is unique.

(2) Culture is stable, yet is also dynamic, and manifests continuous and constant change.

(3) Culture fills and largely determines the course of our lives yet rarely remains in our conscious thought.

Culture and Society

A culture is the way of life of the people, while a society is an organised, interacting aggregate of individuals who follow a given way of life. In simpler terms a society is composed of people, the way they behave is their culture.

Structure of Culture

Man created culture with a view to create his various types of needs. As society passed from simple to complex stage, man's needs also increased and there was greater complexity. In structure of culture also there occurred changes in due course of time. For example, the primitive man with limited or rather only basic needs had limited tools and implements.

The Elements of Culture

Wissler made mention of two elements of culture i.e. culture element and culture complex.

Culture Trait : It is the smallest identifiable unit in a given culture i.e. a watch, knife, table, fan etc. all these are material parts of culture. These items are the smallest and their parts, if removed, become meaningless. Among non-material aspects of culture trait the example could be a word, an idea, any custom etc., these are smallest identifiable units of a culture.

Characteristics of Culture Trait

(1) Every culture trait has a history regarding its origin, growth etc.

(2) Like culture, culture traits are also dynamic and have a process of diffusion.

(3) Among different cultures there is exchange of culture traits.

(4) Several culture element do not live in existence separately rather they exist in combination with each other.

(5) Culture could not be understood without understanding culture elements.

Culture Complex

When several culture elements are arranged in a meaningful way it makes culture complex, or in other words it is a whole set of culture traits that cluster together in a meaningful inter-relationship. In the words of Ralph Piddington, "the aggregate of traits in a complex may be due to functional association or to what is called adhesion, that is the apparently accidental coexistence of culture traits. Sutherland and Woodward stated that the culture pattern is a grouping of trait complexes into a sort of generalized picture of the culture as a whole.

Culture Area: The area in which similar cultures are found is known as culture area. But in modern times, owing to the rapid means of transport and communication, or type of composite culture is emerging everywhere, even in the remote areas which were once unapproachable.

Culture Growth : In the initial stages the nature of culture was quite simple. It has been stated earlier that the culture which is not dynamic or which is static in character ultimately ceases to exist or disorganized. The various theories of culture growth may be summed up in the following.

(a) Evolutionism : Darwin in his famous book on Origin of Species (1859) talked about origin of species. On a similar basis anthropologists tried to understand evolution of society and culture.

Several evolutionists were of the view that the growth of culture has taken place in a definite order. For example, Morgan talked of 3 stages i.e. savage, barbaric and civilized. Similarly, Morgan gave following stages of the growth of family.

(1) Consanguine family

(2) Group family

(3) Syndasmian family

(4) Patriarchal family and

(5) Monogamous family

He gave following stages of marriage

(a) Prosmiscuity

(b) Group marriage

(c) Polyandry

(d) Polygamy and

(e) Monogamy

Tylor gave two stages of religion

(a) Polytheism and

(b) Monotheism

(b) Diffusionism : Diffusionism plays significant role in the changes of culture and in the theories of cultured change. The elements of culture from the place of its origin diffuse or spread to other parts of a geographic region. Culture contact and acculturation causes diffusionism. Geographical proximity encourages diffusionism. Diffusionism, brings lot of changes in the culture.

Indian Tribes : Transition, Contact and Acculturation

The tribes of India are passing through a stage of transition. Though they were not devoid of contact with the outside world in the past, yet they were not in so close contact as they are now at present. The rapid technological advances, increasing means of transport and communication, population pressure, decreasing means of livelihood in tribal areas etc. were some of the facts responsible for contact.

The tribals who lived in remote and isolated areas were socially and economically behind compared to the ordinary villagers. For example, among Bhotias of Kumaon hills, where as the Johari Bhotias had attained education and entered the sphere of non-tribal and non-traditional occupations, the Bhotias of Byansi and Chaundasi were following their traditional occupations and tribal culture during the decade of forties and fifties.

The tribes of Chhota Nagpur region who started working in coal mines, steel industries and had migrated from their tribal villages to the non-tribal areas, forgot their tribal songs. Because these people developed fascination for filmy songs, their tribal songs got mixed up with filmy songs. Thus, tribal songs lost their originality. What ever might have been the reason the tribals had started coming in contact with the non-tribals and the process of acculturation and assimilation started. The process became more rapid in due course of time. The contact had both-positive as well as negative consequences. It gave rise to several problems also. Various aspects of the tribal culture started decaying (disappearing); the tribal social organization started weakening. Some of the traditional social institutions lost their significance. It was also a fact that the tribal people blindly imitated some of the customs and traditions of the non-tribal societies, leaving aside their own customs and traditions which were far better in all respects. Take for example the institution of marriage. Where dowry and marriage at an early age were something unknown to the tribal world. Usually tribal people used to marry at a late age after attaining adulthood. The boys and girls were given freedom of selecting their marital partners and both had right to divorce, and had a respectable position in the tribal society. The culture contact had negative consequences. However after attaining education these people have again reverted to late marriage but the problem of dowry and curtailment in the freedom of women still remains a social evil. Long ago late professor G.S. Ghurye in his book the Aborigines so called and their Future, had called them as backward Hindus and stated that it will be improper to keep them away from the main stream of Indian culture. These views were presented by Ghurye in a seminar on 'Assimilation versus separation'.

Another view was presented by Verrier Elwin who stated that as far as possible the tribal people should be kept apart from the outside contact. Similarly, J P Mills criticized the Christian missionaries for their role in tribal areas in north eastern region. J.H. Hutton believed that the culture contact will make the tribal people landless agricultural labourers and these people will be Hinduised as a backward class. They will be deprived of their tribal festivals and ceremonies. Hutton himself suggested the idea of self-administered tribal regions. S.C. Roy also had initial suspicions regarding culture contact. But later in his book on 'Oraon Religion and Custom' he appreciated the tribal contact with non-tribals. He stated that the Oraons of Chhota Nagpur not only initiated the customs and rituals of Brahmins, rather they became reformists i.e. they became followers of 'Kabir Panth' and started Tana Bhagat movement.

Navendu Majumdar stated that in India's national democratic structure the integration of tribal people should take place in such a way that they do not get separated from their own traditional culture. This was a question pointed toward non-tribals. But the question arises as to who keeps them away from their own traditional culture. Obviously the answer would be their own backwardness, ignorance and contact.

D. N. Najumdar mentioned three stages (levels) of culture growth among tribal population:

(a) The tribals devoid of Hindu influence owing to their habitations at distant and unapproachable places.

(b) Those tribals who have adopted Hindu manners and customs and to some extent are at par with the lower castes.

(c) The tribals who have accepted Hindu religion or have been converted to christianity have suffered after words, because after conversion lower castes (untouchables) and Christian community also did not treat them at par.

After culture contact where as, on the one hand the tribal people benefitted in several respects, on the other they could not save themselves from the customs and usages of the non-tribal societies which have developed so many evils.

Professor Ghurye considered culture contact as beneficial for the tribals. About the Birhor tribe of Chhota Nagpur and Orissa N. K. Bose wrote that after their contact with neighbouring peasant communities they had become more mobile, started making beautiful ropes from the forest produce and there by made some improvements in their economy. Bose also considered culture contact as beneficial for the tribals.

Several tribals in various parts of the country had tried to adopt Hindu caste system also. For example, Johari Bhotias had tried to prove their Rajput origin, established marital relations with local Rajputs (by marrying their daughters). Several reform movements among some of the tribals were the out come of their adoption of Hindu manners and customs. Tana Bhagat movement among Orans was a sort of proof of their assimilation into Hindu civilization. Now a question which generally arises is that can tribals maintain their own indentity ? Or whether it is feasible ? This issue was raised several times in the past few decades or can we force or should we persuade tribal people to retain their tribal culture. The answer at present seems very simple. The tribal people are as free citizens of this independent country as any other person. They are free to choose their education, occupation, place of habitation, language etc. Nothing can or should be imposed on them. The only thing is that they should/ not blindly or unconsiciously out of ignorance imitate the cultures and customs of their neighbours.

Several evil customs like female infanticide among Kader and Eurula, changing 'gotuls' among Maria and Muria, Head Hunting among Nagas, committing theft among Korwas etc have ceased to exist because of their exposure to the outside world. While writing about Tharus, S. K. Srivastava stated that the Tharus had adopted the practices of Hindus, Muslims and Sikhs. At the same time they have maintained some of their original traditions and customs. But it is also a fact that the tribal people at times have blindly imitated the cultural characteristics of the non-tribals, leaving aside certain good aspects of their own culture.

Even the spread of education has helped in increasing some of the problems. With the increase in education, there is more demand for dowry and women by and large continue to suffer. Still bulk of tribal women are deprived of education. Tribals are imitating the cultures and customs of the neighbouring society. Excepting a few tribals of North Eastern Region who agitated for their own language and developed seperatist tendency, the rest of the tribals incorporated themselves into the neighbouring society. Some of them have forgotten even their own Gods and Goddesses. There are a few tribes in India who are now maintaining their tribal cultural traditions while the bulk of these people have adopted the cultural characteristics of the neighbouring non-tribal societies.

References

1. Kroeber, *Anthopology*.
2. Tylor E.B., *Primitive Culture* (1874).
3. Ralph Piddington, *An Introduction to Social Anthropology*.

4. Hoebel E.A., *Man in the Primitive World* (1958).
5. Dube S.C., *Manav aur Sanskriti* (1960).
6. Benedict Ruth, *Patterns of Culture* (1958).
7. Jacob and Stern, *General Anthropology*.
8. Sutherland and Woodward, *Introductory Sociology* (1948).
9. Majumdar D. N., *Races and Cultures of India*.
10. Ghurye G.S., *The Scheduled Tribes* (1963).
11. Hutton, *Songs of India* (1931).
12. Vidyarthi L.P. and Ray B.K., *Tribal Cultures of India* (1977).

❑❑❑

9

Tribal Art

Tribal art has some unique characteristics. As Herskovits states, that search for beauty is universal in human experience. Its innumerable forms have sprung from the play of the creative imagination, and accord some of the deepest satisfaction known to man. Art is a part of life, not separated from it. Specialisation does exist in simple societies also. People apprecitate the work of their specialists.

According to Herskovits, in its widest sense art is to be thought of as any embellishment of ordinary living that is achieved with competence and has desirable form. In the words of Hoebel (1949) the art of primitive people runs a wide gamut from technical clumsiness to high skill, from child like simplicity to confusing complexity, from naturalism and realism to conventionalized abstraction. A primitive man is essentially a man of nature, deriving all his traits and ways of living from natural phenomena.

To a non-tribal layman most of the objects of tribal art may not look beautiful or artistic. But as Leonard Adam (1949) pointed out for the full appreciation of work of art it should be seen as far as possible in the setting for which it was created.

A writer states that 'primitive art is the most pure, most sincere form of art there can be, partly because it is deeply inspired by religious ideas and spiritual person, and partly because it is entirely unselfconscious as art.

Verrier Elwin states that Indian tribal art is almost entirely functional and cannot be appreciated apart from its utiliterian or social significance. There is very little art for art's sake in tribal village.

Much of the art has a religious or magical purpose, much again has social importance. There is very little that is simply decorative or that aims at the creation of beauty and nothing else.

The worship of idols and images which has been so potent a source of inspiration in other parts of the world, is weak in tribal India. Thus, in tribal societies, art has an important place. Though these people have not undergone the stages of science and technology, it does not undermine the significance of art in their society. Tribals and their art has been highly inspired by their environment and geographical surroundings. Thus, their art need to be viewed from their own perspective because these people live in an altogether different environment and are nearer to the nature. Tribals have love for colours. Instances of painting human body with various colours can be seen among these people even today. Thus, to understand tribal values and their art it is essential to know about their particular socio-cultural environment in which they live. Their environment has been altogether different from that of ours. They have an imaginary (view point) attitude for the outside world

According to E.R. Leach tribal people made use of art on religious occasions, decoration of personal belongings, in the memory of ancestors. Thus, art by tribal people was used both for religious as well as secular purposes. It has been both utilitarian as well as ornamental.

Forms of Tribal Art

The tribal art could be visualised in the following forms:

(1) Plastic art

(2) Graphic art

(3) Music and Dance

(4) Oral literature

D.N. Majumdar mentions prevalence of the above varieties of art among the Indian tribes almost everywhere.

Plastic Art : In this sphere the tribals seem to have been motivated and inspired by supernatural belief and other religious notions. Wooden and stone sculptures, the pictures of Gods and Goddess on the walls are made. Some of the tribals were experts in making statutes of Gods and Goddesses. Verrier Elwin did not emphasize the significance of religion in the art. He observed that the worship of idols and images, which has been so potent a source of inspiration in other parts of the world, is weak in tribal India. In rare cases there is representation of tribal Gods. Some of the important tribes namely Gond, Santhals Bhil and Nagas represent their deities if they make them at all, by stones, lumps of earth, bits of unshaped wood etc.

Terracotta animals and the like are popular with many of the Indian tribes and one can see heaps of terracotta figures in tribal villages under the trees. Images are infact made not to represent the Gods but as offering to the Gods. The Murias of Bastar offer at their shrines attractive little brass images of horses, elephants, human figures as magicians in a swing. Other tribes make offerings of birds, horses, and elephants of clay.

Elwin stated that marriage have inspired less art. Yet there are various examples. The santhals used to decorate their marriage palanquines, meant for bride and groom. These were elaborately carved, having pictures of men and animals, friends embracing each other. The carving contained such pictures that were considered auspicious.

Some of the tribal artists are remarkable painters. They make painting on walls. The saoras of Ganjam are almost obsessed with Gods, ghosts and ancestors. Since they believe that these unseen things may interfere with the course of their lives, they have developed an elaborate system of sacrifices and actions to flatter their vanity. Among such actions is the custom of making painting on the walls of the houses. These are usually made in honour of the dead to drive away disease, to promote crops and on the occasions of festivals etc. Most of the tribal painters work under the inspiration of a dream. There are certain instances where a painter sleeps on the floor of a room during the night hours and whatever the dream he sees, he paints the same on the wall.

The Marias of Baster make splendid wooden pillars for the more important of their dead. These are carved with the things that interested the deceased.

Among the soaras of Koraput and Ganjam one can notice the impact of religion on their art. These people have strong sense of reality and power of unseen world regarding Gods, ghosts and ancestors. These unseen things might interfere with their life, therefore they consider it essential to keep them happy and contented. They consider making painting as one of the ways to keep the Gods, ghosts or the ancestor happy. Besides, there is elaborate system of sacrifies prevailing among these people. Thus, soaras have no art that is not inspired and directed by religion.

Among a number of tribes of eastern region viz Changs, the Konyaks the Phoms the Kalyo kengnyus and Sangtams and others head hunting was the main source of decorative and ornamental work. It was a custom that only a man who had taken a head could carve a human figure in the morung, only he could wear the more splendid type of clothes and ornaments. Bamboo drinking mugs were carved with extra ordinary skill but the central motif was always the human head. However, such art is now gradually dying. The cultural contact is obviously responsible for the decay and disappearance of tribal art. It is unfortunate that much efforts have not been made to preserve the tribal art. However, both tribals and non tribal people are equally responsible for such a state of affair. Yet the governmental support and efforts made by voluntary organizations can play crucial role in this direction. Where ever the artistic skill and talents of the tribal people have got ulititarin and economic value it has been possible to preserve and protect the same. For example, beautiful rugs, kaleens, chutkas and wollen shawls prepared by Bhotias of Central Himalayas have not only flourished, rather it has boosted their economy and has generated employment among these people. Similarly, the tribals of Manipur, Nagaland, Mizoram and other eastern region have exhibited their skill in making garment on their traditional looms. Locally available resources have helped in preserving the tribal handicraft and the artistic skills and talents of the tribal people.

The tribal art could be easily saved provided non-tribal people develop a sympathetic attitude toward that. This could be easily possible if the artistic goods have utilitarian value and asthetic notions. For example, among the women of Bastar region viz Marias and Murias art was used to their beauty. Now, after culture contact, it is almost on way to disappearance.

Artitistic ability of a tribal people had found expression in the ornaments made of metals (gold, silver, etc) wooden articles of day today household needs e.g bamboo mats, mugs, buckets, baskets etc. were used. Besides items of personal use e.g. a variety of hair pins and combs made of bamboo and wood are proudly exhibited on the head. Similarly, the decoration of body with flowers e.g. decoration on hair, waist, neck and forehead was commom among some of the tribals. The tribals of north eastern region used to decorate their head-gears made of feather and fibre. The Orans used to make artistic costumes and ornaments from peacock and bhangara feathers. Similarly, the head-gear of Bison-horn Marias of Baster is a rare artistic piece made of the horn of bison. However, the scarcity of bison horn has made it all the more valuable and important. The tribes of Rajasthan used metallic ornaments made of white copper, bronze and silver. The Nagas were expert in making beautiful wooden drinking mugs and spoons. These people (Nagas) decorated the weapons of war. The hunting weapons like bow and arrow of the Bhils and other central Indians tribes and the spears used by tribes of Manipur and other eastern regions are not only kept as utility implement alone but also as decorative articles of show value.

The Todas of Nilgir hills make beautiful earthern wares which show their skill and expertise. However, now these people are generally forgetting their traditional artistic skill. The Kadars of Cochin make beautiful combs. Similarly, the Marias of central India make beautiful combs. The young boys and girls give these combs to each other as a symbol of love. The exchange of combs between a boy and a girl leads them to a marital knot. In several tribes its is considered essential for a boy to present to her would be wife a comb. Similarly, if some person dies among the kukis, then these people destroy their combs as mark of respect to the dead person while mourning his death and burry the comb of the deceased person along with his dead body.

The tribal art reflects both symbolism and realism. An interesting example can be cited that of Chenchus of Hyderabad. These people while making a picture of tree not only show its branches and leaves, rather they make its roots also. The Ho tribe makes the real pictures of their animals.

Verrier Elwin while writing on tribal art has mentioned that in every tribal village there is a special artist and it is believed that he gets inspiration from the dreams and whatever dream he sees, he expresses that by his painting on a wall. These pictures tell a story or are related to some spirits.

Music and Dance

Music and dance have immense significance in tribal societies. Rather, these (music and dance) are part and parcel of the tribal life, otherwise life does not seem to have been possible in such a remote and isolated human group or would have been quite dull and monotonous. Moreover, in such remote and isolated societies there is no other source of entertainment. As such the tribal people have evolved their own means of entertainment through music and dance. On various occasions especially marriage, child birth and similarly on festive occasions of social and economic nature, at the time of harverting or when crops are ready, when there are good crops, these tribal people, (men, woman and children) assemble at a specific place and organize music programme followed by dance. These people have their own simple musical instruments. Some of the musical instruments of the tribal people are, binai and drums, pipes, flutes, horns, brass plates kartals etc. the Maria Mradang, the Bhil Madal, the Naga hol, the Bhilala hol and nagara used in their dances and other ceremonial occasions are examples of excellent craftmanship. Other musical instruments like the special type of drum and the pungi of the Bhils of Maharashtra too are well known for their musical and artistic value. The songs of the tribal people are by and large related to the local environmental condition like forests, rivers, mountains, hailstorm, snowfall and rainfall etc. According to some Anthropologists who studied tribal songs believed that these songs were full of ideas and were meaningful. Like non-tribals these tribal people also have their special songs for various occasions. In every tribal community there are people who have developed skill in music and who initiate the music and dance programme and all people of the community participate. They were not mere collection (assembling) of words. Arthur furer Heimendorf, Elwin and other Anthropologists studied tribal songs. Edwin and Hiwaley wrote a book entitled as songs of the forest. Arthur wrote a book named as The New Grove in which he wrote about the songs of Oraon tribes. Arthur also wrote about the songs of Munda, Kharia, Santhals and Ho tribes. The tribal songs, music and poetry and art are responsible for the existence of tribal culture.

In the beginning a section of Anthropologists considered tribal songs, drama, poetry as meaningless. Some Anthropologists stated that even the tribal people do not understand there meaning. But later on, the studies conducted by Arthur, Edwin, Heimendorf and others dispelled this doubt.

Oral Literature

The tribal people do not have their own script. Rather it should be emphatically stated that there is no tribe in the world which has its own script. Therefore their songs, poetry, folk lores and folktales etc constitute as part of oral literature, which is transmitted from generation to generation. In oral literaturе there is always danger of decay and loss of originality. There is another danger of culture contact and problem of enculturation. The process of urbanisation and industrialisation had negative impact on tribal songs, music and other literature. The tribal people, are by and large very poor and they come toward the cities and towns in search of work. Radio and cinema has affected their tribal songs also. Some Anthropologists who have studied tribal songs, stated that new tribal songs have the combination of original tribal and films songs. Verrier Elwin seemed to be seriously concerned in this regard. In his book on Tribal Art of Middle India, he mentioned that the golden period of tribal art and culture is already over and now there is nothing much left for collection. That is, outside contact has made these people forget their own culture.

The folktales and folk lores, riddles, drama, myths etc also form part of tribal art and culture. Majumdar observed that in the myths and folk tales heard in the tribal villages of the country is enshrined, in a poetic and imaginative garb, the philosophy of these simple folks. Every tribe has several myths, often contradictory about its origin. In these myths Gods and men live together in an amoral world. But there are other types of myths the role function of which is to compel obedience to some customs by pointing out how so and so was punished by the supernatural powers for such and such offences. The world of vegetation, the animal kingdom and man's dependence on them supply the subject matter for many myths current among Indian tribes.

Folk tales are frankly imaginative and more entertaining than awe inspiring. Infact, their main functions appear to be entertainment. They generally deal with human situations in which suspense, ghosts, heroes and heroines have their due place.

Tribal people have taken interest in dramatic stories and poetry also. Riddles, proverbs and sayings are also common among these people.

No doubt that there is much in tribal life that has to be changed. These changes relate to economic and social life of these people. Some of he customs which have proved harmful need to be abandoned. Similarly, some of the tribal laws are deterrent and harmful and forbidden in civilized societies. But it does not mean that every thing is bad in tribal life, art and culture. Some of these aspects of tribal art and culture have great importance and need to be preserved. But, if left to the tribal people alone it is bound to die and disappear soon. Then the question would arise as how to preserve the tribal art. The only way to preserve the tribal music, art and culture is to make it a part of the educational curricula, that is to introduce art and culture as a subject at the school level. We all know that only left to the Anthropologists, we have lost a large part of the tribal art and culture. Even Anthropologists would have taken more keen interest in these sphere had they been motivated by the governmental organizations and their collections would have been given due recognition.

The Role of Dormitories in the Preservation of Tribal Art and Culture

As we shall discuss in one of the chapters, dormitories are a sort of clubs where mostly young unmarried boys and girls meet during the night hours. And one of the important functions of these dormitories is the preservation of tribal art and culture. There are several tribal groups in India viz. Bhotia, Gonds, Muria etc. who give training of dance and music to the boys and girls in the dormitories. These dormitories impart knowledge of art and music to the tribal children which is considered as a major task for the dormitory. All the men and women participate in the programme of the dormitory on special religious and festive occasions. But there are certain exceptions. For example, the women of Andaman do not participate in the dance. Similarly, Tharu women, participate in music and dance programme only with their male counterparts on special occasions. These women consider themselves superior to their men folk and therefore effort is made to maintain some distance. Tharu dance is very popular.

Several tribal groups had devoted large part of their time in war and conflict which affected their art also. 'War Dance' has immense significance among Konyak Nagas. In ancient times sailor dance presented at the court of Gond king was considered as war dance. Similarly, paiki dance of 'Oraons' is an example of war dance in which a girl is forcefully taken away which is known as a form of marriage by capture.

Animal Dance

Animal Dance is common among the tribals of Andaman. Some of the tribals of Orissa were known for snake dance. Animal dance was once popular among the tribals viz Gonds and Baigas. The Juangs of Orissa in their dance used to initiate the actions of animals. Among some of the tribals of Madhya Pradesh the parriot dance had great significance.

Hunting dance: Various tribes viz Nagas, Kharias and Oraons took special interest in war dance. The hunting dance of Mundas was known as 'japi'.

Agriculture Dance: in agriculture dance all the practices of agriculture, right from cultivation, seeding, ploughing, harrowing and harvesting etc. are initiated.

Religious Dance: Almost all the tribals perform religious dance. Tribal people have this faith that dance is not only for dance sake or for the sake of recreation rather it has a special significance. Bondo and Khond tribe consider religious dance as a part of ritual conduct.

Marriage Dance: Marriage dance is full of joy and happiness. People express their happiness on such occasions and liquor consumption, especially among men folk increases. Therefore, many outsiders have criticized these tribal people. Due to excessive drinking habits several other deviant tendencies increase among these people which adversely affects the sanctity of the marriage dance. Therefore, efforts need to make the dance and music free from liquor consumption.

References

1. Hasnain Nadeem, *Tribal India Today* (1983).
2. Adam, L. *Primitive Art* (1949).
3. Boas Franz, *The Mind of Primitive Man* (1963).
4. Herbert Read, *Art and Society* (1946).
5. Radin Paul, *The World of Primitive Man* (1953).
6. Herskovits, *Man and His Works* (1950).
7. Verrier Elwin, *Tribal Art of Middle India* (1951).

❑❑❑

10

Dormitories in Tribal Societies

For centuries the tribal people lived in the isolated, remote and unapproachable places. These people lived in the midst of nature. The natural and environmental conditions made them evolve their own institutions. Tribal dormitory or youth dormitory is such unique institution, though like other social institution viz marriage, family and kinship this institution is not found among all the tribals. Yet dormitories have existed among several tribes in India, almost in all the parts of the country.

Youth dormitories, were usually a sort of night clubs whose membership was by and large confined to young, unmarried boys and girls. Though in certain cases the married boys and girls were also permitted to participate in some of the activities of the night clubs. Some of the famous Anthropologists had taken keen interest in the study of these dormitories. For example, Malinowski, the famous British Anthropologist gave one of the most exquisite descriptions of such dormitories amongst the Trobriand Islander. The detailed studies of dormitories were also undertaken by some of the Indian anthropologists among the Maria and Muria tribes of central India and other eastern tribes.

D.N. Majunder also gave good account of dormitories among Indian tribes. The term 'dormitory has been designated among tribals by various names in their native dialect. For example, the Bhotias of Kumaon and Garhwal Himalayas who, now prefer to be called as 'Shaukas' or the Thakur Rajputs used the term Rang Bang for these dormitories. Among the Maria and Muria tribe of Baster, the dormitories were named as 'Gotul' the Munda and 'Ho' tribes of Chhota Nagpur designated these as 'Gitiora' . the 'Oraons' named them as 'Jonkerpa' or 'Dhum Kuria'; the Bhuiiya tribe called them 'Dhangarbasa' and Gonds used the term gotul for their dormitories.

There are dormitories among the tribals of southern region also. Notable among these are mannams, muthavans and paliyans.

The dormitors are of the two types:

(a) Bio sexual and

(b) Mono-sexual

In Bio sexual type there is a combined dormitory for both boys and girls where as in mono sexual type the dormitories are separate both for boys and girls.

The Origin of Dormitories Among the Tribals

Anthropologists have given their own assumption regarding the origin of dormitories. Some of these factors may be associated with the geographical and ecological setting of the dormitory building, inter-tribal relationship in the tribal area etc these factors could be enumerated as follows:

(1) Protection from the enemy and beasts: Its example can be seen from among certain Naga and other tribal groups, whose dormitory building is located at such a place from where one could keep vigil on any outsider coming toward the village and thereby provide protection to the whole village.

Some of the tribals keep their weapons inside the dormitory where the training of warfare was provided to the youth. Thus, among certain tribes dormitory was a place where the training for warfare, and hunting was provided by senior members to the new encumbuents.

(2) Place for guests and other visitors: Among several tribals the dormitories acted as places for the stay of guests and other visitors during the night hours.

(3) Source of entertainment: As has been pointed out earlier, the tribals did not have any other source of entertainment except their own music and dance. After eating evening meals the tribal youth (unmarried Boys and girls) used to assemble at the dormitory and sing and dance till late hours.

(4) Prevention of tribal cultural heritage: The tribal people have their own culture and customs. Their culure is of oral nature. No tribal group has its own script. Therefore, the problem of survival and transmission of culture arises. In this sphere also the domitories play very important role. The dormitory is a sort of training ground for its members. Here they learn music, dance and other aspects of culture. In this learning process the old members play more important role. Thus, in the absence of any written script it transmits culture from one generation to another. Like folk songs, other aspects of culture ie folk tales, folk stories, riddles etc are transmitted from one generation to next even in the absence of any written record.

(5) Assistance to the community members/villagers: The members of dormitories provide assistance of its community members on different ceremonial occasions like marriage in the family, harvesting, Building of house, worship and similar other tasks.

(6) Planning and management: Various activities were planned inside the dormitory. For example, hunting activity required careful planning ie how many people will participate in hunting programme, who will stay back. Wht will be the time of departure. Who will lead the hunting party-all this has to be planned. Then only success could be achieved.

(7) Selection of marital partner: This was perhaps the most important task of the dormitory. As we have pointed out earlier the member attending these dormitories were usually young unmarried boys and girls, who used to assemble in the dormitory after their evening meals and select their marital partner. Here it is important to point out that the tribals also believed in claan and sub clans, fratry and Moiety etc. At times some tribals even practised village exogamy also. That is, they like non-tribals, also followed certain norms in the selection of marital partner i.e. rules of endogamy and exogamy, incest taboo etc were at times very strictly followed. That is why there was practice of inviting boys from another villages among the Bhotias of Himalayan region. The usual practice among Bhotias was that boys from one village visited the dormitory of another village and the girls remaind in their own rangbang of their village and were joined by boys of another village. In this activity it is the girls who played crucial and leading role. The girls during evening hours (before sunset) used to assemble at a place where from they could be visible to the boys of another village and waved buntings/flags (or a peace of cloth) which was a mark of invitiation.

The match making not only did take place in village dormitory, rather there were several other occasions and places where dormitory activity were performed. For example inter-village fair of Jauljivi in

Bhotia Valley, which used to take place every year and lasted for about a fortnight. In these fairs also the tribal youth used to put a tent and try to give it a shape of ranbang where match making used to take place.

It is also important to point out that among tribal people, the boys and girls were given liberty to select their marital partner but once the marital partner was selected by boy and girl, the parental role began who performed all marital rituals afterwards. The problem arose only when the gotra, frattry or moiety etc were violated. In this case a boy and girl did not get even the support from the community or friends. Among Bhotias the dormitary played very important role in improving inter-village relationship.

The dormitories also acted as the centres of learning. Among gotuls of Marias and Murias and among Rangbangs of Bhotias in Himalayan region the new members were taught dance and songs. Even sex education was provided to the new entrants in these dormitories.

However, the culture contact has brought some of the adverse effects on the tribals, e.g. early marriage and dowry system etc. the tribal were by and large, known for late marriage. The early marriage thus increased parental interference, which curtailed the freedom of the young unmarried girls and boys. Earlier, (before their contact with the outsiders) the parents did not have any objection to their young unmarried children visiting of the dormitories. But, non-tribals (with whom the tribals came in contact) did not approve of free mixing of boys and girls during the night hours in these domitories. Thus, the tribals who came in contact with the non-tribals put restriction on free mixing of their boys and girls before marriage. But the tribals living in remote and unapproachable places had lesser impact in their society and change reached their society a little late. The Marias and Murias of Batsar region, a remote and isolated area had dormitories which gave complete freedom to their youth. Some of the tribals of remote interior who practised pre-marital and extra-marital sexual relationship, even had instances of premarital child birth which did not cause any problem in the marriage of the unmarried mother. The instances of sexual freedom could be noticed among two types of gotuals among Marias and Murias in Bastar region. These were

(1) Paired gotuls and

(2) Changing gotuls

In paired gotuls the boys and girls had fixed partners in the gotul while in changing type of gotul a gotul member was supposed to change his partner after a specified period. If a girl and boy were found together beyond a specified period they were supposed to be violating the gotuls' norms and were likely to be punished. The assumption behind this was that the girls were the property of the gotul and each gotul male youth had equal right on every girl. Among Marias and Murias even the pairing of a boy and a girl and sexual alliance within gotul could not result into marital alliance.

There were occasions when all the community members were invited to participate in the activities of the dormitory. Most of these were related to songs, Dance and other recreational activities on special festive occasions of the community.

Management of the Dormitory

The tribal people also evolved some method of managing the affairs of the dormitory. These were both formal as well as informal. Mostly in dormitory one person especially the senior one) was appointed as in-charge to manage its affairs and every other member was expected to obey his/her order. At times informal committees of the senior club members were also formed and decision were reached at by consensus. In all feeling of cooperation and oneness prevailed among the members of the dormitory. Though the membership of the dormitory was voluntary yet no village youth, boy or girl dissociate himself or herself from visiting the dormitory and always abided by its rules and regulations. Only on rare occasions, the village youth absented himself from visiting the dormitory. These were physical ailments, extreme poverty or other unusual family circumstances. Among Bhotia tribe, an elderly woman was incharge of the dormitory (rang kuri), and every member obeyed her. She used to give training to the new members, and acquaint them with rules and regulations of the rangbang. Through her, the other senior members trained the new members in dance, songs and other activities in the rangbang. All the differences between club members were amicably resolved, through consensus. However, the non-tribals, especially the village folk never liked the free mixing of boy and girl within the club and considered the tribal people as inferior beings.

After reservation the new avenues for education and employment were opened for the tribal youth. Moreover, a sort of process of sanskritization began in tribal society and the tribals themselves did not approve of their age old association of dormitories which met opposition from all quarters of the society. Thus, by and large, after culture contact, the tribals blindly imitated from the neighbouring non- tribals-their customs and cultures indiscriminately.

Functions of the Dormitories

Dormitories had several functions. As we have stated earlier, that their very existence depended on the several important functions they performed. It started with entertainment by songs and dances, folk lores, folk tales, riddles etc., As we have stated earlier dormitories were instrumental in maintaining community harmony. They provided security to the village and over and above these youth houses retained the tribal cultural heritage.

S.C. Roy a renowned ethnographer who has done pioneering work among certain tribal communities, gave an account of Oran tribes of chhota nagpur. He stated that dormitories among Orans had three fold functions:

(a) It served as effective economic organization for the purpose of food quest.

(b) It provided training to the youth in their social and other duties.

(c) And lastly, as a place for the performance of magico and religious ceremonies designed to bring success in hunting and to augment the procreative powers of youngmen.

Thus, in the past these dormitories had immense significance in tribal societies and they helped in the preservation of tribal culture, provided training to the tribal boys and girls in economic and other sphere. Now in modern times, the tribals are rapidly losing their identity, which is now only for name sake and the age old institution of dormitory has almost lost its indentity.

Decline of Dormitories

So far we have already highlighted the factors responsible for the decline of dormitories in the tribal society. To sum up again the following are the main factors responsible for the decline of dormitory.

(1) Culture contact and the process of enculturation: In the process the tribals imitated culture of those with whom they came in contact and abandaoned their own.

(2) The outsiders in neigbhouring non tribal villages (Hindus and others) did not approve of the free mixing of boys and girls in the dormitories during night hours. They considered it as immoral. This had strong impact on the tribal people.

(3) Impact of social customs of the outsiders : the tribals blindly imitated the customs of the people with whom they came in contact. These were early marriage, increasing parental role, dowry system etc.

(4) Earlier among tribal societies (who generally lived at unapproachable places) the dormitories were the only means of recreation and entertainment. Now these have been replaced by modern means like radio, transistors, tape recorder and television and so on.

(5) Education : The education has also proved as a factor for the decline of dormitories. Earlier the tribal youth, after eating evening meals had no other work to do except going to the dormitories. Now education changed their schedule. Schools were opened in tribal areas the children had to complete their home assignment during evening hours. Besides there were adult literacy centres in the tribal villages. Moreover, the tribal youth migrated to the centres of education with a view to get proper education and to equip themselves for employment. The education changed not only their time schedule rather it changed their values and attitude.

(6) Increasing parental control and changes in tribal social institutions: For example, there was increase of the parental interference in the institution of marriage e.g decline in the age at marriage, marriage as a marked parental/family affair, curtailtment of the freedom of boy and girl in marital selection, and introduction of dowry system.

(7) Impact of migration and urbanization: the migration of tribal people to non-tribal areas in search of employment also seversely affected their social institution of dormitory. Gradually the tribal youth got himself incorporated into modern urban culture. They might have lost their tribal identity, even the surnames (after their coming in contact into Hindu society and their inclination to obtain an appropriate place in the caste hierarchy) but for availing the benefits of reservation, they have retained some aspects of their culture. Thus, if they fully assimilate themselves into so called non-tribal society, there would be nothing left with them to prove their own tribal identity and as may jeopardise their chances of availing the benefits of reservation. Even those rich tribes of Munsiary in Kumaon who prior to the announcement of the reservation policy had managed to prove themselves as to descendents of rajput clan and had managed to prepare false genealogy in its support, had to revert to the tribal fold once the benefit of reservation were announced. For example, the Johari Bhotias who were very rich traders, tried to establish marital alliances with the local rajputs. They prepared their false genealogies to prove their rajput origin. Thus, in 1942 itself, prior to independence the Johari Bhotias had established marital alliances with the local Kumaoni Rajputs. Thus, they succeeded to come at par with rajput clan in caste hierarchy. But later on, in 1957, when reservation was announced for Bhotias, these people again succeeded in switching back to the tribal fold and got the benefit of reservation to the maximum extent compared to other Bhotia sub-groups. Because Johari Bhotias were rich, they could provide best education to their sons and daughters at the urban centres and easily availed the benefits of reservation. The other Bhotia sub clans of Biansi, Chaudansi and Darma valley, still retain their dormitories but only for name sake. And these dormitories function only on festive occasions. The old 'Rang kuri' (building) is no more in existence, only some remnants are there. Some of the more accultarised tribal communities have not only forgotten their traditional dormitories, rather they deny its very existence in their society even in the past. For example, Johari Bhotias do not accept the existence of dormitories in Johar valley. Similarly, it has been found that the 'Ho' tribe which had deep urban contacts, constantly denied the existence of 'gitiora', their institution of dormitory.

The spread of christanity also played a pivotal role in the decline of dormitory. The tribals of central and worth eastern region which had been converted into christianity, were motivated to abandon visiting the dormitories. The result of such a systematic and sustained effort was that the youth dormitories almost disappeared from the villages of Christian tribals.

In tribal villages whenever the dormitories existed, its building is now a neglected place and only the remnants are there. Neither is there any hope of the revival of this age old institution. The tribals also seem quite passimistic about the same.

Change is the law of nature. We cannot think of existence of dormitories as they existed several decades ago. The tribals have now became part and parcel of the greater society and there is no doubt about this fact. But if these night clubs are revived in the tribal area (of course in a modified form) for the preservation of tribal cultural heritage, it will definitely enrich the lot of tribal people, Besides, preservation of tribal cultural heritage, it will bring harmony among the inter village and also improve intervillage relationship.

References

1. Hasnain Nadeem, *Tribal India Today* (1983).
2. Banerji, M, *Primitive Man in India* (1964).
3. Bhomik K. L., *Tribal India: A profile in Indian Ethnology* (1971).
4. Bharitya Adim Jati, Sevak Sangh, *Tribes of India* (1957).
5. Government of India, *Adivasi* (1959).
6. Majumdar D. N., *The Fortunes of Primitive Tribes* (1944).
7. Majundar D. N., *Introduction to Social Anthropology* (1967).
8. Madhya Pradesh, *A Study of Tribal People and Tribal Areas of Madhya Pradesh* (1967).
9. Grigson G. A., *The Maria Gonds* (1938).
10. Nakane, *Chie, Garo and Khasi* (1967).

11

Residence System in Primitive Society

As we have stated earlier, man by very birth has been a unique creature. Though in the beginning was very close to other living beings and dependent on nature to a great extent, he utilized his unique characteristics and potentials. In the beginning when man was living in consumption economy i.e. he could not produce what nature had bestowed on him, he was totally dependent on nature. He could not produce neither did he know about. He only consumed things, that is, he could pluck a fruit from the tree and eat the same but he did not know how to plant a tree. Similarly, he could find a shelter which could provide him relief from nature and natural calamities i.e. he lived in caves and could protect himself from rain, heat and cold but had not learnt the art of constructing a dwelling for himself, or to make clothes to cover his body. Though most powerful and intelligent among all the living creatures, he too was a fearful creature. Because of the fear of wild animals he devised means of making a house on the tree and thus take protection from some of the wild and dreaded animals. Even the earliest man who had developed the art of making a dwelling, used all the natural material. The technology was at its lowest level. For example, as lauriston sharp in 'steel axes Among stone age Australians', writes that among the yir yoront tribes living near Mitchill river, the only weapon was stone axe which was used for cutting wood, for building house, for fishing and similar other very important economic, religious, and social purposes. For 'yir yorant' tribe a stone axe was a thing of pride, it was a sign of masculanity and also a source of livelihood.

Gradually, when man started utilizing his unique characteristics, he started making a shelter for himself. Thus, like in all spheres, residence system under went changes along with the evolution of the society.

The primitive societies are more static in character and strictly try to adhere to the traditional norms. There is severe resistance to change or change takes place very slowly. Changes led to the punishment of the individual members of society (who were found guilty of violation of traditional rules or norms) This punishment would vary from simple to severest depending on the nature of violation of the rules. It could be in the form of physical punishment (beating), ex-communication or even ridicule in case of minor violation of the rules.

Residence is one of the basic necessity of human being. A child automatically gets the shelter of his parents or guardian. Man either constructs his own dwelling or inherits the same as per rules prevailing in his society. In all the societies, primitive or modern, there are some sort of residence rules which determine where people (a person) should live. These rules are part of the conceptual system of a culture which determine the residential stay arrangement of its constituent members i.e. who should live where and with whom ? What obligation a person is supposed to fulfill regarding the residence? This is all decided or predetermined by the rules of residence. They are determined by and characterize the mode of relationship. They are closely related to the system of authority, inheritance and descent. These residence rules and patterns are referred to as residence systems.

Residence as per kinship norms refers to the place where a person lives with his spouse after marriage. The newly wed couple in primitive society is supposed to live somewhere either in their own dwelling or with some close kin from either side i.e. either from wife's side or from the husband or in some cases other relatives bound by kinship norms and traditions of a culture. But in most cases these relatives are confined to the husband or wife's side.

Residence norms involve several considerations regarding property inheritance, the custom of lineage and status of husband or wife in the society. For example, in patriarchal, patrilineal or patri local type it is the husband who inherits property, authority or power where as in the matriarchal type the wife enjoys superior position in terms of property inheritance. Some times in certain matriarchal type of societies the status of husband is very low with no say in decision making matters regarding family property, marriages or religious ceremony in the family etc. His position is just like that of an outsider. Thus, residence system involves several considerations like rules of stay (dwelling), property inheritance, kinship and lineage etc. Broadly speaking, on the basis of these considerations the residential patterns could be classified into the following types.

(1) Patrilocal and matrilocal residences: This is one of the most traditional patterns of classifying residence into patrilocal and matrilocal types. In patrilocal type the newly wed couple stays at the husband's place of birth or in other words at the parental house of the husband (at the residence of husband's father). Among all the types of residences, this is the most popular in patrilocal type. In matrilocal type the residence refers to the place of the birth of the wife. That is, in this case the newely married couple usually stays with her parent's (especially mother's) residence. Now, in present times matrilocal types are rare in existence, yet their examples could be found almost in all the parts of the world. Thus, matrilcoal and patrilocal types of classifying residences is quite old and most popular.

(2) Uxorilocal and virilocal type of residences: According to Leonhard Adam the terms matrilocal and partilocal need to be replaced by another terms 'uxorilocal' and 'virilocal' as suggested by him. In the first case (uxorilocal) the sponsor is wife while in the later case, it is the husband. But this classification did not receive much popularity. As Murdock pointed out that this type of classification at times creates some confusion. For example, according to him, 'virilocal' type does not distinguish between (a) residence with husband's father, (b) residence with husband's another brother and the (c) residence newly established by the husband himself.

(3) Unilocal residence: M. Titieve objected to the classification as suggested by Murdock. According to him the term 'unilocal' type of residence presumes that the married couple moves into the already existing household of one spouse or the other.

Titieve, classified three types of residential patterns.

(a) Unilocal matrilocal residence

(b) Unilocal patrilocal residence, and

(c) Near patri and matrilocal residence. In near patri-matrilocal type, the newly married couple establishes its own new residence near residence of the parents' of either spouse.

Murdock's Classification

Murdock in his classification of residences made a reference of Leonhard's terms 'uxorilocal' and 'virilocal, yet he accepted and retained the same old terms. Thus, the classification given by him is as follows:

(1) Matrilocal

(2) Patrilocal

Besides, these above two types of residences he has given five more types of residential patterns.

(1) Local: This is the type of residence which the pair establishes near the residence of either the husband or of the wife. In this type of residence, the choice is determined by the wealth and status of the family of the parents. That is the parents who are socially and economically better off, attract the newly wed couple to establish the residence near their dwelling

(2) Neolocal: Murdock makes distinction between local and neolocal. He uses the term neolocal for the residence which the newly married pair establishes on its own, independent of the parents of the either. The decision regarding place is purely that of the newly married couple.

(3) Avunculocal residence: In this type, as stated by Murdock, the newly married couple moves to the residence of the grooms' mother's brother. Its best examples are found among the Trobriand islanders.

(4) Matri-patrilocal residence: It is a unique pattern where the couple changes its residence. In this type, the couple at the initial stage lives with the parents of the bride, until a child is born and after the birth of the child, moves to the house of the groom's parents.

According to Murdock's scheme the situation of 'tiv' of Nigeria can be called as 'patri neolocal' because among them when man marries first time, he establishes an unconditionally unilocal virilocal residence, that is, he brings his wife to his mothers' hut which is a part of the cluster of huts in his fathers' home stead. The wife joins the production and consumption unit. She works with the husbands' mother and cooks with her. Except that the men usually eat separately, the group forms commensal unit. When the wife bears a child, her husband builds a separate hut for her which is usually behind that of his mother's hut.

(5) Amita local residence: Murdock used amita local for a pattern in which the newly married couple lives with the husband's father's sister.

Ward, Goodenough and John fisher worked on a tiny island for three years. All three people worked separately, independent of each other. They classified the households of the islands into six major categories. These are as follows: matrilocal, patrilocal, avunculocal, amita local, neolocal etc. Goodenough classified the turkese as matrilocal, but Fisher calls them as Amita local.

Goodenough conducted empirical investigation among the Nankani of New Britain and found a recognized pattern in which though the society is considered as matriarchal yet every man takes his wife to live in the village of his father, so long as the father is alive. After father's death, he is at liberty either to continue to stay at his father's place or to move to join the husband's immediate matriarchal lineage where he has his land rights.

Fisher's contribution of residential pattern of primitive people is also quite significant. He says that the question of sponsorship decides their residence. According to him, every person has a sponsor in the household. For example, if after marriage a person moves with his wife to the father's hut then the residence of this type may be termed as patrilocal or if a person after marriage moves to the residence of the mother (i.e. the place of birth of mother where the mother is residing) then in that case the residence is known as matrilocal. Similarly, if after marriage a person moves with his wife to his (independent) own house, it is known as virilocal residence. Thus, the sponsor, or with whom the person is living decides the type of his residence.

Bohanan, has made some modification on the classification made by Fisher. The classification made by Bohanan is as follows.

(1) Neolocal: This type resembles the modern western type of residence in which the couple resides in an independent house. Its examples could be cited among various tribes all over the world. For example, in Africa, the Hausa of northern Nigeria were neo-virilocal. Tiv of central Nigeria were both neo-virilocal and neo-uxorilocal.

(2) Consanguineolocal: These are of the following types in which any of the consanguine is the sponsor:

(i) Patrilocal: In this type father or the male agnate of ascending generation is the sponsor. Among Indian tribes Oraon, Kharia and some other tribes of central India, and Eskimos of vabrodor etc are examples of patrilocal type.

(ii) Matrilocal: In matrilocal type mother or female utrine kinsman of ascending generation is the sponsor. For example in India Nayars of Malabar were the matrilocal. Similarly the Eskimos of Greenland, Dobu of central Africa were matrilocal after marriage until a child was born, after which they became patrilocal and then they had annual movement from one residence (i.e. patrilocal) to another i.e. (matrilocal) and vice versa.

(iii) Filialocal: In filialocal type son or sons's son used to be a sponsor. That is when a person lives with his son or grandson.

(iv) Filia local: Filia local is the type of residence where the sponsor is daughter or daughter's daughter but filia local residences are rarely found among these people. In these cases the grand parents or parents have no where to live except moving to residence of their children.

(v) Avunculocal residences: In which a person moves to the house of mother's brother (maternal uncle) or when the male uterine kinsman of ascending generation is the sponsor.

(vi) Amita local: In Amita local type of residence father's father's sister or female agnate of ascending generation is the sponsor. For example, among Malenesian tribes a man (husband) did not work and had any responsibility toward his wife and children. On the contrary, his maternal uncle had the responsibility of all the household affairs.

(vii) Fratrilocal type of residence is one in which a brother or male parallel cousin of own generation is the sponsor.

(viii) Sororilocal: In this case the sister or female parallel cousin of own generation is the sponsor. Asanti tribe of Africa and Nao of Nyasasand could be taken as examples of this type.

(ix) Nepotilocal: In this type sister's son or other male uterine kinsman of descending generation was the sponsor.

(x) Heterolocal: In heterolocal type of residence any other consanguine is a sponsor.

(3) Affinolocal : Affinolocal type of residence is one in which an affinal relatives almost invariably is a sponsor. These are of 2 type :

(a) Virilocal and

(b) Uxorilocal

In the former case the husband is the sponsor while in the later case wife acts as sponsor. Thus, Bohanan's classification of primitive residence is the most comprehensive and detailed one compared to all other Anthropologists work who have worked in this field. Though this classification was criticized by several Anthropologists the question of sponsorship and problems related to it may vary from person to person under different circumstances. Inspite of all that, his classification is quite significant. Bohanan has recorded families based on five basic relationships.

(1) Societies in which households are based predominantly on husband wife relationship.

(2) Those based on father-son relationship.

(3) Those based on mother-daughter relationship.

(4) Those based on father-daughter relationship.

(5) Those based on sibling relationship.

In the western world of today the households in the civilized society are predominantly based on husband wife relationship, like wise in several parts of India and outside also tribals have this type of residential pattern. Similarly, matriarchal and patriarchal system existed among tribals in India and else where. However, thė matrilocal families are gradually disappearing. Because of changes in the tribal legal system which has been superceded by the law of the country, the sanctity of the mother right and daughter right has been legally challenged by their counterparts in the family. Similarly, in patrilocal system, where the family is of patrilocal type, the female members are no more deprived of the property rights.

However, the changes in the residential system are taking place along with the changes in the family. In case of tribal people the traditional pattern is being affected by culture contact i.e. The impact of education, mobility of the tribal people, modern science, technology etc. yet traditional outlook by and large persists among the tribals.

References

1. Murdock, *Social Structure* (1949).
2. Bohanan, *Social Anthropology*.
3. Lucy Mair, *Introduction to Social Anthropology* (1972).
4. Haebel, *Man in the Primitive World* (1949).
5. Boas F., Race, *Language and Culture* (1896).

❑❑❑

12

Tribal Economy

From time immemorial human beings have been fulfilling their basic needs of food, clothing and shelter in their own way. In the beginning men were living on the nature's produce. This is known as consumption economy. Initially man did not know how to plant a tree or grow crops, built a house or make clothes to cover the body. He had to depend on nature to meet his basic requirements. He used to collect nuts, beans, roots and fruits from the forest. For shelter and protection he lived in the caves or on the trees. He covered his body from barks or leaves etc to protect himself from cold. Perhaps this was the earliest stage, of human evolution, his economic life was simplest and of crude form.

Gradually, in the further stages of human evolution man acquired skills and knowledge for fulfilling his basic needs. He invented culture which altogether changed his life. In the early stages man had to face lot of difficulties for his survival. He was more and more dependent on nature. However, along with the growth of culture he gradually started winning over or controlling the nature. As we all know the culture which only man among all the living creatures, possesses, made him a unique creature. Man fulfilled his needs within a system which he himself created. He is not only concerned regarding his own needs but equally concerned of the needs of the family.

The economic organization of Indian tribes was also like lot of the tribals living in other parts of the world. Basically, their economy was geared to the satisfaction of basic substantial needs hence they fell into broad category of production-consumption economies. That is they (initially) produced only to the extent they consumed. Neither, there was any possibility of surplus production or preservation nor did they ever think about it. Gradually, man learnt the art of surplus production and distribution of goods, the type of economy developed at a later stage and it is known as production consumption and distribution type.

One important characteristic of contemporary primitive economy was that of the absence of currency, yet they managed things by way of exchange of goods i.e. barter system. Thus, the small scale societies also produced, exchanged and consumed goods yet they had poor economic sense and their calculations regarding production and exchange were unlike that of the modern man. By and large the simple societies (tribal) had subsistence economy.

Characteristics of the Tribal Economic System

The tribal economy has been of the simplest nature. Every man is engaged in some production activity. There is usually absence of organisation, planning and control. Family is the basic unit of production. Outside the family the economy is not found in organized form. Thus, the characteristics of the primitive economic system can be stated as following.

(1) Religion and magic are associated in one way or the other in all types of economic activities. For example, there are examples from several tribal societies in India of worshipping Gods and Goddess during the course of agricultural activities. These people believed that through religion and magic one could attain success in economic sphere.

(2) There is absence of technology. For example, in agricultural sphere the tribals used simplest and minimum tools and implements. It is only after their contact with the outside world that these people have started making use of modern technology. Lauriston Sharp in his famous work on *steel axes for stone age Australians* cited the example of yiryoront tribe in south western coast of Australia. The yiryoronts had invented stone axe which were made of stone head, pliable wood, bark and gum. This stone axe was a sign of masculanity of yiryorant men. The stone axe performed economic activity as these people were engaged in axe cultivation (shifting cultivation). Besides, it was the centre of various social and religious activities. It is only after the portugese navigators landed on Australian sea coast that the steel axe was introduced in the life of the yiryoronts. Though, steel axe was much more stronger and useful, the tribals initially accepted it with

strong resistance. This resistance was more from the older generation of the yiryoronts. This is because these people could not associate their social and religious activities with the steel axe. Yet in economic sphere the introduction of steel axe brought marked improvement in the economic life of yiryoront tribe.

(3) The tendency of accumulation was almost absent among the tribal people. They had very little knowledge of the benefits of exchange.

(4) There was absence of any type of currency to motivate the exchange in tribal society. In the absence of medium of exchange it was difficult to evaluate the goods and tribal people's capacity of evaluation was also very poor.

(5) The tendency of profit was totally absent and the economy was linked with a community feeling, therefore it always avoided any sort of profit motive. Though it was natural that after their contact with the outside world, tendency of profit making, developed among these people.

(6) There was relative absence of regular market, competition and monopoly. The family by and large fulfilled the economic needs by itself. There was absence of specialization. A man performed numerous activities by himself.

(7) In tribal societies there was collectivity and cooperation in economic activities. Individual ownership was less and collective owernship was more. The change was very slow. Gift giving or exchange of gifts was based on inter-group cooperation.

(8) The tribal economy may be termed as subsistence economy.

(9) Owing to the absence of means of transport and communication, it was difficult to carry food articles and other goods from one place to another. As a consequence the economic activities were confined to a particular geographical area.

(10) In Primitive society there was almost absence of regular inventions, innovation and change. By and large there was stability. Usually there was no change in the technique of economic productions.

(11) There was absence of specialization and specialists. Specialization was not the basis of division of labour. Neither efficiency or inefficiency was its basis.

(12) So far as property was concerned both types of property, individual and community property was found.

(13) Labour (work) had special importance in primitive economy. It was the medium of exchange also. Among these people labour was rewarded by the goods produced.

(14) According to modern economic system, there is no relationship between political power and economic control.

Thus, in the past the economic system of primitive tribes was not based on individual profit, rather there was community feeling. Along with their own personal interests people were equally concerned regarding the interests of the community. This specific characteristic of the primitive economy disappeared along with the contact with the outside world and these people have also started initiating all those qualities which are prevalent among the so called civilized societies.

Market

Except some collecting and hunting tribes, the institution of market was present among almost all tribals in one form or the other. It is also a fact that among these people there was absence of regular market, only weekly and fortnightly markets were there. People of several tribal villages used to meet at a central place, on a fixed day and exchanged their commodities. As we have stated earlier, in the absence of currency, there was barter system. Generally, locally available commodities like grains, vegetables, animals, salt, agricultural tools, untensils, clothing and other house hold goods were exchanged. There was no fixed method of evaluation of goods in terms of cost. It depended on the availability of the particular item.

The neighboring local non-tribals also used to visit the market in search of the local products. The non-tribal traders also took interest in some of these markets which were visited by them in search of local products at cheaper rate. They also allowed the local tribals for urban goods which were relatively more refined and made in the modern industries. The tribal people took those factory made articles in exchange of their self made goods at throw away prices.

The tribal markets usually used to run for few hours during the day time. But some markets which were held once or twice a year, at times continued for days. In Baster region such markets were known as Marai and held after the harvesting season. The market presented festive look. Men, women and children all used to visit the market. These markets had served manifold purposes i.e. meeting local friends and relatives, discussing politics, establishing marital alliances, perform music and dance etc.

Now the exclusive tribal markets are no more in existence. Industry-made articles have reached the remote corners of tribal habitations, replacing the hand made articles. Most of the tribals now sell their raw products to outside agency and buy factory made articles. Thus, the tribal markets have now become things of the past where only locally made goods prepared by tribals used to be sold and purchased.

Stages of Economic Development

Indian tribes cannot be grouped into one stage of economy, rather they have lived in different stages of economic development at the same time. It depended on natural and environmental development at the place of habitation, approachability of the area and contact with the outside world etc. Before, we talk of the stages of economic development it seems imperative to dwelve into the classification made by different scholars.

Adam Smith was the first scholar who tried to present the classification of various stages of economic organisation. He classified the economic organization as hunting, pastoralism, agriculture and later on he added handicraft and industry.

Ernest Grose put forward the following stages of economic development-

(a) Collection economy

(b) Cultural nomadic economy

(c) Settled village economy

(d) Town/economy, and

(e) Metropolitan economy

Ehrenfels mentioned the following typology of economic development among the early human societies

(a) Food gathers

(b) Higher hunters

(c) Plant cultivators, and

(d) Nomadic herdsmen

Daryll did not agree with the economic stage, rather he believed in the combinations of economies in the growth of cultures. Gordon Child holds more or less the similar opinion. Herskovits talked of four fold divison of economies viz.

(a) Collection

(b) Hunting

(c) Cultivation, and

(d) Stock raising

Thurnwald presented a scheme of various type of economic life which was as follows–

(a) Homogenous communities of men as hunters and trappers, and women as collectors. The befitting example from among Indian tribes could be the Kadar, the Chenchu, Kharia and Korwa who could be placed in this category.

(b) Homogeneous communities of hunters, trappers and agriculturists e.g. Kamar, Baiga and Birhor would fall in this category.

(c) Graded society of hunters, trappers, agriculturists and artisans. Most of the Indian tribals could be placed in this category.

(d) The herdsmen e.g. the Todas of Nilgiri hills are the most befitting example of this category.

(e) Homogenous hunters and herdsmen. The tribes of India do not fall in this category.

(f) Ethnically stratified cattle breeders and traders. The Bhotias of sub Himalayan region, who were once transhumane, are still the best example of this category, and

(g) socially graded herdsmen with hunting, agriculture and artisan population.

Professor Shyama Charan Dube's Classification

Indian anthropologist, Professor Dube has classified the tribal economy into 3 main stages.

(a) Collection and hunting stage

(b) Animal keeping

(c) Agricultural stage.

(a) Collection and hunting stage: According to Dube at the beginning of this stage people barely met their economic needs while at the second stage there was some scope for exchange after meeting the group needs.

(b) Animal keeping was the second stage of tribal economy.

(c) Agriculture stage: He divided this stage into 2 categories:

(1) The first stage was that of horticulture i.e. people grew plants, which provided them food stuff.

(2) In the second stage came the agriculture. He further sub divided the stage into 2 categories.

(i) Simple agricultural stage

(ii) Developed agricultural stage

Thus, broadly speaking tribes in India could be divided into the following categories on the basis of economy—

(a) Food collection

(b) Animal keeping

(c) Axe cultivation/shifting cultivation and

(d) Settled cultivation

(a) Food collection: People used to collect forest produce, nuts, beans, roots, fruits and leaves, besides fishing and hunting. Thus, people without much hard labour tried to manage their living. They used to move from one place to another in search of food. But their movement was confined to a definite geographical region. Among Indian tribes who could be placed in this category are Birhor tribe of Chhota Nagpur region, Jwangs of Orissa, Korwa of Madhya Pradesh, Kadar of Travancore and Cochin and Katkari tribe of Maharashtra. Some of them had been nomadic also in the past. For example, Birhor could be placed in this category. Some were partly agriculturists and semi-nomadic. The Jwangs of Orissa were omnivorous. They even used to kill poisnous snakes and after removing their poison ate the same. Some of the tribes used to collect and cut the wood and sell the same in nearby locality/market. Koya tribe were meat lovers. They used to collect forest produce and also made bamboo mats. Minikoy tribe of the southern coast in south India were dependent on coconuts and fishing. They were expert in the construction of cannoys and were comparatively a rich tribe.

Among 'Ho' tribe, a youth from the very beginning was trained in hunting. The Dombo tribe of Orissa and their other sub groups viz Audia, Onamia, Mandiri, Meergan, kohara used to eat all animals except those one who were their clan animals (as their gotras are by the name of that particular animal). The Malpantram of Transvancore and Pali and Paniyan tribes of Madura were also known for food collection which was their major occupation.

(b) Animal keeping: The tribals of this category make their living by animal keeping. They are mostly in search of good pastures. Sometimes, they moved from one place of another place along with the change of seasons like the Bhotias of Kumaon of Garhwal Himalayas.

Before, Indo-Chinese conflict, they used to go up to Tibet during winder days in search of good pastures along with their sheep and other animals. These people had large herd of sheeps with long hair and they collected wool and prepared wollen garments. Bhotia women equally contributed to the family economy. They are expert in garment making, preparation of wollen carpets, kaleens, shawls etc. Besides, Bhotias are traders also. But their economy is centred around the herd of sheeps and goats.

The Pankhwals of Pankhi Pradesh in Kashmir were once animal keepers which was their main occupation. They used to keep muels for carrying goods from one place to another. The Todas of Nilgiri hills were buffalo keepers. Till recent past their primary occupation was buffalo keeping and their religious rituals were associated with it. Now along with keeping animals, they have started some agricultural work also.

Thus, no tribe is dependent on one particular traditional occupation in modern times. People have been doing several other things along with their traditional occupation. For example, after reservation several hundred Bhotia youths have entered government jobs and several of them have attained very high administrative positions after qualifying civil services examinations.

(c) Agricultural works: Maximum number of tribals are still dependent on agriculture. If we look back about five decades in the past, we find that according to 1951 census, there were about one crore 90 lakh tribal people in the country, of which 1 crore and 70 lakh people were dependent on agriculture.

But now position is changing fast, specially after getting education the change is faster. In the beginning occupational mobility was slow. In 1961 census 1.49 crore tribals were dependent on agriculture, out of which 33.33 lakh people were working as agricultural labourers. During five year plans specially under third five year plan period 47814 landless tribal agriculturists were given cultivable land. Indian tribals followed two methods of agriculture.

(a) Shifting cultivation or axe cultivation and

(b) Permanent or settled cultivation.

Shifting Cultivation

This type of cultivation was also known as axe cultivation because axe was used instead of plough and bullocks. Shifting means change of place i.e. a person after cultivation at a particular place, abandoned the place for a couple of years and did cultivation on another piece of land. This type of cultivation was found in several other parts of the world also outside India. In India axe cultivation was known by several names viz. Jhum, beggar, podu, paida, koman, dalu etc.

This type of cultivation usually took place in sloping, hilly or mountaneous region where sufficient rainfall happened and vegetation/ forests developd at a faster rate. It did not require much hard labour. This was probably the initial stage of agriculture, requiring very little labour, in a patch of land where vegetation/plants had grown, they were cut with the help of axe. After a few days when they dried up they were burnt and then seeds were sown. This task was undertaken usually before the rainy season. Afterwards there was no work in between sowing of seeds and cutting the crops—unlike in plough cultivation where the farmer was busy almost during the whole duration of cultivation. After the crops were cut, the area was left vacant for some period till the vegetables and plants were again grown in the land. During this period, the tribal farmer selected another patch of land and repeated the same process. The instances of shifting cultivation in India can still be seen among some of the tribals residing in remote hilly tracts. Till recently this was very much popular among the tribes of south America. Likewise in some parts of Africa, Mauritius, Malenesia and in Altantic islands, the tribals followed shifting cultivation. The Boro tribe of Amazon in south America was known for this type of agriculture. Bantu tribe of south Africa and several tribes of Magolia practise axe cultivation in the past.

Axe cultivation was named as Jhum among the tribes of Madhya Pradesh and Assam. Some of tribes of MP who followed this practice were Baiga, Gonds, Bhils, Bhil Das, Korku etc. This type of cultivation has now been totally banned. There were several reasons for the same. Some of these are stated as under :

(1) Increase in tribal population and decrease in the forests.

(2) Legislation declaring the forests as the property of the government.

(3) Culture contact—After the tribals came in contact with the outside world, they knew that the facility of the land can be increased and crops in a particular piece of land can be grown on a regular basis.

(4) Decline in religious faith and in the superstitions regarding the plough cultivation.

Disadvantages of Shifting Cultivation

Shifting cultivation had its own disadvantages. This type of cultivation was not possible in modern times because of the following reasons:

(a) It results in violation of law because forests are government property and cutting of trees is banned.

(b) Loss of forests, results low rainfall and environmental degradation.

(c) It has adverse effect on the natural environment, and

(d) It causes landslides and soil erosion.

Tribes in several parts of India, specially in Assam region and in Madhya Pradesh were agitated when forest were declared as government property. Some scholars opposed this type of cultivation, for example Hutton stated that axe cultivation was not beneficial from economic point of view. Instead of profit it could be harmful. While some others supported axe cultivation. According to B. C. Gohen the axe cultivation could be the only possibility keeping in view the geographical situations. Similarly, Verrier Elwin justified shifting cultivation. Some of the tribes did believe that keeping in view the geographical location shifting civilization was the only good method.

About a few decades back after independence some efforts were made for controlling the cultivation. These were as follows:

(a) Opening of Jhum control centres where the officials were supposed to give knowledge regarding agriculture.

(b) Rehabilitation of tribal families and construction of Bastis for tribal families engaged in shifting cultivation.

(c) Economic assistance to those tirbals, (who were following axe cultivation) for the purchase of agricultural tools etc. for adopting the modern method of cultivation.

A broad programme was launched during second five year plan for persuing the tribals to forego shifting cultivation. During third five year plan, money was spent on land reclamation. River valley projects in Madhya Pradesh and Orissa and research centres were started to evaluate and assess the various aspects of axe cultivation. Two such centres were opened in Assam and one in Tripura.

Settled Cultivation (Modern Agricultural System)

At present bulk of tribal people in India is engaged in plough cultivation while some rich and affluent tribals have started use of tractors also. The people of this category are permanent village settlers and resemble the other non-tribals as far as agriculture is concerned. They make use of tools, fertilizers, seeds and means of irrigation etc. They have become part and parcel of the rural India. Now exclusive tribal villages are rarely found. Tribals live in villages along with other non-tribal castes and communities. These people have also adopted and associated various religious activities and rituals along with agricultural activities like sowing, harrowing, harvesting etc. The tribals who are engaged is settled cultivation, most of them live in plain region of the country. In 1961 about 68 percent tribals were doing agricultural work and 20 percent were land less agricultural labourers. The rest were engaged in other occupations.

Handicraft and Cottage Industry

This includes various activities. For example spinning thread, rope making, basket making and pottery, stitching of garments etc. The Maria and Muria tribes of Jharkhand prepare spirit from forest produce Saora, Khond, and Gonds are found engaged in spinning and pottery etc.

Korwas and Augeries are iron smith and prepare iron tools to cater the agricultural and other needs of the villagers. Tharus of tarai in Uttar Pradesh and Uttaranchal are expert in the making of musical instrument, besides they make ropes and baskets etc. the Erula tribe of Tamil Nadu make bamboo mats. The tribals of North coast prepare cotton and wollen clothes. Their women are equally skilled in making cloth. They use various colour and make very attractive clothes. The Bhotias of Kumaon and Garhwal Himalayas prepare wollen garments, carpets, and shawls etc. The Bhotia women have developed expertise in garment making. They prepare various colours also from the forest produce and make colourful dans, kaleens and other garments. Likewise Manipur women are also expert in weaving and garment making. Thus, the cottage industry and traditional handicraft of tribals have survived till date because of the subsidy to the tribals by central as well as state governments.

Industrial Workers

The development of industries, especially in or near the tribal habitation first of all attracted the tribal people. The tribals of Bihar,

M.P. and Orissa started working in coal mines and other iron and ore industries. For example, availability of mineral resources, on the one hand displaced these people while at the same time provided them employment opportunity.

Several tribal people like Santals, Gonds in large number went to North East to work as labourers in tea gardens. Thus, the tribal people got employment in industrial and urban sectors almost in all parts of the country near their habitations whereever such opportunities came into existence.

After independence, planned efforts were made by the government to improve the economic condition of the tribal people. Under five year plans, special efforts were made for tribal area development. In the first five year plan 25 crore rupees were spent on tribal area development. This amount was increased to Rs. 57 crores under second five year plan. In subsequent five year plans, greater efforts were made to improve the lot of the tribal people. Their problem of indebtedness was resolved. In the third five year plan Rs.100.40 crore was spent while in fourth plan Rs. 172.70 crore rupees were spent for the development of tribal area. In fifth plan the target was raised to Rs. 350 crores. Further in subsequent five year plan periods more emphasis was given to the allround development of the tribal people.

Reservation policy attracted the tribal people to government jobs and the educated tribal youth has entered the arena of white colar jobs. Today tribal people can be seen at all the levels of hierarchy in government undertakings yet in some parts of the country these people have not been able to reach at par with other non-tribal population. The benefits of reservataion have not been availed by the poorer sections of the tribal society. Therefore, there is need for distributive justice, not only in case of scheduled tribes, this is equally applicable to scheduled castes and other backward classes for whom also our constitution has made some provision.

For the economic development of the tribal areas, it is essential that they should be made conscious of this fact and efforts should be made to bring changes in their values and attitudes. The tribals today cannot be kept in isolation as had been conceived by Verrier Elwin. The need is to bring them at par with the rest of the society.

References

1. Singh K.S., *Tribal Economy in India* (1977).

2. Singh K.S., *Economies of Indian Tribes and their Transformation.*
3. Singh K.S., *Transformation of Tribal Economy* (1978).
4. Majumdar D.N., *Races and Cultures of India* (1972).
5. Beals and Hoijer, *An Introduction to Anthropology* (1964).
6. Malinowski, *Crime and Custom in Savage Society* (1947).
7. Bose N.K., *Tribal Life in India* (1971).
8. Dabral S.P., *Uttarakhand Ka Itihas* (1966).
9. Pant S.D., *The Economy of the Himalayans* (1975).
10. Kroeber A.K., *Anthropology* (1948).
11. Nash, Manning, *Primitive and Peasant Economic Systems* (1966).
12. Thurnwald, Richard, *Economies in Primitive Communities* (1965).

❑❑❑

13

Religion and Magic

Since primitive period to the modern, religion is found in all the societies of the world. Rather we should say religion has existed in all the societies of the world since the beginning of the man when he became a social being. Though religion has existed in all the societies from earliest days, there has been variation in its mode of observation. This variation may be due to harsh natural and environmental conditions, nature of human society or state of human evolution and existence of social and economic conditions and level of cultural elements that a particular human group or a society has adopted. Non existence of cultural elements would naturally imply the non-existence of religion, because we could not think of a society without culture. In other words, it could be presumed that religion and culture have existed side by side almost in all the societies of the world.

As the society moved from simple to complex so has religion and culture changed too. Even in simple societies it is found in simple form at one place while it seems to have developed a complex form at the other. Anthropologists have emphatically stated that religion is one of the elements of culture which is found every where and whose cultural universality has been emphasised like family, marriage, incest tabaoo, social organizations etc. Tylor was the first Anthropologist who highlighted this fact that religion existed in all the tribal societies in one form or the other. The primitive people may have false notions regarding various worldly subjects, but they have had generally fixed and definite attitude regarding religion which affected their social and economic life to a large extent. According to early Anthropologists there were several reasons for the origin of the primitive form of religion. For example J.H.King believes magic as the cause of the origin of religion. Similarly, he believed in totemism and R.R. Marret believed in pre-animism as the cause of the origin of religion. Tylor emphasised on 'mana' and famous sociologist Emile Durkheim believed in cult of society as the cause of origin of primitive religion.

Definition of Religion

Sir James Frazer in his famous book, the *Golden Bough* (1955, P. 459) stated religion in the following words "By religion....I understand a propitiation or conciliation of powers superior to man which are believed to direct and control the course of nature and of human life". In the words of Edward B. Tylor, "Religion is the belief in spiritual beings. Thus, Tylor believes that there is a power superior to man, and man believes in that power. Frazer talks about three aspects of religion. First of all it is a power, superior to that of human beings. Secondly, this superior power directs, controls and regulates human life. Lastly as Frazer has stated that this power is superior to human being and controls and regulates human life, therefore it is in the interest of human beings to please and propitiate this power.

Malinowski gives equal importance to the sociological and psychological aspects of culture. According to him it is a mode of action as well as a system of belief; more over it is a sociological phenomena and also a personal experience. Thus, in all societies of simple technology, people believe that the process of nature and success of human endeavour are under the control of entities outside the range of every day experience, whose intervention can change the course of events. Lucy Mair has used the word entities for super natural. Religion, in a nutshell, consists of beliefs and practices. Durkheim was the first writer on primitive religion to be an avowed unbeliever, and so to treat all beliefs on a level as far as their truth or falsehood was concerned. Tylor and Frazer did hold that some beliefs were truer than others and therefore also superior, and were advanced. All these can be explained if one supposes that inside the body there is a soul which can leave it temporarily when a person is asleep (because when a person wakes up the soul returns to the body) and leaves the body permanently when a person dies. The idea of survival of the soul gives rise to the cult of dead, particularly in the form of ancestor worship which Tylor saw in the typical expression of animism.

Some writers rejected Tylor's views on the ground that there are people who do believe in spirits yet have ideas that should be called religious. Codrington, a missionary who spent many years in Malensia reported the existence of an impersonal power called Mana which could be both beneficent and dangerous, and which was not necessarily the attribute of spiritual beings, but could be found in inanimate objects.

Thus, religion has following characteristics

(a) Belief in supernatural power

(b) Feeling of sacredness

(c) Religious activities

(d) Absence of logic

(e) Worship and prayer

Malinowski gave following characteristics of religion

(a) A system of beliefs

(b) Religious activities

(c) Social nature of religion

(d) Man's personal desire to believe or not to believe in religion

Theory of Origin of Religion

(a) Evolutionary Theory : Evolutionary theory is individualistic by nature. Kingsley Davis states that this theory has now become unpopular. According to Davis, evolutionary theorists gave too much emphasis to the beliefs and did not pay attention to the rituals and emotions. He states that religious aspects can not be interpreted by one person on the basis of his dreams and on the basis of the consequences of the analysis of nature.

Functional Theory of Religion

William Robertson Smith, Emile Durkheim, R.R. Radcliff-Brown, Malinowski who were structural functionalists, developed the functional theory of relgion. Their assumption is that the religion exists in every known society because it performs certain social functions. They believed that society is an emergent whole, which can only be understood in totality.

Durkheim believes that society itself is the source of religion has played important positive role in history. Religious notions are born and conceived of when we find social groups collecting together for festivals at other social gathering. He says that the source of religion is the society itself.

Malinowski Studied religion among Trobriand Islanders. According to him it is essential for the social existence of man. Religion in the society develops according to human needs. Religion is such an agency which made adjustment in all types of situations like hatred, greed, anger and love etc. The function of religion is to keep human mind free from tension and presence. The function of religion in an unbalanced situation is to maintain coordination between man and super natural power. Thus, according to him religion is an instrument through which man attains stability in his mental and physical life.

Radcliffe-Brown's Theory of Religion

Radcliffe-Brown stated that the existence of society is more important than the existence of the individual. If man wants his existence possible in the society he will have to make some sacrifices. Its adherence to behavioural norms is essential for social survival. And it is the fear of super natural control and punishment, as also the anticipation of support in case of socially approved conduct that brings this adherence.

Belief and Ritual: According to Tylor belief is the central characteristics of religion. According to Frazer and Tylor, some believes were truer than others, and therefore, also superior and more advanced. For Tylor belief was more important than the actions. He introduced the word 'aminism' (ANIMISM) to cover all forms of belief in spiritual beings and divided these into 2 main classes- (i) The doctrine of soul- the idea that human beings have souls which survive their death and the doctrine of spirits the idea that the other spiritual (personalized) beings exist.

Frazer wrote that religion consists of two elements (i) Belief in powers higher than the man and an attempt to propitiate or please them. Durkheim stated that beliefs and rites are the basic components of the religion. Belief is static part of religion and rites are the dynamic part. Malinowski also stated that religion is a mode of action as well as a system of belief, and a social phemonena as well as personal experience.

Religious ritual is the active side of the religion. Like the belief it comes to have a quality of sacredness attached to it.

The Sacred and Profane

It is evident that sacred is the heart of religious system. It is the attitude which makes a things holy or sacred. It is a feeling that certain thing are above and apart from the ordinary matters of every day life. Belief and ritual are two aspects of the sacred.

Religion and Magic

Religion and magic are the two ways of tiding over crisis. They are closely interwoven and intertwined. There is a close relationship between the two. Magic is also a system of manipulation of the unknown. It is a pseudo science based on false conception of causality, assuming a control over powers, not understood.

Majumdar and Madan while comparing magic and religion stated that both magic and religion are tools of adaptation, the objective being to help man out of difficult situation and relieve his tension. The two approaches seem to have always existed together and sometimes they come so near each other as almost blend into each other.

Magic is a means to pursue definite end. The end is generally immediate, practical and usually private. According to Frazer magical formualas are based on 2 principles.

(a) Like produces like, and

(b) Once in contact always in contact

Majumdar and Madan have presented the views of Frazer in brief. Frazer called the first principle the law of similarity and magic associated with it, homeopathic, imitative or mimetic. The second law is called by him the law of contact and the magic associated with it is contagious magic. All the magical rites found in primitive society are based on these two principles and laws.

Like modern science magic is also based on observation of and experimentation on cause effect phemomena. Frazer sums up these conclusions as given below-

Magic

(a) Theoretical or magic as pseudoscience

(b) Practical or magic as pseudo art

(i) Positive, sorcery, witchcraft

(ii) Negative, taboos etc

Differences between religion and magic

(a) Religion is the belief in the supernatural, where as magic is the belief in the natural.

(b) The power that underlay have natural and supernatural forces needed to be controlled for social and psychological adjustments.

(c) Religion is based on submission to supernatural power and magic is based on coercion.

(d) The technique of both religion and magic is ritualistic. The entire performance is governed by a traditional order, which must be strictly followed, otherwise the efficacy of the rite is lost.

Tribal Religion in India

Tribal life and society can not be properly understood without religion. Religion pervades all aspects of tribal life.

Religion of a tribe is simple in so far as it is expressed in everyday language and experienced in everyday life. Without understanding tribes' religious notions we cannot understand tribal life style. In the following pages we shall discuss the religious notions of some of the tribes of India.

Todas: Todas are a pastoral tribe of Nilgiri hills in south India. They keep buffaloes. By their own account the Todas and their long horned buffaloes were created on the hills of Nilgiri Hills by the great Goddess TEIJIRZI. Their settlement is marked by the unique barrel-vaulted houses and dairy buildings. The dairy buildings are temples.

The Todas are socially organized into two endogamous sections, named Tarthoral and Tievaliol. The division is based on ritual specialization. Tarthoral alone can own to most sacred dairy temples with their associated herds, the Tievaliol men called the servant of the Gods fulfill the highest priestly tasks associated with them. Their social and economic life are centred on the buffaloes. The greater part of their religious observance is also focused on this animal. The buffaloes are ritually guarded. These people (Todas) observe a number of special ceremonies related to the dairies, buffaloes and pastures. They purify the dairy through rites when it is defiled and make offerings to it. They protect dairy from pollution associated with several social customs. Thus, the religious life of Todas revolves round one major economic activity of buffalo keeping.

Santhals

Among Santhals religion has an important place which keep the whole tribal community in a bond of social unity. They too have very strong faith in religion through which they control and dominate the unknown powers. For different religious functions, there are different persons, known by different names, Ojha, Jungur, Kamguru, Rerenik,

Atonek, Kudamnek etc. the witch doctor among these pople occupy important position. They believe in ancestral spirits and worship them. Besides they believe in house Gods (orek Bongo) and tutelary spirits.

Before they leave for hunting they worship a bonga. There are other village Gods (deities), main of them are as follows

(a) Jaher era

(b) Gosai Era

(c) Turko Muruko

(d) Morung Buru

(e) Perganet

Besides on the village border there is a God named as "Seema Bonga' and at some distance from the village (within the village territory) is the deity named as 'Bahare Bonga'.

Thus Santhals have immense faith in religion and spirits and religion governs their social and economic life.

Religion Among Bhil Tribe

The following are the characteristics of the religion among Bhils

(a) These people believe in Hindu Gods and Goddesses, whom they consider as powerful and not harmful.

(b) They have faith in ancestral spirits.

(c) They believe in several natural spirits also and worship them. They propitiate these spirits by sacrifice and alcohol.

(d) They have immense faith in religion. According to them magic has such a power which can harm others and can cause destruction.

Bhil's believe that a dead person's soul hovers around the place of his death and takes active interest on the living persons of the family. Those people who have natural death and had good and normal life, their soul is quite satified. On the contrary, a person who had unitimely and unnatural death his soul may be harmful. Among some of the Hindu Gods and Goddesses whom they worship are: Mahadev, Ram, Kalika, Hanuman and Ganesh etc. their followers are the Bhils who are relatively more progressive and have relatively attained higher social and economic status. They consider "Mahavdev' as the great God. Other Gods and Goddess are lower to him in hierarchy. They consider 'INDRA RAJ' as the God of the sky who controls rain and crops. Bhil consider Kalika as the mother of all universe, who protects them from ghosts and wild animals. Some times they sacrifice goats to please her. Besides, these people worship their tribal Gods and Goddesses which are related to crops, illnessness, animals etc. The culture contact has brought Bhils quite close to Hindus. As such primitive tribal deities are almost on the verge of extinction.

Tharus and their Religion

Like Bhils, Tharus also have started worshipping Hindu Gods and Goddesses. Besides, muslim, sikh and other religions have also laid their impact among Tharus. Tharu Gods and Goddesses and ancestral souls are both beneficial as well as harmful. They worship them with a view to please them. As there is a saying among Tharus that their women who belonged to superior racial stock, enjoyed higher status in the Tharu society so among deities also Goddesses are considered as superior to Gods and are worshipped more. They worship ancestoral spirits also. These spirits are placed in one corner inside the house. These people worship their ancestors who were popular and important in their life. These important ancestors are remembered as Gods and Goddesses. Another important thing among Tharu tribe is that Tharu women are considered as very skilful in magic.

Dabla Tribe

Dabla tribe has too much faith in evil spirits and ghosts. At the same time they believe in tribal Gods and Goddesses. So far as any disease is concerned they associate it with the displeasure of any God and Goddess. The religious priest is known as 'Bhagat'. Bhagats are both, among men and women.

Tribes of Andaman and Nicobar

There are various tribal Gods and Goddesses among these tribes. According to them, after death, a man's soul becomes spirit. If a person has special position/status during the life time, after death also, his spirit attains same rank. According to them spirits reside in the sea and forests. These people, do not make any sound during night hours as it would mean calling the spirits from the forests. On the other hand they have faith that the spirits run away with the sound of music. They believe in dreams and consider them as forecast. Dream-predicts about auspicious (good) or inauspicious (bad) events or news. These people also give too much of importance to magic.

The Soara tribe of Orissa have also been very much influenced by Hindu religion and culture. They have given due place to various Hindu Gods and Goddess in their religion. The 'Fear' has an important place in their religion. They make use of black magic also to harm the enemy while magic is used for illness, impurity, solution of crime etc. They follow moral rules to get rid of crime, theft, incest taboo and impurity. Verrier Elwin in his book, 'Religion of an Indian tribe', has said that Soaras spend too much money on religion and its ceremonies. Elwin also mentioned that one of the causes of their indebtedness is the money spent by these people on religious activities. Besides, money, they devote too much of time on religious activities which ultimately adversely affects their economy. But Elwin also writes at one place that religion is the cause of their good economy. He writes that some of the most important religious ceremonies take place only when there are better crops, therefore they work hard for good crops. The performance of religious ceremonies is considered as auspicious by them. All important religious ceremonies are followed by community feasts. These community feasts are beneficial for unity among these people. Thus, the tribals of India who are in a state of transition, have by and large adopted the religious values, practices and mode of life of the non-tribals to some extent. Those tribals who have attained higher degree of acculturation and integration have to a great extent adopted the religious values and practices of the non tribals, while those tribes, who are relatively more backward and live in unapproachable places having little culture contact, have more faith in tribal Gods and Goddesses.

The tribes, who follow Hindu mode of religion have developed hierarchical notions regarding Hindu Gods and Goddesses. It prevails among Hindus itself in the caste ridden society.

The tribal man has developed the ritual language consisting of

(a) Estoric word, mantra

(b) Gesture, dhvani, and

(c) Everyday language of interaction

Ritual space: In the tribal perception the space is filled with spiritual beings. Some spirits/ Gods according to tribal people dwell in the sky while some others occupy space near the settlement i.e. the physical space. For example some deities live in sky, some in mountains, others on the trees and else where.

Ritual time : Tribals also have in mind their ritual tune i.e. the time of blossoming of plants and trees, the position of stars and moon, various specified days, occasions etc. On such occasions, these people perform their rituals.

The forms of ritual may vary from one tribe to another but the basic ritual code of esoteric word (mantra), sound (dhvani), gesture (mudra) and everyday language of interaction (vyavhariki) is applicable to all the cultures.

The impact of Hinduism among Indian tribes has been very widespread. Tharus of Tarai region studied by S K Srivastave and Khasas by D N Majumdar reveal the fact that both these tribes have adopted Hindu mode of life by adopting Hindu caste names, wearing sacred thread, inviting Brahmin priests etc. similarly Hinduism has been adopted by Chero Kharwar in middle India, Paharia of Bihar, Bhumij and several other tribes of Madhya Pradesh. The Oraon people worship Hindu Gods and Goddesses.

Looking at the situation in south India we find that belief and practices of the neighbouring Hindu castes have been adopted by Chenchu, Kadar, and Muthavan etc. Hindu Gods and Goddesses like Aiyappan, Maruti and Kali are usually worshipped.

Hindu castes too have been influenced by the contact with the tribals. We find the impact of tribal religion prevails on certain Hindu groups living in tribal villages. For example, process of tribalisation in Bastar region of Chhatisgarh is reflected in the acceptance of tribal morals, rituals and beliefs among high caste Hindus. Majumdar mentions the concept of transculturation among the Ho tribe of Singhbhum, signifying reciprocal impact of tribal culture on local castes. Hutton long back stated that Hinduism and tribal religions share a common base, while Bose stated that the tribal population of India contributed to the making of Hinduism.

Impact of Muslim and Buddhism

Tribals have also been affected by muslim and Buddhism. For example, in upper Lahul and the Ladakh region the tribals are mainly Buddhists. Similarly, the Gujar of north western Himalayan region and some of the Bhils of Rajasthan and Gujarat have close contacts with Muslim groups and are affected by their beliefs and practices. But the number of tribals embracing Islam and Buddhism is very insignificant.

Christianity and Tribal Religion

The process of tribal's conversion to Christianity started in 1813 among the Khasis of North Eastern region. Similarly, the Orans of Chhota Nagpur in 1850 and the Bhils of Madhya Pradesh in 1880 accepted Christian religion. The missionaries played key role in the conversion of tribals to Christianity. The process was widespread and all over the Indian subcontinent. After Hindus, the largest number of tribal population accepted Christian religion. An interesting thing was that the missionaries concentrated on numerically strong tribal groups for their conversion. Such tribals constituted very important segment of the tribal population. Other very important tribal groups, whose members largely followed Christian religion were Mizo, Garo and Nagas.

Similarly, in south India, Hill Pulayan, Malayarayan and Palliar tribes of Kerala accepted Christianity. Thus, the church organization, western education, values and morals reached the tribals through Christianity.

The conversion changed the mode of life of the tribal people. For example, it brought considerable changes in the celebration of festivals, village organisation, economic life and other aspects of their culture. Some scholars went to the extent that they viewed Christianity as a source of disintegration of tribal religion.

No doubt that the Christian tribals got early benefit of modern education and were more progressive in outlook in accepting the modern western values. But alienation from tribal culture and its way of life at times created the rift between the Christian tribals and the non-Christian tribals within the same community, where the economic allurement was the cause of accepting the Christianity. Thus, during British rule the Indian Christianity spread its roots in the tribal habitation and the 'missionaries' who were entrusted with the task of reform in tribal areas, opened educational institutions. In these schools at times the medium of instruction was kept 'English'. The use of roman script was made, but behind this was the hidden motive of the spreading of Christianity.

References

1. Boas, Franz, *Race, Language and Culture* (1896).
2. Bose, N.K., *Cultural Anthropology and other Essays* (1953).
3. Fridel, John *Cultural Anthropology* (1976).
4. Hoebel, *Man in the Primitive World* (1949).
5. Pritchar, Evans, *Nuer Religion* (1956).
6. Lowie, R.H., *Primitive Religion* (1924)
7. WHR, Rivers, *Medicine, Magic and Religion* (1924).

❑❑❑

14

Primitive Political System

Any society, primitive or modern, requires some sort of regularity and a mechanism of control over its individuals so that it could maintain an order. An uncontrolled situation causes disorganization and disorder in the society, making its survival impossible. The mechanism or the institution which brings law and order situation in the group can be termed as political organization or political system. This directly or indirectly acts as a sort of control mechanism or acts like a pressure group in the society. The nature of political system varies from society to society and from simple to complex. In modern times, the political institutions have become highly specialized and have a specific role to play. These institutions are specifically created for the maintenance of law and order and for the maintaining harmony in the society. Where as in the simple societies it is more and more of informal nature, being most informal in small, acciphalous or the face to face societies. The face to face societies are those with the small number of population. In such type of society, every person knows every other person and every one performs multiple roles. There were certain primitive societies which had no state but these too had some sort of political system. There were small scale societies of hunters/wanderers which also had some sort of political system which was based on kinship and descent.

There were small tribal groups in several parts of Africa and elsewhere which lived in food collection and hunting stage. Their judicial and administrative institutions were quite unclear. Even the law and order or the social control mechanism used to take place through an informal arrangement. In relatively larger tribal groups, with several clans and sub clans, the political power was inherited through kinship and descent. Rarely there used to be specialized political agencies or institutions. It was to be determined by kinship or age set.

Beals and Hosier divided primitive political system into three categories :

(a) Those societies which had in true sense no political system. In these societies there was no definite leader other than head of the family.

(b) In the second category of political organization those tribals can be placed who had relatively more population, had more developed economic base but no savings. These tribals groups were often involved in conflict with each other. Victory was given due importance. The victorious groups succeeded in ownership of resources and area.

(c) In the third category, were those who were victorious. They levied taxes on and obtained goods from the defeated territory. There were elites in the group who were incharge of administration.

But this classification has its limitations because it does not include all the types of primitive political system.

Political System Among Indian Tribes

Because of cultural and economic variations different political models can be seen among Indian tribals. On the one extreme there are tribes such as Kadar, Eurula and Chenchu who till recently were in food collection and hunting stage and from the point of view of development they were very backward. On the other hand, there were Khasis and Garos of Meghalaya who had adopted developed form of agriculture and horticulture. Their economic life was quite comfortable.

The tribes in India and their political systems have been affected by their contact with the outsiders, especially Hindus and Christians. For example, the large number of tribals of central and western India were affected by Hindu culture. while on the other hand the tribals of North Eastern region were greatly affected by Christianity.

North-Eastern Region: This region includes tribals of Assam, Meghalaya, Arunachal Pradesh, Nagaland, Manipur, Mijoram and Tripura. The political nature of these tribes is by and large democratic. The collective ownership of land is given due importance. The individual right to property is not given importance. In this region there are certain tribal groups like Khasi, Garo who are matriarchal in character. This naturally has affected their political institutions also. For example, among Khasi tribe the leadership vests with the elder son of chief's sister. Among Khasis the chief has no separate right over land and forest. All decisions are taken by consenens by the elderly members of the group in their meeting. The presence of all members is considered essential. Khasi chief can not levy any tax or make any law on his own.

The tribals of northern Kachar distt. believe in the principle of inheritance along with election. All the matters are resolved in the presence of all the villagers (especially, the male members). The judgement taken against any criminal is considered as right. In such decisions the role played by elderly members of the village is very important.

Among Garo tribes the democratic norms are observed in the functioning of political institutions. These people do not have any definite 'head' and all the important matters are resolved by the village council, whose membes are head of the family and senior members of the village.

Stephen Fuch (1973) in his study of Mikir tribe stated that in tribal villages the administrative organization is tripartiate. At the lowest level the senior influencial member of the village who is well conversant with all the customs, norms and traditions of the Mikir tirbe and his authority is confined to the boundary limits of the village. He is appointed by senior office who is known as 'Heb'. Similarly, Heb is appointed by 'pinpo'. Pinpo is appointed by the rulers of Jayantia, for the Mikir hills. Thus, the administrative system is hierarchal and the nature of appointment is hereditary or kin based.

Naga Tribe

Among Nagas the political nature is of diverse type. Some of the Naga chiefs are too bureaucratic where as in some other Naga groups democratic norms are followed. The village chief has limited powers. He is chief for name sake. All decisions are taken collectively.

But by and large most of the Nagas are considered as militants and history testifies this fact that they were very often involved in war like situations.

The villages of Konyak Nagas are large social units. These villages are divided into wards. These wards are more closely knit social units than the villages. Each ward has a number of patriarchal clans. These are again sub divided into lineages.

Konyak Naga chief, administers over several villages. He is regarded with respect and fear.

Among Angamy Nagas the basic unit of administration was not village but a part of the population having common ancestor. They do not marry amongst themselves (within their gotra or clan) rather they marry outside this segment. Thus, the political system of Nagas has been full of conflicting situations, factions and groupism. Konyak Nagas were divided into three unequal social classes as chiefs, commoners and intermediate group. The village community consisted of a chief and ten morung officials known as Niengba. The council settled disputes and used to punish the offenders on breach of taboos concerning the community as a whole. The council also used to take decisions regarding rituals and ceremonies. All the posts of the council were hereditary.

The Ao Nagas were another important Naga tribe. The village affairs of the Ao Nagas were organized in two ways.

(a) The various communal duties were assigned to different age groups.

(b) The council was empowered to control the various activities of the village. It was entrusted with the task of setting up all the disputes and quarrels arising in the village. The method of selection of the councellors as well as their tenure of office, varied in different groups.

Santhal

In Santhal village the chief is known as 'Majhi'. Marriage etc were celebrated in the village under his leadership. He is assisted by a council of elderly male persons in the village. If the chief of the village is not a santhal and a person of other tribal group was the chief, then in that case santhals also appointed a chief of their own caste. He was known as "hadi Majhi' who except collecting taxes and other administrative responsibilities, does all other social tasks. The taxes are realized by the village chief.

Village had three assistants also who help 'majhi' in its administration. They are appointed by him. The main assistant is known as 'Parmanik majhi'. Then there is jog majhi who visits the village chief ('Majhi') during social activities and other functions. He resolved the matters relating to marriage and on the occasion of birth and marriage the villagers seek his advice. Jogmajhi too has an assistance who is known as 'Jog parmanik'. Then there is 'godet' who acts as assistant for majhi and communicates the decisions of the majhi to the villagers. He arranges the meeting of the villagers for discussion.

Perganet : He is chief of several villages. Like majhi perganet too has assistants who are known as 'Desmajhi', one who assists the 'desh majhi' is known as 'parganet chakladar', who conveys the messages of parganet to all the villagers.

Banglow : This is the highest organization among Santhals. It has administrative functions over certain villages. It has two councils. The higher council is known as Panchayat whose highest officer is parganet of Banglow and village chiefs are members of this panchayat. This panchayat deals with all the matters relating to the villages. The lower body of the council is known as 'Kulidrup'. In this meeting, the village chief represents all the families and all villagers are its ex-officio members. This council decides about issues of minor nature whereas all the major problem are decided by the upper council. These are the matter relating to two or more villages. Or in other words, the inter village issues are discussed in the upper council, where as intra-village matters are discussed in the lower council.

Law and Order Situation Among Santhal Tribe

A particular traditional method is used for maintaining law and order situation among Santhal tribes. There is a custom of 'Bit laha' according to which, if a person admits his crime he is made an out-caste. This punishment is given to specific types of crimes, for example in violation of incest rules among close relations. This is particularly done with a view so that social order could be maintained in the society. To determine the crime, first of all the meeting of the villagers is called which is known as gram sabha. If at the initial stages the crime is not proved or if there are not sufficient/convincing evidences then the suspected person is discharged after giving warning. If the crime is of serious nature and is proved, then the decision of 'bitlaha' is taken by calling a meeting of the villagers. First of all the chief (majhi) of the village goes to meet the parganet and makes him aware of the decision taken by the villagers regarding the crime and requests him to invite the meeting of the five village majhis so that their consent for 'Bitlaha' could be sought. This meeting of majhis is known as Disamhor. Withouth the consent of the 'Dihamhor', bitlaha cannot be performed. After this sabha has given the consent of 'Bitlaha', the decision of 'Disamhor' is communicated to a local officer. On a particular day, fixed for 'bitlaha' by the disamhor all the villagers protest in front of the house of the victim who is to be punished. He is publicity humiliated and then excommunicated and people stop eating or drinking with him and avoid talking and going to his house.

'Jop': It means taking back person who has been excommunicated. After all a man canot remain in isolation for long. Some people are even compelled to leave the village and go elsewhere. Some people bear the humiliation but after some time express the desire to return to the society and be pardoned. As a result of penance he has to give a feast to the village on an appointed day. On this occasion the senior most (elderly) parganet declares that the victim is being taken back to the community. He (the victim) peforms certain rituals and provides a feast to all the villagers. After the feast ceremony is over, he is considered as a normal member of the village/tribal community. Thus, among santhals, 'Bitlaha' custom is an example of maintaining law and order (social control) for punishing and pardoning a victim. It was direct, cheap and quick method of punishing a person, contrary to the modern judicial system which takes lot of time, money and resources for getting justice.

Oraon Tribe: Among Oraons of Sundarban there used to be both village panchayats and Farah-inter village councils, but now the later is gradually disappearing. Once upon a time Farah panchayat used to act as judicial, social and political institution. Several villages had one Farah panchayat. In the Panchayat the village chief (Rajparak) or 'Mantri' or any member of the panchayat used to represent the village. Any one member was elected as its chief. If there was any intervillage dispute, it could be settled by Farah Panchayat. If the Farah chief is himself involved in any dispute or party to any dispute then in that case some other peson acted as chief. In the past these panchayats were very effective and powerful. During the British rule these traditional leaders were given considerable power and prestige but later on the government withdrew the power of police and revenue collection and these panchayats gradually lost their significance.

Village Panchayat: At the village level the panchayat settles all the minor issues. The influencial and senior male members of the village are its members. The scope of panchayat is quite wide and its decisions are respected but with the growing influence of courts and judiciary, the influence of panchayats have gradually decreased.

The organisation of Oraon panchayat is like this

(1) Chief (Rajmoral) (one)

(2) Mantri-Assistant or Adviser of chief (one)

(3) Members (Number not specified)

(4) Peon (messanger) one

Usually the chief of panchayat is hereditary. After chief's death, his son acts as chief of the village panchayat. Rajmoral(chief) appoints his secretary (mantri) and later on with his consultation he appoints the members. In some matters he consults elderly persons of village also. The village panchayat settles disputes relating to conflict between two or more persons, matters related to land, matters related to marriage and similar other social and economic issues or violation of traditional tribal norms. If Rajmoral is involved in the dispute then in that case the secretary acts as the chief and if Rajmoral (chief) and secretary both are involved in the dispute then in that case any senior member acts as chief. Thus, by and large the panchayat succeeds in the settlement of disputes at the village level. But as has been said earlier, now the people have started going to the courts for the settlement of disputes and feel themselves more secure because now panchayats are not very effective.

Ho Tribe

Among the 'Ho' tribe the headman is known as 'Manki'. He is selected on the basis of the influence he has in his neighbourhood. The general consent of the inhabitants of the village people over which he is to be placed is also taken into account. Now a days a Manki decides only the cases of adultery and desertion by a wife. Earlier he used to try civil and criminal cases also.

Kharia Tribe

There are several sections among Kharia tribe. These are Hill Kharias, the Dhelki Kharia and the Dudh Kharia. The inter village panchayat of the Hill Kharia is known as Bhira. Its head is known as 'dandia'. The eldest and wisest of all village headmen is selected and called 'Dandia'. The Dhelki Kharia do not have a permanent panchayat. They only have occasional intervillage gatherings called Farha or Kutumb Farha. The Farha of Dudh Kharia consists of villages of different clans. The village head man is known as Kartaha. The office of 'headman' is hereditary. The main function of these panchayats among all the sections of Kharia is readmission of ostracized persons into tribal fold.

Munda

The Munda have two kinds of village unions:

(a) The Bhumhari Patti, which became part of the realm the king of Chhota Nagpur and

(b) The Khut katti patti which consisted of people who wanted to be free of king rule. In the Bhumhari area, the Farah panchayat is a fixed body and acted as a ruler or its officer. In the Khut kati area, the panchayat was not a fixed body.

Juri System Among Dabla Tribe

Judicial system among Dabla tribe, who are found in Gujarat region, have been very strong and powerful. These are a sort of panchayats. The organization of panchayat is found at three levels.

(1) At the lowest there is village panchayat. Its area of power (administration) is the entire village. The villagers decide its rules and regulations and accept the decisions taken by village panchayat.

(2) At the second level is the Dabla panchayat which deals with the problems relating to the Dabla tribe. These problems are of internal nature. Dabla panch provide the leadership and try to resolove the matters.

(3) At the third level there is panchayat of different Dabla tribal villages, which has maximum powers and authority. A chief of the panchayat is selected on the basis of age, education, status and experience. Dabla Panchayat tries to resolve their matters, disputes etc at their own level. The chief who is known as 'patel' is given due respect by all the members. His advise, and decisions are highly valued and respected.

Conclusion

Thus, on the basis of the political organization of few tribes of India the following conclusions could be reached at.

(a) There are still tribal groups residing in the remote and less accessible places where traditional authority structure is still dominant. But such tribal groups are very few in number. The outside contact has weakened tribal traditional authority structure.

(b) The powers of traditional tribal chiefs have been replaced by modern panchayats or modern arrangement of law and order situation.

(c) The power of administration, collection of revenue etc have now been replaced. Only in social and cultural sphere, the traditional tribal head yields some influence.

(d) There is a change in the decision making system too. Earlier in tribal society, decision making process was either by consensus or it rested with the chiefs and the committee appointed by him. But with the introduction of new system it has been replaced by majority decision in place of consensus or an individual one.

(e) Individual having political powers along with religious one still carry their influence among traditional orthodox sections of the tribal society. The illiterate or semi literate tribals still have strong faith in superstitious elements.

References

1. Radcliffe-Brown, *Structure and Function in Primitive Society* (1956).
2. Lucy Mair, *Introduction to Social Anthropology* (1972).
3. Hunter David and Whitten Philip, *Anthropology : Contemporary Perspective* (1985).
4. Fortes and Evans, Pritchard (eds) *African Political Systems* (1940).
5. Shapera I., *Government and Politics in Tribal Societies* (1956).
6. Lewis H. Morgan, *Ancient Society* (1958).
7. Mair L.P., Primitive Government (1962).
8. Gulliver P.H., *Social Control in an African Society* (1963).
9. Line hardt R.G., *Social Anthropology* (1964).
10. Evans, Pritchard, *The Nuer* (1940).
11. Fortes M., *The Dynamics of Clanship among Tallensi* (1945).

❑❑❑

15

Socio-Religious Movements Among Indian Tribes

Tribal people, barring a few exceptions, have been very simple and peaceful. They were least ambitious, and contended with whatever, they were provided by the nature. But this was the situation at the very early stage of the evolution. Gradually, the times changed, there were changes in the man nature relationships. A stage had reached where nature had not cooperated enough to satisfy man's basic needs of survival. Thus, the primitive man who was initially satisfied in his natural surrounding, had no alternative but to come out of it. This brought him in contact with the outside world.

Even man's dependence on nature varied from one natural surrounding (one area) to another. There were regions where nature provided enough to satisfy basic human needs. Even these were too on a decline. The outside environment at times met with hostility also. But by and large, the tribal people's movement outside their native surrounding was in search of means of livelihood, in which to a certain extent they succeeded also. At times, the outsiders also entered the tribal territory, which, on several occasions disturbed the harmony. For example, forest employees, road construction workers, mine workers etc. had met with encounters in the tribal area.

Social movement is a social phenomena which requires social or collective endeavour. A social movement is a sort of change in the existing social order. It is a by product of collective social behaviour,

Mc Laughlin finds social movement as the byproduct of socio-political development. Social movement according to Herbert Blumer is a collective enterprise to establish a new social order.

Paul Wilkinson explains the movement as follows: the English word movement derives from the old French verb 'movior', which means to move, stir or impel, and the medieval movimentum (turn); and then reproduces the definition of movement from Oxford Dictionary as 'a series of actions and endeavours of a body of persons from a special object. Thus

(a) A social movement is a collective social endeavour to promote change in any direction.

(b) A social movement must envince a minimal degree of organization.

(c) There is commitment to change and active participation on the part of the followers.

Thus, according to Wilkinson the major characteristics of social movements are:

(a) Conscious commitment to change

(b) Minimal organization

(c) Normative commitment and

(d) participation

Social movements are multidimensional-

Mahapatra believes that a social movement occurs when a fairly large number of people are bound together in order to alter some position of existing culture or social order or to redistribute power of control within a society.

Mclaughlin identifies two main types of social movements.

(a) Revolutionary movements, and

(b) Reform movements

According to him both seek to influence social order but the revolutionary movement attacks existing social norms and values and attempts to substitute new ones while the reform movement accepts existing norms and values and uses them to criticize the social defects it opposes.

So long as the tribal people were happy and contended, they did not resort to any type of movement. The movements started when

(a) These people came in contact with the outsiders and the outsiders tried to impose their values beliefs and practices, directly or indirectly, or when tribals themselves wish to enculturate the values, beliefs and practices of outsiders.

(b) When the tribals had their own internal problems and these had reached the maximum ie extreme poverty due to absence of means of livelihood in their native area.

(c) The enforcement of law against the rights and monopoly of the tribals on the forests and their resources.

(d) Out migration of tribals and their exploitation by the outsiders.

(e) Emergence of minerals, mines etc in the tribal area and increasing outside interference. For example, banning the forests and shifting cultivation, exploitation of tribals by forest contractors and money lenders.

Thus, the above factors made to tribals angered and restless. The agitated and disturbing situations led to some sort of movements. By and large, the tribal movements were based on local issues and wished for an early and quick solution of their problem.

Tribal Movement in India during Colonial Period

During the British rule in India several tribal movements took place. As the main aim of the British rulers in India was to collect more and more wealth by exploiting the natural resources and by levying taxes in the form of revenue. The colonial government's policy was responsible for several tribal movements.

Another factor is that after the contact with the outside world, the tribal people got attracted toward greater tradition. The process of acculturation began irrespective of their exploitation,. For example, the the caste hierarchy, the caste Hindus ranked these tribal people at the lowest ladder, in the category of untouchable castes. Even then these tribal people preferred to adopt the religion and culture of outsiders. Majority of them embraced Hinduism, some of them were motivated to adopt Christianity. Whereas a very few of these people adopted Islam. During colonial period the role played by Christian missionaries by converting the tribals into Christianity, at times created certain problems. For example, a tribal group was divided into two; Christian tribals and non-Christian tribals. Thus, in the grab of welfare activities the Christian missionaries changed the religion of these people. This also complicated the situation.

Thus, by and large tribal movements took place in all the parts of the country but the North East, Chhota Nagpur, Maharashtra, Gujrat were the pioneering centres for tribal movement. In other words, tribal movements started along with the awakening and growing consciousness among these people. From the very beginning of the British rule in India Chhota Nagpur region has been the centre of various tribal movements. Some of these were

(a) Rulers of Dal Bhum (1779-84)

(b) Chhuwar tribes of Midnapur (1799)

(c) Bhumij chhuwars of Chhota Nagpur, Santhal pargana and Manbhum (1795-1800)

(d) Kol, Munda of Chhota Nagpur (1831-32) and

(e) Santhal Revolt (1855-57)

All these above movements were due to exploitation of tribals (especially economic exploitation of these people). A stage came when tribals had organizd themselves against the exploitation which they were facing. As we have stated above, in India tribal movements took place almost in all the regions of the country. They were hundreds in numbers. Some of them were very successful. Others did not meet much success and were of minor importance. The following were some of the prominent tribal movements.

(1) Jharkhand movement

(2) Chipko movement

(3) Santhal unity movement

(4) Social movement among Ho tribe

(5) Mahato kurmi movement in Chhota Nagpur

(6) Gond movement

(7) South Gujrat tribal autonomy movement

(8) Socio-religious movements among tribals in south Gujrat

(9) Tribal movement in Andhra Pradesh

(10) Naga movement

(11) Ethnic movement in Manipur valley

(12) Mizo political movement

(13) Khasi unity movement

(14) Cultural and political movement among Bodos of Assam

(15) Tribal movement in Tripura

(16) Movement relating to language and script in Darjeeling Himalayas.

(17) Nebula movement for regional unity

In addition to these movements, several others had also taken place from time to time.

Movements Among the Tribes of Eastern Region

The tribes of this region were politically more active than the tribes of other regions of India. Some of the important tribes of this region are Naga, Garo, the Khasi, Mizo, Mikir, Kuki, the Kachari, the Dafla etc. Though they share common geographical area, yet culturally and linguistically they maintained independent identities. Many of them were known for traditional hostilities and feuds. These had bearings upon the tribal politics and the emergence of new states in the region after independence. No doubt missionaries brought several changes in the tribal life. These missions imparted education to these people, provided them economic support, and changed their religion. All this provided base for social change among the tribals. The Britishers arrived in this area in 1832. Even before that the local kings who had harassed and maltreated these tribal people, may be held responsible for discontentment among the local tribals, which had already sown the seeds of political movements. Political movements acquired slogans like 'political autonomy', 'Naga nationalism', nothing sort of sovereign states' etc. These movements were supplemented by varied organizational activities like the Naga club, the Naga national council, the Naga youth movements, the Naga women's society. The Naga club in the year 1929 had put the demand that their region should be under the direct administration of the centre and later on, be granted independence at the time of departure. Britishers from India. Thus, independent socio-political identity, was the main demand of these people.

Such demands did not cease after independence. Rather they were intensified. The Naga national Council, the Assam Hill Tribal Union, the All Party Hill Leaders Conference, all were striving for autonomy. And many of them adopted violent subversive methods. These movements led to the emergence of Nagaland in 1961, upgradation of Manipur and Tripura to full state (1972) and the emergence of new state of Meghalaya in 1972. The process does not end here. There are several other such demands even right now.

Movement among Tribes of Chhota Nagpur

Unlike the tribal movements of Eastern hill region the movements in this area were mostly associated with particular leaders, having charismatic powers. The movements were by and large the reactions against rulers and land lords or were against the rules laid down by the government which were interfering with the interests of the tribals. The movements of Chhota Nagpur were more of a reform type. Two movements of this region ie Tana Bhagat Movement among the Oraons of Bihar and Birsa Munda Movement which emerged in and around Ranchi distt. and Singhbhum in Chhota Nagpur division were of great significance. Here, Jatra Bhagat and Birsa Munda, the tribal leaders of the respective movements eventually fought against foreign exploitors, landlords and contractors.

Birsa Munda Movement : This movement was named after Birsa (1874-1900), a Munda by birth. He gave a lead to his people for socio-political emancipation and religious reform. During the second half of the 19th century the whole Chhota Nagpur region under went a tremendous change. The old Munda system of tenure gave way to a new and alien system of exploitation by the landlords, known as jagirdar and thekadar. Under their greed and cruelty the tribal population was squeezed out of their land and other possessions. These people suffered economically and politically and were assigned low social status. Though later on the missionaries gave them some of the socio-economic benefits but it was at the cost of religious conversion. A large number of Mundas did convert to Christianity but they soon realized that this was not the solution. In 1895 Birsa Munda started a movement. In him the Mundas found the embodiment of their aspiration. He gave his people leadership, a religion and a code of life. He held before them the prospect of Munda raj in the place of foreign rule. Under the influence of a learned Satnami pandit, Birsa Munda became a vegetarian and he preached, both Hinduism and Christianity to his people. He preached people that religion would end their misery. His followers started treating him as embodiment of God 'Birsa Bhagwan'. They believed him to the extent that he could infure life into a dead person. He had magic touch and cured people of all ailments. Thus, Birsa was seen as the provider of new and better life for his people.

But later on his movement assumed quasi-political and militaristic shape as he organized a force to fight oppressive land lords, Christian missionaries and colonial officals (British officials), he was imprisoned. His people believed in his magical/supernatural powers, they did not ask for his release, rather they wanted to go to jail with him. Their belief was that he would come out of jail within 3 days, but he was released after 2 years.

After his release he again organized his people. He organized a force to fight oppressive land lords. He trained his army to attain the goal of self rule. He was however arrested and later died in jail. But the seeds of unrest were already sown among his people and they continued to fight against injustice. Jharkhand movement had its roots in this movement.

Tana Bhagat Movement

Like other Bhagat movements, in Tana Bhagat movement an attempt was made to emulate the way of life of Hindu upper castes. This movement had emerged among the Orans of Chhota Nagpur. It was started in 1913-14, under the leadership of Jatra, an oran by birth. There were other Bhagat movements like Memha Bhagat and Bachi dan Bhagat. The term 'Bhagat' was employed in many parts of Bihar to refer to sorcerers and magicians. Among the orans it was however applied to a distinct section of the tribe which subscribes to the cult of Bhakti.

Jatras' message to his people was to abandon meat, alcohol, have faith only in one God, give up faith in witchcraft and so forth. The movement aimed to raise the status of its members in the eyes of the surrounding Hindu society and to incorporate Hindu beliefs and practices into its ideology. The leader of the movements Jatra oran in 1914 announced that Dharmesh, the high God of oran had revealed to him that people would have to give up worship of ghosts and spirits and practice of exorcism. He told his people to refrain from animal sacrifice, eating meat and liquor consumption etc. Even cultivation by plough with the use of animal power was rejected.

Tana Bhagat wore khadi and participated in the non-cooperation movement by non payment of land taxes.

The Sibu Bhagat, the Balram Bhagat, the Devamania or 'Bom Bom', the Newala Bhagat, the Bachi-Dan Bhagat and Kabirpanthi Bhagat represented local sectional variations within a broad common framework of oraon socio-religious movements.

Khasi Unity Movement

Khasis live in the Khasi and Jayantia Hills of Meghalaya. It is an important tribe with distinctive culture and tradition. These people are divided into sub groups. In addition to that there are two more sub groups in Jayantia hills. These people are divided into various gotras (clans) and subclans. Each of them is endogamous in character like other tribal groups of Assam region. The Khasis also accepted Christianity in large number. The conversion to Christianity caused conflicting situation. The problem was with regard to the customs and traditions of khasi people. The church had banned some of these customs for the converted khasis. The church did not permit the converted khasis to participate in their tribal traditional dance. This was the situation at the beginning. But gradually there was change into situation. The Christian khasis also wanted to retain their tribal identity. The efforts were made to establish unity between Christian and non-christian khasis by clan welfare committees which came into existence in the year 1965. In 1969 the Christian khasis participated in the traditional dance as both two group (Christian khasis and non-christian khasis) desired to maintain their traditional tribal identity.

The religion has played important role in khasi leadership. It will not be out of place here to reveal this fact that the Christian khasis were educated and socially more enlightened than the non-christian khasis. The political leadership was in the hands of christian khasis but the social and cultural movement were led and initiated by the non-christian khasis. Though Christian khasis were smaller in number, they were educated and since the British period, they had succeeded in attaining high position in the government It does not mean that the non Christian khasis had not participated in political movement, but the Christian khasis had upper hand in this sphere.

The beginning of khasi movement was from the year 1923 when the first political party, named as 'khasi National Darbar' was formed. This party demanded independent khasi state. The demand was reiterated in the year 1934 thought he khasis did not meet any success to their demand but, it had made them more conscious and enlightened.

After independence their contact with outsiders increased. The non khasi officials came to their area. In the field of trade and business also the outsiders migrated to their area. This resulted in the exploitation of the tribal people. The outsiders purchased the tribal land and other stable property. Though the khasis opposed the purchase of their land by the migrants, it did not meet with much success. As a consequence the conflicting situation developed between the government Administration and the tribal chiefs. This situation continued for sometime and demand for separate state came up. At last on 21st Jan. 1972 the separate state of Meghalaya was established and congress emerged as a major political party in the new state. But again the internal rift between Christian and non–Christian khasis come up at the forefront. The differences were with regard to the khasi tribal culture. The non Christian tribal khasis blamed the Christian khasis for the loss of tribal culture. Thus, both the groups blamed each other.

The Khasi tribe has certain characteristics. It is matriarchal and matrilineal. The custom of marriage has been some what different i.e. in the form of institution of visiting husband. According to this custom, the girl after marriage used to stay back at the place of her birth and the husband was considered as an outsider and used to visit his wife (at her residence). He had no say in family matters. After cultural contact and after their conversion into Christianity, there has been a gradual decline on this customs and the husband after marriage lived at wife's place more or less on a permanent basis. This change is specially due to the impact of Christianity and these people continued to have their faith in Christian religion. The presence of outsiders especially Bengalis, Marwaris, Sindhis, and others in Meghalaya had created some problem for the khasis. They after migrating to Meghalaya had captured the trade and business. The khasis blamed the government who had encouraged these outsiders to open industries and thus neglected the interest of the local people.

Thus, inspite of several differences, the movement succeeded in bringing unity among various khasi groups and the political agencies played, successful role in bringing out awareness among various sub groups at social and cultural level. Thus, where the movement was succeeded in the creation of a separate state, it also paved way for the emergence of traditional tribal leadership to strengthen their tribal social and cultural life. The uniqueness of their cultural practices and social traditions prevails even today, of course in a modified form. One characteristics of khasi movement was that unlike Naga and Mizo tribe these people did not have separatist tendencies in their movement. The khasis always considered themselves as part of the Indian sovereign.

Naga Movement

There has been discontentment among various Naga sub groups of Naga hills. From time to time these people had started movement for autonomy. Because after independence these people could not adjust with the changing situation. Their feeling was that during the British period these people had been given more facilities and after independence they felt that they were loosing their tribal identity. The contact with the people from the plains and their loss of the ownership of the forests, also aggravated their discontent. The outside contact directly or indirectly started interfering in their cultural autonomy in Naga hills. All Naga groups depend on agriculture for their livelihood. They practice shifting cultivation also, along with plough cultivation. They also partly depend on forest produce for their livelihood.

Missionaries had great impact on Nagas. Most of these people accepted Christianity. These missionaries provided them formal education and economic assistance also. The Naga people did not like the interference of non tribals (outsiders) in their native region, which had already started during the British period. It developed a feeling of insecurity which multiplied after the independence.

Traditionally, various Naga groups were not organized, were hostile to each other but in the eyes of outsiders the Naga groups were like one tribal group. Naga movement started in 1918, along with the formation of 'Naga club' at Kohima. Its members were Naga elites and the government officials also. In addition to that, the presidents of the neighbouring villages were invited to the meeting of Naga club when social issues were discussed. The members of this club had submitted the letter of demand before the Simon Commission at Kohima in 1929. The demand of this Letter was to keep the Naga hills separate from British Administrative reforms. In this letter the feelings of independence for Nagas were expressed. The letter, further said that Britishers were the only people who had defeated Nagas and when they leave their country, they should leave Nagas on their own. This letter of demand was signed by 20 members of the club. This indicated that feeling of unity had started prevailing among to various Naga sub groups.

Naga hill distt tribal council was established in April, 1945. In 1946, its name was changed as Naga National Council. It tried to lay the foundation of political unity among the Naga tribal groups and tried to develop the concept of Naga nationalism. In 1946, the British government prepared a scheme in which the Britishers wanted to make a trust territory by combining Naga hills and some territory of Burma. The trust territory would be directly under the control of British government from London. But the educated Nagas, opposed this proposal. The Indian National Congress also vehemently opposed this proposal and raised slogan that Britishers should quit Naga hills also once they leave India.

In addition to Naga club, various Naga tribes established various organizations. For example, Ao council was established. Lother council had already come in existence. Thus, in the decade of forties several Naga organizations had come into existence. In 1948 after the merger of Naga Hill Distt. Tribal council with other tribal councils, a larger organization named as (NNC) National Council came into existence and this organisation demanded more autonomy.

After 1947, Naga movement took place in several stages. The period between 1947 and 1954 was by and large calm and peaceful. There was no violence. Nagas did not accept Indian constitution and boycotted the first general election. No Naga candidate contested the election. In 1954, the demand of independent Nagaland (as a sovereign state) was raised. In 1956, a new organization, named as 'Naga Central government', was established. Its activities were all underground. The active leaders were all underground, for fear of being arrested. Later on, the Nagas were divided into 2 groups and those who were liberalists kept themselves aloof from the other groups who had gone underground and resorted to violence. Afterwards several conferences took place. In 1957, two leaders of the church also appealed for peace. The outcome of various meetings and conferences was that a separate state as 'Nagaland' should be made within the Indian union and it should be under the department of external affairs of the government of India.

In 1960, the prime minister of India declared the acceptance of the parliament regarding Nagaland as the 16th State of Indian union, though Nagaland was established in December 1963. The Naga extremists who were associated with the Naga movement remained underground from 1954 till 1964. Their leaders were in London. Further, there was division among their leaders and a section of which was for peaceful negotiations within government of India.

In Nov. 1975 there was a formal meeting between Naga leaders and the government and shilong treaty was signed. According to this treaty the Naga leaders agreed to accept the Indian constitution and to lay down arms. Among the leaders who signed the treaty, were the representatives of the underground leaders also.

The leadership of Nagas was from the beginnings in the hands of educated and those who had been converted into Christianity. And among several Naga sub groups, role played by "Ho", seema and 'Angami Nagas' was very important. Nagas had this fear in their mind that after their merger with the Indian union, their Christian life style might be adversely affected. Thus, Nagas from the very beginning could not adjust with the non-Nagas/outsiders. As a consequence, always there arose a conflicting situation. The outsiders also left no stone unturned in exploiting them. In the beginning the Naga movement was peaceful but later on it took a violent turn. Naga Church, Naga Peace Council and government of India all the three played important role for a peaceful compromise. As a result of movement unity developed between various sub groups and internal differences were sorted out.

As a result of movement, the separate state of Nagaland came into existence. After the merger of Naga council into Indian National Congress, the path of unity had already been opened.

Bodo Movement

Bodo kachari is the largest tribal group of Assam. Bodo movement was primarily political and cultural. Economically, Bodos are very backward. The leadership of the movement was in the hands of Plains Tribal Council of Assam (PTCA). Bodo Sahitya Sabha and Bodo Sahitya Parishad (Bodo Literary Parishad) also played pivotal role in the movement.

Initially the region was very peaceful. But after the migration of people from East Bengal, the process of exploitation had started. The migrants gradually purchased their fertile land. The Land Ceiling act also had negative impact on the economy of these people. The Bodos, being poor, were less educated as compared to Nagas and Khasi, who had attained success at political end. Gradually, they had been conscious of this fact that they might achieve success only by resorting to path of movement.

Bodos wanted to revive their language and there by wanted to organize their people. Thus, the movement was started with a view of revival of their own language. In Assam language was a political issue. After the 1960 act of Assam government regarding language, several tribal groups had started agitation.

In 1963, the government had recognized the need of Bodo language in schools in the Bodo dominated area of Assam. Thus, in 1975, the movement for the separate Bodo script was launched. And secondly, another movement was started for separate state (udyanchal state) comprising of Bodo region with the state of Assam.

In this movement, the role played by Bodo Sahitya Sabha has been very significant. The basic demand was that Bodo language should be the medium of instruction in schools in Bodo dominated area. In principle the state government accepted this demand in 1963. In 1968 the matter relating to Bodo language was accepted in secondary schools. In 1975, a movement for separate Bodo script was started. At the same time another movement for separate state 'Udayanchal Rajya' (Udayanchal state) was started.

The role of Bodo Sahitya Sabha was very significant in the movement in which language issue was very important in the Bodo dominated areas the medium of instruction should be Bodo language.

In 1968, the Assam government, in principle accepted the demand of Bodo language. After that, sahitya sabha was engaged in the preparation of text books so that announcement made by state government could be implemented. After sometime of the language movement, the demand for autonomous state was also raised. As we have pointed out earlier, the movement was under the leadership of PTCA (Plains Tribals Council of Assam). Thana Bodo Sahitya Sabha and Bodo Sahitya Parishad had also played important role. Their role at the beginning was non violent in which these people boycotted the election in 1968 for the M.P. from Kokrajhar. After the release of the PTCA leaders from Jail in 1969, the movement took a different turn e.g. fielding their own candidate in the election in 1971 and 1972 against the candidate of the ruling party, raising demand for separate state of 'Udayanchal Rajya in 1972 and opposing Assamese language which had by now become the medium of instruction at the university level. PTCA supported English as medium of instruction at college/ university level so that the interests of the minority communities could be protected.

In 1974, the movement was started for Roman Script and Bodo Sahitya Sabha played an important role in this regard. In support of this demand, the Bodo Sahitya Sabha put forward the following facts-

(a) Kothari commission agreed for the adoption of Roman script

(b) Garo tribals of Golpara adopted Roman script

(c) Renouned linguist Dr. A.K. Chatterjee and Dr. kakati considered Roman script most appropriate for Bodo language.

(d) This was not a new script for Bodo language. In 1904 also the Roman script had been used for the text books of primary classes.

Thus, the movement started with (Dharna) Satyagrah and strike etc. The movement affected non-Bodo population also. Ultimately, the state government put the issue before the central government The central government after discussing the matter with the Bodo leaders, decided that the 'DEVNAGARI script' should be used in Bodo language as medium of instruction. Thus, in Bodo movement, the youth played more important role than the people of other age categories. The leadership was in the hands of educated Bodos. Though the demand for separate state was raised, some people supported. The state government also or opposed to demand of 'Udyanchal state' directly or indirectly.

The cultural aspect of the movement was as important as political because to educate the people, preparation of literature in their own language and to keep alive their own culture was also the aim of the movement. These two demands were closely interlinked. The cultural aspect was a means to attain the political one. The purpose of separate state was that people would maintain their socio-cultural identity. Though, the movement was confined to Assam state only, the activities of the Bodo Sahitya Sabha had its impact on the neighbouring states also. The movement was well organized, both structurally and functionally. The Bodo literature and the published material played important role in the movement, the top Bodo leaders were quite educated and enlightened. They had full knowledge regarding their aim and programme. The Bodo movement achieved success in attaining the goal of medium of instruction at the secondary level. They accepted Devnagari script in place of Assamese script. In Bodo movement, their traditional folk songs and folk literature also played important role which made the movement more effective.

Garo Political Movement and the Role of Garo National Council

Garos lived in the vicinity of Garo hills. They did not have any traditional political organisation. Garos were divided into various clans and sub clans. The people of a particular clan sub clan lived in a particular region consisting of several villages which did not have any traditional political significance.

Before Britishers came to the area, there was no political leader even at the village level. The village matters were resolved by mutual discussion and consensus. The people of a clan/sub group lived in a particular village.

In Garo hills the political changes came along with the arrival of Britishers. Officials were appointed at the village level for the collection of revenue. These officials were given some powers. The whole district was divided into several revenue zones. The distt. level official was a Britisher or the officer trusted by British government and the village level official used to collect revenue from the villagers and deposited the same with the distt. level officer. The British government constructed roads and bridges in the area. Till that time, the Garos were not in contact with the outsiders. The outside contact was by and large confined to the missionaries.

The first instance of political activities can be noticed in 1902 when a Garo leader opposed the ownership of land by an outsider in their area and put their demand of reserved forests and other forest produce. The British government officials sympathetically considered their demands and gave certain concessions.

The feelings of unity arose among Garos when during the 2nd World War an army unit consisting only of Garo youth, was sent to Burma. The army unit consisted of youth from various Garo tribes (groups and sub groups). The soldiers from different groups and sub groups met for the first time and developed the feeling of unity. The feeling of unity persisted even after their return to Garo hills. There were educated Garos also in the unit who were lower level officers and they played more important role in this regard.

In 1946, a Garo leader, who was Ex-soldier, established Garo National Conference. After sometimes its name was changed to Garo National Council. The main aim of this organisation was to bring reform in the social life of Garo people. The political ideology of Garo National Council had its affect in 1952 general election. The council put their candidate for the state assembly and distt council. Out of 4 candidates who contested election of state assembly, three were successful. Similarly, they attained desired success in the election of distt council. The Garo National Council emerged fully as a political force.

After 1952 general elections, the demand for a separate state was raised. The demand was put before the commission in 1954-55. In 1957, the movement was at its peak. The council fought 1957 election on the issue of separate state and the council won all the 4 seats. In 1957 distt council elections, out of 22 candidates who contested the election, 17 were declared elected, two were elected unanimously.

After the passing of Assam Language Act in 1960, the demand for separate state was further intensified because these people were against Assamese language as a medium of instruction. The Garo elected members resigned from assembly and from the cabinet and participated in the movement for separate state. Garo leader capt Sangma called a conference of all the tribal hill leaders at Shillong. In this conference the leaders of Garo, Khasi, Jayanta, tribes were present. But this combined organisation was not free from internal differences. Even then the all party hill leaders conference emerged as a common force under the leadership of Captain Sangma. In 1962 elections, under the leadership of All Party Hill Conference, Garo candidates won one of 4 seats. Later on, on the issue of Assamese language as a medium of instruction, all the members were asked to resign. In response to this call only Capt Sangma resigned. Thus, internal differences had cropped up within the conference. The GNC (Garo National Conference) was also not free from differences.

Again the demand for separate state was made in 1967 and it became a matter of discussion in Delhi. All people hill leaders conference once again attained very good success in 1967 elections. In 1968, the government of India accepted the demand of a state within the state of Assam, which was a step for attaining the full statehood. The new state was named as Meghalaya, which consisted of three distt. of Assam state namely Garo hills, Khasi hills and Jayantia Hills. The process of attaining full statehood for Meghalaya was peaceful and there was no further movement.

As we have discussed earlier, Garo National Council was not free from internal conflicts. Its leaders, at several times faced problems. Later on, educated Garos came forward and their 2 associations. Garo Graduate Union and Garo Unions came into existence. Naturally these organisations affected Garo National Council. In spite of seversal ups and downs, Garo National Council was the only active organization of the Garo common people. One significant reason was that from the very beginning it had the effective leadership of Capt. Sangma. Garos gave him respect and affection.

Thus, the political movement led by Garo National Council played the role in the formation of the state of Meghalaya.

Nebula Movement

This movement was related to three groups i.e. Nepali, Lepcha and Bhotia. Until 1935, there was a conflicting situation between people of Bhutan, sikkim and Nepal. Here the term 'Bhotia' has been used for the people coming from Bhutan to this region or the people of Bhutan origin and should not be confused for 'Bhotias' from Garhwal and Kumaon Himalayas. All three Ethnic groups migrated to Darjeeling region and settled there. After the coming of Britishers the Nepalis who were basically agriculturists migrated to this area in large number. Where as Bhotias were basically traders and the Lepchas were engaged in axe cultivation. In the beginning, the Britishers, as usual, adopted the policy of non-interference.

The Nebula movement had its roots in language and religion. In this region the government opened schools, having English and Hindi medium. The Bhotias and Lepchas had no problem in picking up Hindi language. As the number of Nepalis had multiplied in number, there was a demand for introduction of Nepali language. In 1910 a 'gorkha' magazine started and in 1918, Nepali as a subject was recognized from metric to B.A. This highly encouragd the Nepali educated youth and they started the movement to make Nepali as a medium of instruction. In 1925 a Nepali newspaper (Fortnightly) was launched. A committee was constituted consisting of the members of all three ie Bhotias, Lepcha and Nepali. Which the members of the first two communities ie Lepchas and Bhotias opposed the Nepali being the medium of instruction. The opposition met with counter opposition and the number game started. In 1927, a committee headed by deputy commissioner Grifith, recommended the introduction of Nepali language as medium of instruction in some schools. This was opposed by the other two groups.

An influencial leader, Sardar Bahadur Laden La, who had once aspired to become member of the legislative assembly of undivided Bengal, tried to establish unity among these three groups. He established an organisation which was known as 'Hill People's Social Union' in 1934. Its aim was to generate employment, social development and also to undertake welfare activities among these people. Gradually the efforts were made to bring unity among these three groups and remove the differences in terms of language and religion.

Gond Movement

Gonds are the largest tribe, spread over the large part of the central India, from Satpura to Godavari river. In the past, their habitation was known as Gondwana. In ancient times, the area had several Gond rulers having their own small territories. Till recent times the Gond landlords had monopolised the area. That is why Gonds were in more prominence, compared to other tribal groups of the area.

The movement of the Gonds was related to land and forest. The Gond rulers (like other) used to take revenue from others in the area. Though like other landlords, the Gond rulers also crushed the movement in 1857, but at that time, all the Gond peasants did not participate in the movement. In the decade of Forties, the Gonds started the movement for their monopoly over the forests. The movements was confined to forest. It had following reasons-

(a) The king who was owner of the land, was religious head also. The Gonds who were God fearing, were afraid of religious powers of the king.

(b) The Gonds therefore, never started agitation for the land.

(c) The forests were also their important source of livelihood and government control was gradually increasing in the forests and their traditional rights over the forests were gradually on decline.

(d) Forests and their resources were continuously on decline and tribal people had become conscious of this fact.

Because of these stated factors, Gond movement was centred around forests. During forties, the Gonds of Adi Aabad started movement but it was short lived. Actually Gond tribe was organized in 1950, under the leadership of Dharmdas. The activities it started were regarding the welfare of the people. This organisation was non-political in nature. After Dharam Das, a person of Raj Gond tribe-Lalshyam shah took the leadership. He was influenced by the rural reconstruction programme as envisaged by Gandhi ji. Later on, he started taking part in politics as he believed that politics is the most powerful weapon for bringing social change.

During the fifties and sixties several events took place in Gond region, which caused unrest among Gond tribe. Some of these were as follows.

(a) Undesirable events in Bastar

(b) Launching of Dandkaranya project. In this project one important task was the rehabilitation the refugees who had come from east Bengal and the government interference in forest had increased. The tribals opposed the rehabilitation of outsiders in their area.

(c) The exploitation by forest contractors. For example, tribal labour was hired at cheaper rates.

(d) Restriction on the collection of forest produce by the tribal people.

(e) Unemployment among educated tribal youth and the demand of these educated unemployed people was that they shall be provided employment at Bhilai and at other government establishments.

Thus, various factors were responsible for Gond movement and they started agitation for separate state. For example, in 1941 Gond leader 'Kurma Bhimu' started the demand of 'Gond Raj'. In 1963, the Gond leaders demanded separate state for the tribals. The demand was put before state reorganization commission on the occasion of the meeting of all India Congress Committee at Raipar in the year 1960, about 40 thousand tribals staged dharma in support of their demand. As a consequence of which Dhewar commission was established, which nominated a member from Gond tribe in its committee. Again the demand for Gondwana state was raised. The tribal leaders, asked their people to stop animal sacrifice, have their own temples (religious centres), respect women, religions unity and several other social reconstruction programmes were launched. But, because several tribal leaders were arrested the movement was unsuccessful. Moreover, Gonds were themselves internally divided and could not muster courage to oppose the Gond landlords and when ever they opposed they met with failure.

Role of Bhotia Tribe in Chipko Movement

This movement was started in Garhwal Himalayas, basically by savarna hindu castes of the region and the women played significant role. Likewise the Bhotia men and women also played important role in this movement. 'CHIPKO' means embracing the trees ie saving the trees from cutting. Its sole aim was to save the forests. A similar movement had started in Jodhpur district of Rajasthan, but these two movements had taken place independent of each other. In Rajasthan the movement was crushed by the then rulers, where as in Garhwal Himalayas it met with great success. Actually, Chipko movement had started in 1930, during the British period but it did not meet any success. But it revealed that the people of Himalayan region had become conscious enough regarding the preservation of forests. However, the modern 'chipko' movement started in chamoli (Gopeshwar) Garhwal in the year 1973, under the leadership of Chandi Prasad Bhatt. He organised the villagers, who directly or indirectly benefited from the forests.

The policies of the British government, gradually caused unrest among the villagers. There were several reasons. Some of these were given as below-

(1) Government's increasing control over the forests, auction and sale of forest property.

(2) Increasing restrictions on the native people (local people) regarding the use of forests and their resources.

(3) Decline of forests and its adverse ecological effects e.g. decline in rainfall, soil erosion, scarcity of water and scarcity of grasslands.

(4) The development of Hill areas in the form of construction of roads, exploration of mineral resources in hill areas etc also had negative effect on the forests.

The government's policy to earn more money and the development of hill region both had negative effects on the forests and their resources. It is worth remembering that after 1962 (Indo-China conflict) the government had taken initiative for the development of hill areas. It established an organization, named as Border road organization. This organization tried to build roads at a large scale in the region. Though, this was appreciated by the local population, it also resulted into the decline of forests. Moreover, once the transportation network in the region developed, it also resulted in the theft of forest wealth and illegal cutting of forests increased. Even after independence the local and central government, continued the policy of making forests as a good source of revenue. All this led the people to organize themselves for an agitation with a view to protect the forests from further loss. These above stated factors led to Chipko Movement which was widely appreciated and had moral support not only at the all India level rather ecologists from all over the world gave moral support to this movement.

The Bhotias who lived in the out skirts of the Kumaon and Garhwal distt, were traditionally traders and shepherds. They used to keep goats, sheeps and other animals which were their source of livelihood and which provided them raw wool, transportation facility etc. The Bhotias were trans-humane and moved from one place to another, in search of pastures. The loss of forests and pastures affected their source of livelihood also. The Bhotia men and women were made aware of this fact and these people also entered the agitation. Thus, the Bhotia tribe also had its contribution to Chipko Movement which is known all over the world for the environmental preservation. In Chipko Movement the contribution of women has been more significant than that of the men, though the leadership was basically in the hands of men. This is because in Kumaon and Garhwal Himalayas women play more important role in the domestic chores e.g. collection of grass, fuel and forest wood etc. As these were in scarcity due to the loss of the forests, it was easier to motivate the women, first to help in the availability of these resources in the area and later to have their share. This movement started at the villages level. It spread in Bhotia villages or Bhotia dominated villages also one woman of a Bhotia village played very important role in organizing the other village women in embracing the trees from further felling. She organized the other Bhotia women and motivated them to protect the forests.

Tribal Movement in Rajasthan

From the point of view of tribal population, Rajasthan is an important state. Out of 12 important tribal groups Bhil tribe is well known, not only within the state but all over the tribal world, for its particular characteristics. Bhils have an important place among Indian tribes. Bhil social movement can be associated with Bhagat movements. The historians have in their writings termed them as political and reform movements. The following are some of the important tribal movements in Rajasthan

(1) Moti lal Tejawat Bhil movement (1921-22)

(2) Govind Giri movement

(3) Garasia unity movement

(4) Meena social reform movement against 1871 criminal tribes act.

However, this fact has to be noted that the role of sociologists in the study of tribal social movement in Rajasthan has been negligible. Yet there are a few, which are worth mentioning. These are:

(a) Tribal unity movement (adivasi Eki Andolan) Moti lal Tejawat a non tribal person was the founder of this movement. The purpose of this movement was to organize the tribal people, provide them social justice and to make them free from the clutches of feudal lords who had exploited them for a long time. Tejawat was in favour of structural unity among all sections of society, especially the tribal peasants. The movement started from Jhadol state of Mewar region. Gradually the tribals of neighbouring region joined the movement. Tejawat wanted to establish unity among Bhils, Meenas and Garasias, the three major tribal groups. He being himself from agricultural background knew the plight of a poor farm labourer and landless peasants and how and to what extent they were being exploited by feudal landlords. He lodged complaints to the ruling authorities regarding the exploitation of the tribal people but did not meet any success. On the contrary, he was punished and put in jail. In prison he was given in human treatment. In the year 1921-22 Moti lal toured the villages of the region and tried to organize the poor villagers against the exploitation by feudel landlords (jagirdars). The authorities were not at all happy with his activites and they wanted to get rid of him. Motilal had at times, remain underground and the villagers, especially Bhils always stood behind him. On June 3, 1929, he was again arrested and sent to Jail for 7 years. His activities were strictly watched. He was arrested in 1938. Again he was arrested during quit India movement and was released from Jail in 1945. Thus, a non-advasi played a significant role in mobilizing tribals.

Social and Cultural Movement among Bhils

Bhils are an important tribe. Numerically also Bhils are the largest tribe of western India. In Rajasthan, they have ruled over certain regions of the state like Kota, Banswara and Dungarpur state. History testifies to this fact. Among Bhils the priest (bhopa) who is also known as Gameti has a special status in their society. All the members of the clan give him due respect and obey his orders. In the past when Bhils were rulers, they were challenged by Rajputs and Marathas. They were defeated by the later in the battlefield and forced to take shelter in the forests. As a result a new cultural homogeneity emerged among these people. Their dwellings were in the form of barracks which were locally known as pals.

Bhils were divided into two parts-

(a) In this category were those who used to live in remote areas, kept themselves away from the non tribal people (outsiders). These people never accepted the authority of non-tribals.

(b) the second category was of those people who accepted the superiority (authority) of the outsiders (non-tribal people) and started adopting their way of living. Both these groups of Bhils used to claim superiority over each other. Gradually, Bhils started realising that social, cultural norms of Hindu society were at higher plane. As a result the emergence notion of 'Bhagat' took place. Bhagat was a person who had lost his faith in primitive religious traditions and had developed belief on Hindu Gods and Goddesses. Bhagat movement was responsible for tribal people's loss of faith in primitive religious practices. Thus, among Bhils, one section for a long time resisted these ideas.

Bhagat Movement

First this movement started more than 500 years ago among Bhils. Besides Bhils other castes such as Bhoj, Kurmi, Kumhar even Brahmins also participated in the movement. Bhagat Bhils adopted vegetarianism. They stopped taking bride price, abandoned marrying elder brother's wife. Efforts were made to avoid remarriage of any type. They adopted new norms of greeting. For example, Bhagat Bhils used the respectable term of 'Jai Maharaj. Bhagats used to wear white clothes which they considered as sign of truthfullness. Another leader Govind Giri started preaching Bhils for establishing a new society.

Bhagats were devotees of Mahadev and lord Krishna. The followers of Govind Giri observed the following rules.

(1) Observing rules of not committing theft.

(2) Avoid drinking and eating flesh.

(3) Observing path of non violence.

(4) Avoiding polygamy, following the rules of marriage.

(5) Taking bath everyday and observing fast on special occasions.

(6) Observing rules of etiquette in the norms of greeting.

(7) Instead of cremating burying a dead person.

In addition to that Bhagat panthis started wearing sacred thread. Bhagat panthis had some differences with Non-Bhagats ie those Bhils who were against this sect. For example, under developmental programme some Bhils had started fishing and poultry farming which was opposed by the Bhagat Panthis but in all the followers of Bhagat Panthis played important role in bringing social, cultural and religious changes in Bhil society.

References

1. Patel M.L., *Tribal Development* (1984).
2. Thomas and Taylor, *Tribal Awakening* (1965).
3. Singh K. Surendra, *Tribal Situation in India* (1972).
4. Verrier Edwin, *Philosophy for Nefa* (1960).
5. Singh K.S., *Tribal Movement in India.*
6. Meclanen V., *Studies in Social Movement* (1969).
7. Hasnain Nadeem, *Tribal India Today* (1983).
8. Wilkinson Paul, *Social Movements, London* (1971).
9. Joshi M.M., *Bastar: India's Sleeping Giant.*
10. Martin Oraon, *The Santal: A Tribe in Search of Great Traditions* (1965).

❑❑❑

16

Tribal Women in India

Tribals in India have an important place. They are among the most backward people in the country. These people are known by various names. Risley, Sobert, Martin and others used the term 'aborigines' for these people. Hutton called them 'Primitive tribes'. Sir Baines used the term 'Hill tribes'. Else where he called them as 'Jungle people' 'forest tribes' or 'folk'. G.S. Ghurye called them 'so called aborigines' or 'backward Hindus'. Later on, Ghurye himself proposed the term 'scheduled tribes' for these people which was accepted under section 342 of the Indian Constitution.

The term 'tribe' was first used by the British Census officials cum Anthropologists for the purpose of enumerating social groups in India. In the eighteenth century the term caste had often been used synonymously with the term tribe. Later on, it was used to differentiate certain social groups from the caste Hindus. The Government of India Act 1935 used the term 'Backward tribes'. The Indian Constitution 1950 has retained the terminology of 1935 Act, with a slight alteration, using 'scheduled' instead of 'backward'. Articles 342 and 342-A of the Indian constitution empower the president to specify certain groups as 'scheduled tribes'. Article 366 (25) of the constitution has defined 'scheduled tribes' as 'such tribes or tribal communities or parts or groups within such tribes or tribal communities as are deemed under Article 342 to be scheduled tribes for the purpose of this constitution.

According to S.C. Dube the term tribe has never been described precisely and satisfactorily. It was used at one time, to denote a bewildering variety of social categories that were neither analogous nor comparable. He has given the following characteristics of the tribal people:

(1) Their roots in the soil date back to very early period; if they are not the original inhabitants, they are at least some of the oldest inhabitants of the land.

(2) They live in relative isolation of the hills and forests.

(3) Their sense of history is shallow for, among them, the remembered history of five to six generations tends to get merged in mythology.

(4) They have a low level of techno-economic development.

(5) In terms of their cultural ethos-language, institutions, beliefs and customs- they stand out from the other sections of the society.

(6) If they are not egalitarian, they are at least non-hierarchic and undifferentiated.

In India at present there are several hundreds of tribal groups, spread over almost throughout the country, mostly sporadically but with sizeable concentrations in major areas. The tribal people living in different parts of India, belong to various linguistic, economic, social and religious categories with a heterogeneous cultural pattern and variegated economic conditions and activities largely based on ecological settings. The tribals constitute about 8 per cent of the country's total population with wide regional variations. There are states like Nagaland, Mizoram and Arunachal Pradesh with overwhelming tribal population. On the other hand the states like Uttar Pradesh, Punjab, Tamil Nadu and Karnataka, have less than one per cent of the tribal population. Among other states and union territories, Punjab, Chandigarh, Delhi and Pondicherry have the lowest proportion of tribal population.

Sex-ratio in India is one of the lowest in the world. There are about 935 females per one thousand males. But if we look at male-female sex ratio among the tribals in India we certainly find a different picture. The number of tribal women per one hundred tribal men was 98.2 according to 1971 census—a ratio indicating good stability and balanced composition of sex for healthy growth and survival. In this respect the Indian tribals are at a vantage point a matter to be envied by the general Indian population. What emerges is a real accomplishment of adjustment and progress by tribal women in contrast to the general female population of India. Their growth has been incredibly massive and perhaps unprecedented, but with a very balanced sex ratio pushing them to a situation which is certainly advantageous for a viable existence. But, all said and done, one may well ask: how long can the tribal women keep up their demographic pace. For such a healthy sex ratio one would like to give due credit to the tribal social structure and the culture which blossomed independently in the midst of nature which always valued and kept women at par with the men folk. But now the old tribal norms are gradually fading away and the picture is not alike every where One can easily notice great complexities and contradictions in the Indian tribal groups. While on one hand women are far more independent and free in certain isolated pockets, on the other hand they have been subjected to certain forms of inequalities and oppression. The social structure and culture of these tribal groups is in a state of transition. The contact of the tribals with the outside world and the gradual process of acculturation and assimilation has to a great extent, played a decisive role in determining the status of women.

In the words of Rizvi, "Anthropologists have paid scant attention in studying the role of women in tribal economy. What one infers from available studies on tribal economy is merely a sex wise division of labour described in a ritualistic fashion. The economy of the tribe is a projection of tribal society, a response to the eco-system in which it is placed, its functions of production and distribution are governed by the bonds of kinship within or between families, clans or kindred. Production is based on the expoitation of resources locally and easily available with a crude technology largely for consumption.

The tribal people could be placed at different stages of economic development beginning from hunting and food gathering to the stage of industrial growth. But whatever has been the stage of economic development and whatever be their position in family economic affairs, one thing is certain that the tribal women, by and large act as labour machines. They not only exercise their authority in the internal chores of the households, even in external domestic economic affairs, at times women play significant role. Barring a few economic activities, women have been taking part almost in all the activities, at all the stages of economic development. In some of the tribal groups, the rules of inheritance and succession have put women in a superior position compared to their male counterparts. In the tribal world, there are also instances of patriarchal domination where women have been reduced to a much inferior position as chattels. They have been prohibited from property rights and have been living on the mercy of their men folk. But the general picture does not indicate such a pathetic sight. Poverty and hardships are widely prevalent in the tribal world but women are not much discriminated against as one can view in the lower stratas of the Indian society.

Economic Life of Tribal Women

Gujar women of Himachal Pradesh work harder than their men folk and play double role in earning bread for the family. Regarding Gadulia Lohar women, Misra states that these women have immense capacity to work and tolerate. At one moment she might be pounding red hot iron in hot sun with a hammer weighing not less than 5 kg. In a minute she might be feeding her 10 day's old child, in another she might be grinding grain or making chapati and rushing back to hammering work.

The Kota women of Nilgiri hills are considered as economic assest. Their contribution to the family economy is no less than that of their male counterparts. They keep themselves busy in domestic chores round the clock. But the hard tasks performed by women do not raise their status. The male domination is discernible even customarily. For example, cooking is generally done by women and if the meals are to be prepared in milk or milk products—this is the prerogative of men folk.

Among the 'Ho' tribe men are known for their idleness and by and large depend for their livelihood on their women folk. Regarding the idleness of their men folk. D.N. Majumdar wrote 'so long as it is indispensable for Ho men to work, so long as they depend upon the labours of their women folk, they prefer to remain idle and content with hand to mouth existence. One of the ways Ho males utilize their female folk to maintain them is by sending their wives and sisters to work in the mines, themselves remaining in the village.

While stating about the economic role of Dafla women, Shukla stated that though Daflas practise polygyny and do not permit their women to participate in religious ceremonies, each Dafla wife has a separate hearth by which she lives. She has a plot of her own which she cultivates. She has a poultry of her own and many have pigs and goats. Thus, each Dafla wife does all the tasks to maintain herself and her children. The husband's role is of secondary nature. 'for some of the Daflas privileged with eight or ten wives, it is easy to have a comfortable life. A rich Dafla, therefore, can often be seen living an idle life or settling?

Some of the tribals have developed mythical notions regarding feminine tasks. One such myth about drinking water and fire is associated with Birjhia tribe of Chhota Nagpur. 'situated as the Birjhia habitat fetching drinking water for the house, which is a feminine task, poses a hard problem. The women have to traverse long distances down hill slopes with pitchers and similar containers to reach the stream to collect drinking water. The people say that the women have been condemned to this labourious task due to the original sin committed by their women ancestors by disbelieving Mahadeo.

N.C. Choudhary believes that tribal woman is an economic asset and considerable value is placed on a hard working, industrious and dutiful wife. There is a clear division of labour between a man and a woman. Her life is spent in working in the field, raising the children and attending all domestic chores. But her important economic role does not give her a very high position in the society at par with man......her loss in position is compensated because she enjoys sufficient freedom in her movement.

Jyoti Sen while highlighting the economic role of women concluded that:

(a) In Khasi society women take an active part in trade which elsewhere is usually in the hands of men.

(b) Many women maintain their families by engaging in different types of occupations.

(c) There are many women petty traders who shift from one occupation to another within a short span of time.

Land has special role to play in the economic upliftment of the tribals because they are basically interested to live on it due to their affinity with forest and love for nature. Culturally, forest and land are interwoven in the daily life of the tribal people. Their happiness knows no bounds when, they sing songs of forests while working in their own fields. Women folk join hands with men folk in forest and farms to make the hard work quite charming.

With the growth of industries in tribal areas, a large number of tribal women have been drawn into occupations unknown to them. Their status in labour market has changed. They are now employed in such jobs which give them ready cash. Sachchidananda writes about tribal women working in Hatia, 'most of the women work to supplement family income. In certain cases they are the only earners in their families. There are, however, at least 12 per cent of them, who work for some extra income and self fulfillment. The idea of pin money is expressed in terms of self comfort and better dressing. It is related to the traditional concept of pleasure. Pleasure in tribal life is virtually synonymous with dancing, singing, eating and drinking, festivity and implicitly sexual activity. Since the scope of pleasure in the form of community event is now minimum, pleasure in present context is associated with visiting cinema, restaurant, listening radio and so on. Thus, the idea of pleasure shows an emerging importance of individuality and this is a departure from the accepted norm of community in which group interest is dominant."

Thus, as we have stated earlier, the economic life of the tribal women in India presents a vivid picture. Bulk of the tribal people residing in the plains having closer cultural contacts with the non-tribals have more or less adopted their cultural norms and practices. Their women folk now enjoy lesser amount of freedom and equality and now their position is similar to that of the rest of the women. But most of the tribal women in North East India do not suffer from inequality. In economic pursuits, women do not lag behind their men folk. Biman Kumar Gupta writes: 'In Manipur especially it is difficult to find a male seller in the market. At Imphal there is the Ama market (market of mothers) where about 99 per cent of the sellers are women. In Meghalaya, even hawking of commodities are mainly done by women pedlars. In Arunachal the girls cover miles and miles of hilly tract to exchange essential commodities.

Thus, the tribal women in India have maintained the long tradition of working shoulder to shoulder with men in almost all the areas of the productive system at various stages of the economic development. They have maintained this pace even in the sphere of industrialization. But the industrial sphere has put more burden of economic role on tribal women as the new order formally separates the two types of work roles which at times creates the problems of adjustment. It can be concluded that the involvement of women in economic activities and their control over property is responsible for their status in tribal society.

Property Rights : In primitive society, the idea of individual or family property came quite late. In the beginning the property was community based. The property rights are by and large traditionally determined. In patriarchal type of society, men enjoy all the privileges where as in a matriarchal type the property rights are transmitted from mother to daughter. However, in both the types there are certain exceptions also. For example, Bhotias of Kumaon and Garhwal Himalayas are patriarchal but in economic and other social matters, women are at par with men. Bhotia women not only enjoy economic independence, at times, they are the custodian of the family purse, and their contribution to the family economy is much more than that of their men folk. This is because of their expertise in weaving, garment making and preparation of various kinds of rugs etc. all the skills have been developed by the women and men are largely engaged in unskilled kinds of jobs. Similarly, women in patriarchal Tharu community enjoy a status which is not inferior to that of their male counterparts.

Among matriarchal Garos and Khasis the inheritance rights are enjoyed by women. The rules of primogeniture and ultimogeniture are also observed. Among Khasis, the major part of these rights belongs to the youngest girl. She claims the biggest share in the property. Important parts of property like House and Jewellery are owned by her. But she can not dispose off this without the consent of other sisters. They are entitled to a share too. They also have the obligations like the maintenance of the family property.

Among Garos, generally, any of the daughters who pleases the parents by promising pattern of behaviour may be selected as an hairess. The youngest one has the best chance of being selected as the hairess if she does not otherwise disequalify herself. In the absence of a daughter the family selects one from the extended family. Since the Garos are matrilocal and uxorilocal the selected daughter inherits the family residence and household properties and stays with her parents after marriage. These people, however, do not permit their widows to inherit the property. But if a widow remarries within a specified period after the death of her husband, she can retain the property rights which otherwise, she has to forfeit. As the property is to be transmitted from mother to daughter and if the daughter is married, the only option left for the mother (who is a widow) is to marry her daughter's husband for the retention and smooth transfer of property.

But among the majority of tribal groups, women customarily do not enjoy property rights like the lower caste Hindus. At times, their only property consists of a few clothings and ornaments. The ornaments too they have to part with in case of a divorce.

Social Structure : For analysing the position of tribal women, it is necessary to understand the tribal social structure. There are several hundred tribal groups in India with distinctive social structural characteristics. To understand the position of tribal women an attempt has been made to analyse their various social institutions namely family, marriage, religion, and political institutions within the group structure. This would give an idea in understanding the position of tribal women in their native setting.

Marriage: Unlike Hindus, marriage among the Indian tribals is more of a contract and less of a sacrament. Among these people we find various types of marriages and ways of acquiring marital partners, from most civilized modern criteria of mate slection to the most primitive or barbarian way of acquiring a mate. On one hand, we find marriages taking places by mutual consent of a girl and a boy or arranged by parents, on the other hand there are instances of marriage by capture, marriage by intrusion and marriage by service. Usually, the marriage of a girl used to take place after attaining puberty (prior to their contact with the non-tribals), child marriages were almost unknown to these people. However, after their contact with the outside world, child marriages have started taking place, which has curtailed the freedom of the marital partners and now marriage is becoming more and more an affair of the parents.

The tribals consider marriage very essential from economic point of view also. Some of the tribals viz. Garasias, Bhotias, Tangsa, Nagas and Kukis still follow the norms of late marriage. But most of the tribals following late marriage are those who reside in geographically isolated regions.

Probationary marriage is something which is traditionally absent among other sections of the Indian society. Kukis practice probationary marriage, these people permit free mixing of boys and girls and pre-marital sex relations are not taboo in probationary type of marriages. The boy and girl who have lived together before marriage but later refuse to marry each other, do not bring any disgrace to the family or to the community at large. Nor are their marital chances decreased (minimized) owing to premarital sex relationship and subsequent child birth.

Marriage by trial which could be noticed among Bhils and Angamy Nagas has its instances in the Hindu epics, which was looked upon with great respect.

The marriage by service was practiced by Baigas, Gonds, Birhors, Gujaras of Himachal Pradesh and others, a crude method of getting a marital partner, indicates the fact that the girl was precious commodity in their society which could fetch wealth to the family in cash or kind. Rendering service at would be wife's parental home for a specified period is a sort of substitute for one's inability to pay the bride price.

The 'marriage by purchase' is practiced by Santhals, Ho, Oraon, Kharia and Gond etc. and marriage by capture is popular among Nagas, Bhils and Gonds. Marriage by intrusion as practiced by Santhals and Kamars, is one of the most primitive ways of acquiring mates among the tribals.

There are instances of monogamy, polygyny and polyandry among these people. Where as Hos are strictly monogamous, Bhotias Nagas and several other tribes of north-eastern region practiced polygyny. Polyandry was popular among Tiyans of Kerala, Todas of Nilgiri hills and Khas tribe of Jaunsar Bhabar in Uttaranchal.

Custom of levirate and sororate is also popular among these people. Only a few Indian tribes viz. Adiyana, Muduvars and Malavedars of south India do not observe liverate. The sororate as a custom at times takes the shape of polygyny for which the anthropologists have used, the term 'contemporary sororate'. In this type of marriage, the younger sister of wife become a cowife. This custom was common among Kannikars, Kadars, Mala kuduvars, Mala pulayars and Uralis. Among palliyars, a man who wanted to take a second wife could only marry the younger sister of his first wife. However, the Chingathar and Kalanadis who practise sororate, forbid levirate.

The tribals also follow various practices in the marital selection. They also observe incest taboos. For example among the Bodos of Assam offenders against the incest rules are punished. Boys and girls are generally free in the choice of their marriage partner though they must ask for the approval of their parents before wedding can take place. No marriage is celebrated, without the payment of bridal wealth which consists of animals and agricultural products.

Among Garos (having matriarchal type of family) the girl possesses more power than a boy. She selects a boy as her husband. There are certain unique practices in the marriage among certain tribes. For example, among the Khonds, it is the bride and her party that goes to the bridegroom's place and there, the marriage is concluded.

While considering the qualities of the girl, the tribals give less importance to the physical appearance and more to her abilities and skills. Choudhary states, "A strong and hardworking girl, clean and properly dressed with lots of ornaments is considered beautiful by Murias. Bride price of a Sema girl depends on her capabilities. A girl who is thrifty, works hard in the field and home and adapt in weaving commands higher bride price. Personal appearance and physical beauty have very little to do with marriage price. Among Bhotias, the beautiful garments prepared by the girl and her expertise in weaving etc. were treated as the main considerations in deciding the marriage.

Ramesh Chandra believed that the economic hardship among the North western Himalayan dwellers was the cause of the prevalence of polyandry. Even love marriages are not known among most of the Indian tribes. Now the marriages by intrusion and elopement are lacking social respectability and love marriages are being discarded by these people. These people have developed very high preference for arranged marriages.

Thus, the institution of marriage regards tribal women in their society quite significant with full consideration of self-identity. They play important role in deciding their own affairs. But the process of acculturation and assimilation has started bestowing several vices upon women. The child marriage has been introduced. The freedom of women has been curtailed. Marriage is becoming an affair of the parents and family. Some more assimilated and Hinduised tribals like Meenas of Rajasthan and several others, have introduced dowry also which has adversely affected the position of the women.

Widow Remarriage: Unlike Hindus, widowhood is almost absent among Indian tribes. Almost all the tribal groups provide traditional sanction for widow remarriage, mostly through levirate. The consent of the widow is of course given due consideration. Thus, widow and widower remarriages are widely prevalent among the tribal people. It is a sequel of a socially accepted principle that no adult individual should remain without a mate. Replacement marriage is obligatory. Widowhood is a temporary phase. For a woman, the widow's position hardly arises in a Bhil family, for she remarries after a period of mourning. Only old women who do not take recourse to remarriage, remain as widows. As a widow she is revered by the family. Among the Oraons a widower is customarily supposed to marry a widow or a divorced woman and not a maiden.

In the past there was a custom of inheritance of widows among the 'Daflas'. After the death of the father, the son used to inherit his step mothers. Now such a custom has died out. However, there is a custom of levirate which provides that if a man dies, his widow may remarry one of his younger brothers. The rules of leviration, the younger brother marrying the widow of the elder brother are quite evident in Birjhia social life but the widow's consent for remarriage is a necessary condition.

Thus, a widow is not debarred from any activity normally done by a married woman. She works in the field, raises her own family and exercises all the authority of a woman of her age. There is no social stigma attached to the widows. However, due to the limitation of the Hindu customs some discriminations are at times discernible among some of the tribals of the plains. Such a discrimination is noticeable on auspicious occasions. The more accultuarised Meenas of Rajasthan do not permit their widows to participate in marriage rituals.

Divorce: Divorce among tribals is practiced more simply and less inextricably as compared to the non-tribals. Generally, it is on account of failure in marriage and among most of the tribal groups women are granted equal rights in seeking divorce. For example, a santhal woman is entitled to seek a divorce if her husband is unable to fulfil her basic necessities. The cruelty on the part of a 'Tharu' husband (a tribe of Tarai region in Uttar Pradesh) entitles his wife to seek divorce. The wife can also divorce her husband if he is impotent and has lost his social prestige. The Khasis separate so frequently that children often do not know their fathers. The procedure of divorce is short and cheap. The Garos only demand a repayment of the bride-price. The bad effects on the children usually resulting from divorce are largely absent in matriarchal societies as children always remain with the mother and her family.

Among the Bodo tribe divorce and remarriage are quite easy affairs. In case of divorce (if there are children of the divorced couple), sons go with the father and daughters with the mother. There are certain tribal groups whose rules of divorce are tilted in favour of males. This is indicative of the fact that if a Birjhia wife is seeking divorce and trying to get another husband, her prospective second husband has to obtain formal permission of the first husband before solemnizing the marriage. Only after admitting the divorce, the marriage could be soleminsed.

Divorce is a recognized affair to break the marital relationship among the Lahaulis. The procedure is simple. The husband and wife seeking divorce hold a piece of thread and break it by pulling in opposite directions. If both partners agree to divorce no money is paid to any body, but if only one party is interested in it, the payment is made to the other party.

The Dafla tradition (custom) is silent over the rights of women. But as the wife is obtained for a specific payment, the husband claims full control on his wife. She cannot leave her husband according to the tribal custom, unless some one compensates him for the loss. Among the Gonds divorce is permitted with the assent of the payment. The husband normally requests for divorce although wife is equally permitted to do so. If the wife does not want to leave the husband's family she is provided with a house and maintenance till her death or remarriage. The separating wife can take her children. Among Khasis divorce is brought about by a formal ceremony in most cases. Among the Santhals divorce is performed through a 'leaf tearing' ceremony in the presence of the villagers.

Among Mizos a man can legally divorce his wife by saying 'I divorce you'. Divorce often takes place at the insistence of the members of the husband's family, if they are not pleased with her. Although, it may be initiated by the either party, divorce usually takes place at the insistence of the husband. The status enjoyed by men in this respect can be easily appreciated from the old saying that 'A wife and a bad fencing can be changed at any time." Divorce can also be affected by the wife by refunding the marriage price. This is resorted to only when the wife finds her situation intolerable. If the wife leaves her husband in this manner, it lowers the prestige not only of the unwanted husband but also of the husband's family.

There are also some instances of wife beating and harassment among the tribals. For example, among the Dublas of Gujarat if a man does not like his wife he persists in beating or treating her badly to such an extent that she runs to her natal home and never returns. At the same time there are examples also where women have free and at times upper hand in the dissolution of marital ties. The divorce is quite easy affair among the Apatanis of Arunachal Pradesh and the most usual case for divorce is the wife's dissatisfaction with the treatment she received at the hands of her husband or her mother-in-law. If the wife wants to leave her husband's house she is given the dowry she brought with her. While writing about the tribals of Bihar working in an Industrial setting, Sachchidananda writes that there were about 9 per cent women who were divorced on conventional grounds viz. barrenness, unfaithfulness, laziness, evil eye, quarrel some, impotency and so on. He states, 'there are some cases of dissertion by their non-tribal husbands. Some non-tribals who have come to Jamshedpur or Hatia, marry tribal women and live with them so long as they are here. As soon as they leave the work place, they forget all about the marriage. In many cases, the deserted women have children also. Since marriage with non-tribal is forbidden, those married women are outcasted and not taken back into the community after desertion,'

Thus, in simple societies the problem of divorce is not of a serious nature and women do not suffer on account of this problem. Neither is there any social stigma associated with problems of divorce.

Family: Various forms of family can be noticed among the tribal people in India. These family structures can be noticed on the basis of:

(a) Number of members of the family

(b) The nature of marriage and

(c) Lineage and habitation

On the basis of number, we can classify tribal families into nuclear, joint and conjugal types. Hos who are strictly monogamous, have nuclear type of family, consisting of husband, wife and their unmarried children. While Kharias have conjugal families in which along with married couple and their children some relatives also reside with the family.

According to marriage there are again two types of families.

(a) Monogamous and

(b) Polygamous

Khasas, Santhals and Hos are monogamous. The polygamous family types can be further sub-divided into:

(a) Polygynous and

(b) Polyandrous

In polyandrous type of family there are more than one wife in the family. Several tribes like Bhils, Nagas, Bhotias and Gonds etc had the tradition of polygyny. But now it is confined to the economically well-to-do persons in these tribal groups.

Polyandrous families can also be sub-divided into two types:

(a) Fraternal polyandry and

(b) Non-fraternal polyandry

In the fraternal polyandry, only the real brothers had a common wife or wives. While in non-fraternal polyandry a husband (other than the real brothers) lived in the family (usually a cousin-near or distant), sharing a common wife. Economic hardships and disproportionate male female sex-ratio seemed to be some of the important factors responsible for the prevalence of this custom. It is interesting to note that the position of women in polyandry is certainly better than that of women in most of the tribal groups. But in polyandrous society a woman losses her status and prestige if she remains barren.

Some of the tribals who now practise monogamy, had no customary restrictions in keeping more wives. The Birjhia is an example of this type. However, in Birjhia family, the wife nevertheless exercises certain rights in regard to some household matters which no husband would normally challenge.

Another type of family forms can be noticed from the point of view of lineage and habitation. Actually speaking, the roles of tribal women can be comprehended in the context of two basic forms of social structures. One is represented by matrilineal social structure and the other is patrilineal type. The Khasis and Garos fall in the former category. In matrilineal type where the property, and lineage transmit from mother to daughter, the position of woman is undoubtedly superior.

It would be incorrect to presume that in patriarchal type of family, the position of woman is inferior every where. There are certain tribal groups, which fall in this category and give utmost freedom to their women folk. For example, patriarchal Bhotias give ample freedom to their women folk but now the process of Hinduization has adversely affected the position of women. Actually speaking, the position of women in tribal society was better when the property and economy was more community based. With the growing individualistic notions of property, the institution of family has become more powerful and there is some decline of community influence on the individual to some extent, which has negatively affected the position of women.

In matriarchal type of societies women, who were enjoying the privileges of inheritance and succession, have started meeting the challenges from the male members of the agnate group, over the question of right to property. There are even cases pending in the courts of law, but the tribal customs of matriarchal societies have put women at an advantageous position.

Dormitories (Night Clubs) : It was a pivotal social institution among several tribal groups in India which used to have multifarious functions, right from guarding the village to drinking, dancing and merry making. These gotuls were by and large an abode of unmarried boys and girls. Match making, security of the village people and preservation of tribal cultural heritage were some of the important tasks of the gotuls. Among Bhotias these Gotuls which were known as 'RANGBANG' used to function under the charge of an old woman, with whose permission only a new member could be admitted into the gotual during the night hours. She used to maintain the discipline of the club, besides imparting sex education to the young unmarried boys and girls.

The institution of Gotul by and large acted as an outlet for premarital and extra marital sexual relationships, economic cooperation and group cohesiveness. With the spread of education along with growing contacts of the tribals with the non-tribal world, the Gotuls are loosing their significance and people have stopped sending their sons and daughters to these night clubs. It is significant to note that Gotuls gave ample freedom to the woman and always tried to uphold her dignity in the tribal society. Through the institution of gotul, better understanding and group cohesiveness always prevailed in their society and women were always treated as an equal and important partners in all the walks of life. Thus, the decline of the institution of dormitory has adversely affected the position of tribal women.

Political Matters: The tribes have been viewed as a part of the larger political system of the country. Within this political system the tribes enjoy certain special privileges. In this sense, the tribes constitute a separate category within India at the political level. At the civilizational level, however, they form many separate entities in a larger spatial mosaic. Traditionally, the tribal women had very little say in the political affairs. Even in certain matriarchal societies where the descent is traced through the female line, women were rarely allowed to take part in the traditional political institutions. But we can notice a few exceptions. For example, Tharu women were consulted by their male members on several important issues. The sansi women hold a good position in the community. They enjoy much influence in the tribal council in which they can speak freely, bear witness and give advice. The status of women in the tribal council is more important as due to the natural aversion of the sansis to apply for the protection of the law, these councils practically regulate all affairs and disputes of the community.

In simple societies, politics was not refined and it lacked patience, tolerance and wider participation. It was more aggressive and violent, the participation of women in politics was considered least desirable and therefore, they (women) remained at the periphery.

Religion : In the sphere of religious practices and rituals, the position of the tribal woman is somewhat inferior to that of their men folk. Usually the office of the priest is controlled by males. Among some of the tribal groups, where women enjoy same position in economic and other social spheres, in religious matters they enjoy secondary position. The Santhal women are not allowed to participate in community worship. Similarly, the Dafla women hardly have any privileges in religious matters. A Dafla woman does not take part in religious ceremonies except in the preparation of beer for ceremonial use. She may watch but does not participate. Yet we have a few exceptions in the tribal world were women enjoy position similar to that of their man folk. For example, the Lepchas have female priests also. The Lepcha priestess knows various mantras and tantras through which she cures a patient or even kills an enemy. The santhals believe in evil spirits, demon or ghost. There are witches among women as well. But by and large men hold supremacy in religious matters and women play only preferal role.

Tribal Women and Purdah : The Purdah was originally unknown among the tribals. These people do follow the custom of avoidance, but unlike Hindus-between those two persons who practice avoidance, the purdah does not exist. The acculturation and assimilation of tribals into larger Hindu society has introduced purdah among some of the tribal groups. For example, among the Meenas and Damors of Rajasthan, the purdah is widely practiced but the same is absent among the neighbouring tribes viz. Bhils and Garasias.

Husband-wife Cooperation : The existence of man as a social being is based and centered around the cultural norms and practices which people adopt in a particular social setting. Culture is the most important embodiment of man's survival and existence as a social being. The tribal societies have devised certain cultural practices which reflect cooperation as well as close association among its members. One of such cultural practice is known as 'Couvade Relationship' which is observed among some tribal groups in India. For example, among the Khas tribe of Jaunsar Bhabar, if a wife is pregnant, during that period she has to observe certain restrictions like abandoning heavy tasks, not washing clothes, not crossing the river, abandoning cooking and not touching the drinking water. Likewise, her husband is also not supposed to perform these tasks and imitate his wife in all the social restrictions. Similarly, while writing about the Dublas of Gujarat, Shah states that the husband of the pregnant woman has to observe several restrictions if an eclipse falls within period of pregnancy. Anthropologists are of the opinion that such a custom strengthens the bond of affection between husband and wife. It is a symbolic gesture which reminds a husband that he has to cooperate and sympathise with his wife when she is in dire need. The non-performance of such a custom brings social humiliation to a husband. It may appear as a crude device and to the civilized world it may appear as ridiculous but these symbolic gestures indicate the bond of cooperation which the husband and wife used to have. It also reflects the attitude of the tribal society toward women.

Aesthetics : The tribals have deep sense of beauty. Nature has enhanced their knowledge in art and craft. They too have desire to look better and therefore they decorate their faces and other parts of the body. The role of decoration mostly belongs to women. In the decoration of body, tattooing once was widely practiced art. This was generally done by women on certain ceremonial occasions. The Gond and Baiga women were often tattooed all over the body, but for each tribe the pattern was different. On a few occasions, the painting of the body was also done. Among the Gonds and Baigas a special decoration of hair was the comb. Unmarried boys and girls who had developed liking for each other, used to exchange combs, indicating their love.

The Island dwellers and various tribals of the sea coast, collect sea beads and other shell ornaments to decorate themselves. Women are better than their men in this task. The Garasia women are beauty conscious and are fond of decorating themselves with red colour which they often apply on their cheeks. The Garasia and Bhil women get their bodies tattooed in different designs. Sometimes they make flowers and birds on the body.

The aesthetics is also reflected in their art and craft. Among the Lakhers, basketry is a very important handiwork in which the role of women is quite outstanding. Among these people all the pottery work is done either by unmarried girls or widows.

Thus, the nature and the surrounding environment has played crucial role in the development of aesthetic values among the tribals. Tribal women have always shown greater adaptability in the retention of such values. Long back Verrior Elwin had hinted toward the possibility of the decline of tribal art on account of their contact with the outside world. His apprehension was that there is now very little left to be preserved. The reason is that the culture contact has brought inferiority among these people and they have started abandoning their own things.

Thus, the tribal people are in a state of transition. No doubt, the preservation of tribal cultural identity and cultural heritage is certainly a difficult task in the face of dominant cultural values. The process of acculturation and assimilation is also inevitable. But this process at times seems to be doing more harm to the tribal people, especially to the women. All the privileges which women were enjoying in their own native social structure are being taken away from them. Their social structure has adopted several customs and practices which have victimized the women. Rather, one can say that they have been quicker in adopting vices than virtues.

References

1. Shah Ghanshyam, *Economic Differentiations and Tribal Identity* (1984).
2. Duhe S.C., *Tribal Heritage of India* (1977).
3. Shashi S.S., *Tribal Women in India* (1978).
4. Singh K.S. (Ed) *Economies of the Tribes and their Transformation* (1982).
5. Shashi S.S., *Tribal Women of India* (1978).
6. Shukla Brahma Kumar, *The Daflas* (1999).
7. Das Gupta S. B., *Birjhia* (1976).
8. Choudhary N. C., Womanhood in Tribal India, (in) *Tribal Women in India* (1978).
9. Jyoti Sen etal, "Roles of women in Tribal economy in K.S. Singh (ed) *Economies of the Tribes and their Transformation* (1982).
10. Biman Kumar Gupta, "Tribal woman in North East India" *in Tribal Women in India* (1978).
11. Sachhida Nanda and Mandal, *Industrialization and Social Disorganization, A Study of Tribals in Bihar* (1985).
12. Verrier Elwin, *Tribal Art of Middle India* (1951).

❑❑❑

17

Problems of Indian Tribes : Some Remedial Measures

It may appear out of place to discuss the problems of Indian tribes after more than 6 decades of independence. Now the tribal people do not have a separate identity. They have been fully assimilated into larger Indian society. Of course, a few exceptions might be there in the remote interior and isolated hill tracts where these people have maintained their identity, that too partially.

In this chapter, the tribal problems would be discussed in Historical context, that is what were the problems and how these problems originated. What has been done to solve them. As we all know human society has never been problem free. People have suffered and faced problems at every stage of human development. Problems have been there to some extent. The natural conditions have troubled human society more at the initial stages of social developments, when man was ignorant about the productive economy, he depended more and more on nature for his livelihood. Problems have also been man made i.e. they originate from the social arrangements i.e. customs, habits and traditions etc. These 2 factors i.e. natural and social are relevant for non-tribal society even today. For example, in the sphere of nature e.g. draught conditions, affect our economy and social sphere has given rise to so many evils like untouchability, from which we have not been able to get rid of, even after several centuries. The problems of tribals have been quite different compared to that of the non-tribals. Their contact with the outside world, multiplied their problems. They were exploited and met harsh treatment at the hands of money lenders, contractors, feudal lords and administrators.

Broadly speaking the tribal problems could be divided into two categories:

(a) In the first type are those problems which were confined to the tribal area i.e. some of their customs and traditions like shifting cultivation and customs relating to marriage eg. Marriage by capture, marriage by elopement and marriage by service, custom punishment etc.

(b) In the second category those problems could be placed which were the outcome of the revenue system during British period and other rules and regulations which were not confined to tribals alone.

A few eminent Indian sociologists considered the second category of problems more important than the first one.

Causes of the Origin of Tribal Problems

The following may be the causes of tribal problems

(1) Residing at approachable places : For centuries they lived at such unapproachable places where there were no means of transport and communication. These places were cut off from the outside world. Even today there are certain places in Rajasthan and else where in India where even a doctor has to cover long distance of about 10 km by foot. Tribals in such remote areas have lived under economic hardships. Thus, those unapproachable habitations have made the tribal people suffer for a long time.

(2) Contact with the outside world : Of course, contact with outside world have both positive as well as negative consequences but it is also clear that for a long time these pople did not come in contact with the outside world because of many reasons. For example, the problems of communication (language), fear, superstition etc. The contact gave rise to several problems.

(3) Administrative system and reform : Originally tribal were owners of large areas of land. Some of the tribals were once the rulers of certain parts of the country. For example, the Gonds, Bhils and Meenas etc had been the rulers of certain parts of this country. They had full control over the forest produce. They used to practise axe cultivation. Later on, during British period, the rights of tribals over forests were curtailed, axe cultivation was banned, and new taxes were levied. All these reforms, made during British period gave rise to several problems.

(4) Availability of mineral resources in tribal areas : Though this should have improved the lot of tribal people but these people at times had to leave their homeland and move to farther places. They were given poor wages. The outsiders started entering the tribal areas and this was the beginning of several problems.

(5) Exploitation of the tribals by the outsiders: As we have stated earlier, the contractors, money lenders, administrators and businessmen took full advantage of the backwardness and illiteracy of the tribals. All these people played role in making their economic condition further complicated.

(6) Religious conversion by Christian missionaries: The Christian missionaries entered the tribal area during the British period. They gave economic allurement to the tribal people and thus persuaded some of the tribals to embrace Christianity. This, at several places, divided tribals into 2 segments—Christian tribals and non-Christian tribals. The problem arises when one section apposes such a move. As has happened recently in Gujarat and else where, the religious conversion created problems. Even, during early days among some the tribals of north East, the Christian tribals were asked by the church to dissociate themselves from the tribal dances on certain occasions and this had caused problems.

The British government's policy of non-interference did not have any positive effect on these people. Rather, there was not any improvement in the condition of the tribal people excepting that the converted tribals got more opportunities for education and employment during those days (preindependence days)

Contact and problems: Tribal's contact with the outside world was inevitable which could not have been avoided at any cost before British came to India, the tribal's had already come in contact with the non tribals. At several places tribals had confrontation with non-tribals and the former were forced to leave for the remote forests for survival. But during the British rule for the first time the non-tribals (either missionaries, officials forest contractors or others) entered the tribal area. Thus, during this period contact between tribals and non tribals increased rapidly.

The Christian missionaries, moneylenders, business men, contractors, even Brahmin priests all had their personal gains in mind and each of them wanted to the benefitted by the contact with the tribal people. For example, the Brahmin priests of the hill region of Himalayas exploited Bhotia tribe in their own way. The Bhotias of

Munsyari region of distt Pithoragarh in Uttaranchal state were once rich traders and wanted to have marital alliance with the local Rajputs. In this regard the Brahmins helped them by preparing their false geneologies, indicating their Rajput origin (these geneologies traced their Rajput origin from Chittorgarh (Rajasthan). For preparing these false geneolgoies, the Brahmins charged huge sums a money. The money lenders charged high rate of interest. The forest contractors used them as cheap labour, the business men grabbed their level and other immovable property.

The availability of mines and other mineral resources in tribal region forced them to leave their own home land. There was discrimination in wage rates so far as the tribals vis-a-vis non-tribals were concerned. In the social and cultural sphere the contact had several adverse consequences.

The contact made these pople give up their own tribal customs and traditions and to adopt the culture and customs of the non tribals. For example, the tribals used to marry after attaining puberty (adult hood) and child marriges were almost absent in their society. After their contact with Hindus and other non tribals they adopted child marriage, there was increasing parental interference in marital matters, dowry system and bride price etc. similarly, untouchability and inequality emerged in tribal society also. Tribal songs, art and tribal judicial system all gradually disappeared. The non tribals especially the Hindus placed these people at par with the lower castes (scheduled castes). It is not that there were no problems in the tribal society, yet it is also true that new problems were added to the tribal world.

The Christian missionaries entered the tribal area as social reformer but their other motive had been to convert the tribals to Christianity. The result was that a tribals who embraced Christianity, left their own culture and started adopting the others (western) culture. These missionaries started giving education to Christian tribals through roman script. The result was that these people forgot their own dialects/language.

Economic Problems: As a result of contact, the tribals gradually adopted the economy of non-tribals and the introduction of money economy resulted in the disappearance of Barter system. The increase in tribal population, and decrease in material (forest) resources resulted in the deterioration of tribal economy. Some of the important problems were as follows-

(a) Problem of shifting cultivation: This type of cultivation was banned by law during the British period. Axe cultivation resulted in loss of forests and caused soil erosion. Control over forests by the government consequently debarred these people from their rights over forest produce. As axe cultivation was associated with some of the religious customs and rituals, the introduction of plough cultivation in place of axe cultivation, had problems in the initial stage and was vigorously opposed by some of the tribal groups.

(b) Problem related to land: Since ages the tribals had controlled large areas of the land. Forests were their property and the tribals used them indiscriminately. Now forest came under government control and tribals had limited control over government land. Restrictions were laid on collection of forest produce, grazing of animals, and even collection of dry wood etc.

The other problem was that businessmen and moneylenders grabed the best-land which tribals had in their possession.

(c) Indebtedness: Because of illiteracy and poverty they fell easy pray to the moneylenders and other businessmen. In case of non payment of loans their land was grabed. The bonded labour was the result of poverty and indebtedness. The debt carried over from generation to generation and they could at the most pay back the interest only. Thus, the indebtedness continued for generations.

(d) Problems of industrial workers: The tribals left their native place in search of work in coal fields, tea gardens and in other industrial establishments. There they faced the problems of accommodation, low wages and retrenchment etc. At times they returned back to their native places. Because of illiteracy, they immediately adopted all the social evils e.g. alcoholism, gambling and prostitution etc.

(e) Problems relating to health and education : The tribals were very suspicious as far as the medical facility is concerned. Instead of going to a doctor they used to go to a 'shamon' (priest). They used to take illness as a divine curse and therefore it was thought as proper to appease the divine spirits. Illiteracy was the root cause of all such notions. Had they been literate they would not have been exploited by the outsiders so easily.

(f) Alcoholism: Drinking among tribals has been widely prevalent. The indigeneous beverage prepared by rice and millets has been the favourite liquor of the tribals. It is called by different names in different regions. They consume liquour on festive occasions, marriages, funeral and other ceremonious occasions. The liquour consumption among tribals has proved disasterous to the tribal economy. Many of the tribal communities are aware of the evil effects of liquor addiction and consequently in tribal areas strong movements have taken place from time to time. The Bhagat movement in Gujrat, The Tana Bhagat movement in Bihar may be cited in support of this argument. Education and social movements can further reduce this problem. Further the administration also need to play effective role by banishing the liquor magnates from the tribal areas. Several efforts have been made to solve the tribal problems. Some of these can be stated as below.

Constitutional Provisions

Under Indian constitution the tribals have been given special rights and facilities. These people have been listed from all over the country. Some times, some of the tribes had put in hard struggle to get themselves included in the list. Under article 342, the president of India in consutation with the governors of the concerned state regarding the listing of those communities or part of the community whom they deem as appropriate to be included a scheduled tribe. Similar other provisions have been made under article 338, 16(4), 35 and 245 (2).

Under the tenth part and section fifth and sixth schedule, special provisions have been made for the administration of tribal region. Under article 46 of the 4 th part of the constitution it has been treated as the duty of the state government to give special emphasis to the education and economic interest of the scheduled tribes. For a long time these people were exploited as cheap labour. They have even been used as bonded labourers. Under article 23 of the constitution it was considered as illegal. Article 27 states regarding the protection and preservation of the tribal culture by the state government

In some of the states Madhya Pradesh, Orissa and Bihar, provisions were made under article 164 to have separate Ministry for the welfare of the tribals.

Thus, India's constitution, along with security, provides facility for the social and economic development of the tribal people.

There have been diverse opinion regarding the assimilation and integration of Indian tribals. The process of acculturation is inevitable once the tribals come in contact with the non- tribals. There have been scholars like Verrier Elwin a famous Anthropologist, who was tribal adviser to the government of India; wanted a separate identity for the tribal people. He went to the extent of suggesting a separate home land for the tribes. Though it was an extreme and impractical suggestion, but efforts can certainly be made to protect and preserve the positive aspects of the tribal life and its culture.

Late Pandit Jawahar lal Nehru stated the following five principles:

(a) People should develop according to their capacity. We should not impose anything on the tribals. We should encourage their art and culture.

(b) We should respect the rights of the tribals regarding land and forest.

(c) We should select people from amongst them and train them for running the administration and developmental activities. Though at all initial stages some efficient persons (non tribals) may be required, but our efforts should be that a minimum number of non-tribals should be involved in tribal administration and other developmental activities.

(d) As far as possible every work in tribal areas should be done through their own social and cultural institutions.

(e) We should not evaluate the results through the money spent or by the statistics rather from the point as to what type of human quality (character) is being developed there.

Similarly, Professor Shyama Charan Dube in his book 'Manav aur Sanskriti (man and culture)' has given some of the anthropological suggestions—

(1) Availability of knowledge of values and social organization through scientific study.

(2) Minute study of the tribal problems at the level of different technical, economic and cultural development.

(3) Study of the factor and forces of integration in tribal life.

(4) The analysis of easily changeable aspects of culture.

(5) The study of inter connection and inter dependence of different aspects of culture.

(6) Special arrangement of training for social workers and administrators who work in tribal area so that they could be acquainted with the tribal life and culture.

(7) Construction of such developmental scheme which could coordinate between the needs of tribal groups with the regional and national needs.

(8) Study of the activities of these schemes and abolition of the harmful elements.

Thus, the tribal problems could be solved by keeping in mind the humanitarian point of view and feeling of respect and sympathetic view.

Welfare Schemes

Only after understanding the background of the tribal life a welfare scheme could be made successful in their region. We should not keep the tribals in a zoo, rather we have to keep in mind the positive aspects of their traditional values. Welfare schemes should be related to the overall development of the tribal life which can improve when economic, cultural and educational-all aspects could be kept in mind. The spread of education can bring change in their ideas.

In economic sphere the development of agriculture is essential as bulk of tribal population is engaged in agricultural activities. Now tribals, who once practiced axe cultivation, understand its ill effects. They understand that the loss of forest, soil erosion, scarcity of rainfall has adversely affected their economy. At the initial stages banning of axe cultivation was a major problem for these people however it has now become a thing of the past.

In several states multipurpose cooperative societies were established to provide loan to the tribal people.

Government of India launched various schemes for the welfare of tribals. Some of these are as follows:

(a) Formation of multipurpose development blocks for the development of the tribals.

(b) Establishment of training and production centre and to provide grant for the development of cottage and village industries for providing employment to the tribal people.

(c) Permanent rehabilitation of those tribals who moved from one place to another and were doing axe cultivation.

(d) To provide educational facilities, scholarships and other related facility to tribal students.

(e) Establishment of tribal cultural institutions to studying the cultural problems which affect tribal life.

(f) To reserve the seats for the tribal people in government jobs.

(g) To make legislation to prevent money lenders for charging interest on exorbitant rates.

(h) Appointment of a commissioner for scheduled castes and scheduled tribes under central government to evaluate various welfare schemes and to implement various proposed schemes for the security of scheduled tribes under the constitution.

Tribal Research Institution

In several states the tribal research institutions have been opened where efforts are being made to study tribal art, culture and customs etc. The purpose of such institutions is to preserve to the tribal art and culture. Such institutes can only truly depict the tribal life.

Five Year Plans and Tribal Welfare

After Independence government has made special efforts to bring improvement among tribal life and to solve their problems. Especially, the north Eastern states were given special facilities. In the first five year plan Rs. 17.36 crore was spent on the scheme relating to the welfare of the tribals. Under the plan, the developmental programmes in tribal region were broadly divided into four parts –

(a) Communication

(b) Education and culture

(c) Economic reforms

(d) Health, housing and water supply

Under second five year plan there was provision of Rs. 91 crores for the development of backward classes, out of which Rs. 48.33 crore was spent for the tribals.

Under third five year plan provision of Rs. 60.43 crore was made and the following voluntary organisations extended their cooperation in the tribal development programme.

(a) Bhartiya Adim Jati Sevak Sangh

(b) Tata Institute of Social Sciences, Bombay

(c) Indian Council of Child Welfare, New Delhi

(d) Andhra Pradesh Adim Jati Sevak Sangh, Hyderabad.

(e) Ramkrishna Mission, Cheera Punji, Shillong

(f) All India Backward Classes Federation.

(g) Bhartiya Ghumantu Jam (nomadic) Sevak Sangh, New Delhi

According to 1961 census report 1.49 crore tribals were engaged in agricultural activities, out of which 33.33 percent were working as agricultural labourers. In the first 3 years of third five year plan 51017 Acre land was distributed among the landless tribals, which benefited 47814 families.

Under five year plan, following measures were undertaken for the rehabilitation of axe cultivators (shifting cultivators) and to engage them in settled cultivation.

(1) 3 piolet farms and 5 agricultural units were opened in Andhra Pradesh and for this agricultural work, appropriate assistance was provided.

(2) Land reform by land reclamation took place in Assam region and there was introduction of cash crops.

(3) Money was given for the purchase of agricultural implements in Madhya Pradesh.

(4) Axe cultivation control scheme in Orissa was started and development of colonies for tribal people took place.

(5) Financial assistance for tarraced farming and small irrigation schemes in Manipur.

(6) Development of colonies in Tripura.

Besides, small scale industries and cottage industries were developed in tribal areas, barren land in tribal area was made cultivable. Training centres were established. Different types of cooperative societies viz forest labour cooperatives, consumer cooperative societies, worker's cooperative societies etc were established.

Under Second Five Year Plan, 43 tribal development blocks were started for the development of tribal areas. In third five year plan 450 such blocks were established.

Thus, every possible efforts were made for the solution of tribal people and there is no doubt that there has been improvement in the social and economic life of these people. The tribal people are accepting the change in giving their cooperation to the innovative schemes and in their implementation. Though certain tribals of the north eastern region (under the influence of some foreign element), have raised some anti-national issues. But it seems essential to curb such elements in the interest of the nation. The question of national unity is of utmost importance and it is hoped that all the tribals will become an important part of the national life.

Tribal people cannot be kept in isolation, the process of acculturation is inevitable and natural. If the social distance between tribals and non tribals is reduced then most of the problems of the tribals would be automatically removed. Even after retaining their tribal culture, these people can be brought near the so called civilized society. What the tribals need is education and self enlightenment. Once the tribals attain this level then the question of acculturation can be left to themselves. We cannot make tribal society problem free. If the non tribals themselves suffer from the stigma of inequality, high and Low social status etc then it would be too much to expect from the tribals to keep themselves free from those evils. Culture contact, assimilitation, acculturation and integration may give rise to certain problems among the tribal people. The loss of cultural identity, language, habits, manners, customs and traditions etc. should not be taken as a problem. This is as true in case of Indians coming in contact with the western society, as tribals coming in contact with the non tribals. Both situations give rise to certain amount of problems.

But the tribals are relatively simple, and even ignorant about their own good things. therefore, the need for them is to develop such awareness and to differentiate between right and wrong. We all understand that the culture contact will lead some sort of assumiliation and integration. The problem of integration is not only the problem of tribal people, but it is the problem of whole society. Yet it is good in the interest of the tribals and for the whole nation.

References

1. Sharma Kailash Nath, *Indian Society and Culture* (1958).
2. Vellign Elwin, *A Philosophy for Nefa* (1958).
3. Dube S. C., *Manav aur Sanskriti* (1961).
4. Arora G.S., *Tribe, Caste Encounters* (1972).
5. Majumdar D. N., *The Affaris of a Tribe a Study in Tribal Dynamics* (1950).
6. Mahalotra L. K., *Transformation of Tribal Society in India* (1970).
7. Mathur H. S., *Development Administration in Tribal Areas* (1976).
8. Patel M. L., *Changing Land Problems of Tribal India* (1974).
9. Sachhidananda, *Cultural Change in Tribal Bihar* (1968).
10. Shrinivas S. K., *The Tharus : A Study in Cultural and Dynamics* (1958).

11. Singh Parmanand, *Inequality, Reservation and Discrimination in India* (1982).
12. Thaper Romesh, *Tribe, Caste and Religions* (1977).
13. Thomas and Taylor, *Tribal Awakening* (1966).
14. Singh Surendra, *Tribal Situation in India* (1972).
15. Yogesh Atal, *Adivasi Bharat* (1965).
16. Majumdar D. N., *Races and Cultures of India* (1961).

18

Tribes of Rajasthan

From the point of view of tribal Population Rajasthan has an important place. In the year 1971 Rajasthan state had approximately 12.13 percent of the tribal population. In 1961 census Rajasthan ranked fifth in tribal Population in the country. In Rajasthan bulk of tribal population lives in few regions. For example in Banswara distt. 73 percent of the population was tribal. The tribal percentage in Dungarpur district was 53.64. Similarly, Sawaimadhopur, Udaipur distt, Sirohi and Chittorgarh districts have significant percentage of tribal population. In 4 districts, alone viz Udaipur, Banswara, Dungarpur and Jaipur, about half of the state's tribal population resides. So far as the tribal population in urban areas is concerned, according to 1971 census data only 2 percent of the tribal people were residing in urban areas where as 98 percent lived in rural areas.

Tribal Population According to 2001 Census

There has not been any change in the percentage of tribal population in Rajasthan for past 3-4 decades as its percentage in 1971 was 12.13 where as in 2001 it was 12.6 percent of the state's total population. Total number of tribal population in 2001 in the state was 7097706.

The main tribes of Rajasthan are: Bhils, (Bhil-garasia, Dungari Bhil, Dholi Bhil, Mewasi Bhil, Rawal Bhil, Tadki Bhil), Dungari-Garasia, Mangalai, Bhilala, Pawara, Basawa, Bhilmeena, Damor, Dagaria, Dhanka, Garasia, Kathod, Katkari, Kokna, Kokani, Koli Dhor, Tokre Koli, Kolcha, Kolga, Meena, Nekda Mota Nayak, Patelia and Saharia. The Census of 1971 mentions about 13 tribes in Rajasthan out of which about 6 tribes are more or less insignificant in terms of population number as according to 1971 census their total population (population of 6 tribes) was 359. Out of remaining 7 other tribes Bhils and Meenas are the most important. Numerically also they constitute about 94 percent of the state's tribal population. Among these two also Meenas are at number one in terms of population as they alone constitute about 49 percent of the state's, total tribal population. While Bhils are at number two with 44.9 percent of the total tribal population.

In 1981 census Rajasthan's tribal population was 41.83 lakhs which constituted about 12.12 percent of the state's total population.

So far as district wise distribution of tribal population is concerned, as we have stated above that distt of Banswara, Dungarpur, Udaipur and Jaipur constituted highest number of tribal population where as some districts like Bikaner, Nagaur, Jaisalmer and Churu had very little tribal population.

Geographical Location

The following points are significant in the distribution of tribal population in Rajasthan.

(a) The tribal people lived on the borders of princely states.

(b) The areas were for long time un-approachable and did not have any means of transport and communication.

(c) Till recently the tribals were least affected by the impact of urbanization.

(d) Because of poor (inadequate) means of transport and communication in their area, these people till recently remained immobile.

From geographical point of view the tribals of Rajasthan can be divided into 3 regions.

(a) Southern Rajasthan: This region includes Banswara and Dungarpur distt., 7 tehsils of Udaipur district viz Fasalia, Dorwara, Sarada, Kotra, Chirawa, Lasaria, Salumber), Pratapgarh tehsil of Chittorgarh distt and Abu Road tehsil of Sirohi distt. In this region about three fourth of the population, consists of tribals. In other words, 43.8 percent of the state's total tribal population resides in this area. The main tribes of the region are: Bhil, Meena, Garasia and Damor etc.

(b) South Eastern Rajasthan: About half of the state's total tribal population resides in this region. In this region Bharatpur, Alwar,

Jaipur, (including Dausa) Sawai Modhopur, Ajmer, Tonk, Bhilwara, Kota, Bundi and Jhalawar distts are included. Besides, some tehsils of Udaipur, Chittorgarh and Sirohi distt are also included in this region. The main tribes of the region are Meenas, Bhils, Saharia and Meena Bhils.

(c) Western Rajasthan: The following distts. constitute this region, Sikar, Jhunjhunu, Churu, Ganganagar, Bikaner, Nagaur, Pali, Jaisalmer, Barmer, Jalore and Jodhpur. The tribal population in this region is very less. This area has about 7.14 percent of the state's total tribal population. Bhils and Meenas are the main tribes of Western Rajasthan.

Tribal Population Distribution According to their Places of Habitation

From the above point of view we find that about 70 percent of the Bhils reside in Banswara, Dungarpur and Udaipur distt. Remaining 30 percent are scattered all over the state. Similarly, a little more than half of the total of the Meena population is found in Jaipur, Sawai Madhopur and in Dausa distts. Remaining are found in Alwar, Kota, Bundi, Chittorgarh and Dungarpur distt.

About 56.73 percent of the Garasias are found in udaipur district. In Pali and Sirohi their percentages are 20.11 and 19.74 respectively. Thus, in the three districts alone the total population of Saharias was about 96.48 percent.

96.82 percent of the population of Damors reside in Dungarpur district alone. Their number is maximum in Segalwaie panchayat region. 99.47 percent of the Saharias reside in Kota district. In Sahabad Panchayat Samiti their number is maximum. 61.94 percent of Bhil Meenas are found in Jalore distt, 18.07 percent in Banswara, 7.95 percent in Ajmer and 6.38 percent in Dungarpur districts.

Other tribes are Marwa, Tadvi, Valvi, Kathodia, Kalidheer, Nexda, Patilia, Bhilgarasia, Dholi Bhil, Pawra etc. These tribes are mostly found in Sirohi district. The percentage of different tribes according to 1961 and 1971 census was as follows:

Tribes	1961 census	1971 census
Meena	49.14	49.03
Bhil	38.56	46.01
Garasia	2.66	1.67
Damor/Damaria	0.62	0.47
Saharia	0.99	0.86

Bhil Meena	0.09	0.55
Others	-	0.01
Unclassified	7.94	1.40

Though Bhils are most important tribe of Rajasthan and one of the most important tribe of India, numerically Meenas could be placed at number one. Bhils are the second largest tribe in terms of number. But population wise, Bhils could be placed at number three in the country because they reside in Gujarat and Madhya Pradesh also where as Meenas have (by and large) Rajasthan as their habitation. So far as district wise population of tribes in Rajasthan is concerned there are districts with less than one percent of the tribal population. On the contrary certain districts have more than half of the tribal population.

The census data 1971 gives distt wise percentage of the tribal population.

S.No.	Name of Distt.	Percentage of tribal population in the total population of the distt.
1.	Ganga Nagar	0.08
2.	Bikaner	0.07
3.	Churu	0.39
4.	Jhunjhunu	1.77
5.	Alwar	7.99
6.	Bharatpur	2.96
7.	Sawai Madhopur	22.68
8.	Jaipur	11.14
9.	Sikar	2.50
10.	Ajmer	1.34
11.	Tonk	11.37
12.	Jaisalmer	4.13
13.	Jodhpur	2.11
14.	Nagaur	0.16
15.	Pali	4.70
16.	Jalore	7.81
17.	Barmer	5.74
18.	Sirohi	2.48
19.	Bhilwara	9.36

20.	Udaipur	33.66
21.	Chittorgarh	19.27
22.	Dungarpur	63.64
23.	Banswara	72.93
24.	Bundi	19.27
25.	Kota	14.54
26.	Jahalawar	10.30

Thus, we find that in terms of tribal population the Distt of Banswara, Dungarpur and Udaipur are first, second and third respectively. During the decade 1961 and 1971 there was 32.9 percent increase in the tribal population. The Highest increase was in Jaisalmer district which was 50.7 percent.

From social, economic and educational point of view the tribals are far behind the non-tribals. According to 1971 census only 6 percent of tribals were literate where as this percentage was only 4 in 1961. A comparative analysis of the percentage of literacy among tribals and non-tribals have been given in the following table.

The percentage of Literary According to 1971 Census

Population	Literacy		
	Males	Females	Total
Tribals	12.03	0.49	6.47
Non-tribals	31.02	9.57	20.81
Total State	26.74	8.46	19.07

Even today educationally the tribals are far behind non-tribals. Among tribals the condition of women is the worst. Among tribes the situation of Meenas is better in comparison to other tribes. For example, in 1971 census the percentage of literacy among Meenas was 8.3 while this percentage in Bhils was 4.7 only. There was variation in the percentage of literacy rate among of rural and urban population. The percentage of literacy among urban based tribals was 19.7 where as the percentage of literacy in rural areas was 6.2. According to 1971 census tribal Population was 2.05 percent of the total urban population where as the percentage of non-tribals was 18.-12. Thus, 97.95 percent of tribal people lived in villages.

The Scheduled tribes in Rajasthan constitute about 5.35 percent of the urban population of the states' total tribal population, where as 94.65 percent are rural.

The Percentage of Urban ST to total S.T. Population in Rajasthan

So far as the percentage of scheduled tribes population to the total S.T. population in the state (as per 2001 census) is concerned the scheduled tribes have attained a growth rate of 49.36 percent during the period 1991, 2001 where males accounted for 46.01 percent and females 53.50 percent at the state level. The highest growth rate has been found in Ganganagar distt. with 367.67 percent, followed by Bikaner at 122.07 percent. Barmer has registered a negative growth rate of 24.15 which is the lowest. The highest growth rate among males has been registered at Ganganagar with 348.83 percent, followed by Bikaner distt with 103.76 percent. Among females the highest growth rate was found at Ganganagar distt with 391.45 percent, followed by Dhaulpur at 175.74 percent. The state had registered a sex-ratio of 944 for scheduled tribes in 2001. At the distt level the highest sex ratio of 1028 has been registered in Dungarpur, followed by 985 in Udaipur and Lowest in Bikaner district (817).

District wise Male-Female Literacy Rate among Tribal, According to 2001 Census

Educationally, the tribals in Rajasthan lag far behind the non-tribals. For example, according to 2001 census the general male literacy was 75.7 and female literary rate in the state was 43.9 percent. This percentage among the tribal males was 62.10 and among tribal females it was 28.20. However, there are regional variations in the literacy rate. It was found lowest in Banswara, Rajsamand, Pali, Jodhpur, Sirohi and Jalore region and higher in Sikar, Jhunjhunu, Alwar, Bharatpur, and Jaipur district. The distt wise data have been presented in the following table.

District Wise Literacy Rate (in percentage)

Distt/States	Persons	Males	Females
Rajasthan	2480331	62.10	26.20
Ganga Nagar	6709	68.94	40.27
Hanumangarh	4641	69.29	42.03
Bikaner	2557	47.49	35.71
Churu	5801	83.29	57.06
Jhunjhunu	21573	85.73	55.64
Alwar	107367	75.24	32.83
Bharatpur	25603	85.56	44.79
Dhaulpur	20955	77.98	31.74

Karauli	134239	78.82	41.60
Sawai Madhopur	110102	77.60	30.14
Dausa	161967	76.63	36.90
Jaipur	196722	78.14	38.88
Sikar	33874	82.57	50.05
Nagaur	3039	75.11	37.65
Jodhpur	16128	40.54	12.33
Jaisalmer	7510	52.77	17.70
Barmer	40271	59.03	28.83
Jalore	24427	38.74	11.10
Sirohi	52248	47.83	17.20
Pali	25414	47.26	13.62
Ajmer	18018	58.85	25.25
Tonk	49378	64.42	18.45
Bundi	76867	67.58	28.11
Bhilwara	45826	46.79	16.05
Rajsamand	33169	49.84	15.51
Udaipur	416544	59.64	25.71
Dungarpur	217784	57.82	21.83
Banswara	299467	52.33	18.88
Chittorgarh	102932	49.26	18.07
Kota	78612	77.43	46.42
Baran	83943	65.97	29.80
Jhalawar	56444	68.05	31.14

Occupation of the Tribals: Most of the tribal people are agriculturists. They make their living either by cultivating their own land or by working as agricultural labours. Of the total rural based tribal people more than 90 percent were associated with agricultural tasks in one way or the other. Out of those 81.67 percent were doing agricultural work on their own land and 11.45 percent worked as agricultural labourers. Besides, they were engaged in building and road construction work, forest labourers, petty business and cottage industries etc. But such people constituted only 2.21 percent of the total rural tribal population. Now occupational mobility is clearly discernible among the tribal people especially after reservation, it has increased. The following table shows the occupational classification of tribals in Rajasthan according to 1971 census.

The Occupational Classification of Tribals in Rajasthan

Occupation	Percentage
Agriculturists	81.7
Agricultural labourers	11.5
Animal keeping	2.4
Mining workers	0.4
Cottage Industry	0.2
Construction work	0.4
Transport and communication	0.3
Other services	2.5

By and large the tribals are engaged in agricultural activities. Their percentage in non-agricultural tasks is insignificant.

Sex Ratio: Sex Ratio in India is one of the lowest in the world. It was 933 in 2001. But sex ratio among tribal was slightly higher. It was 951 according to 2001 census. In Durgarpur woman out numbered men. Their number was 1031 females per 1000 males followed by 985 at Udaipur and lowest was seen at Bikaner with 817.

Studies undertaken on Tribes of Rajasthan

First of all BH Baden Powel in 1899 wrote about the Aryan races of Rajasthan in the Journal of Royal Asiatic Society of Great Britain and Ireland. Later on, in 1907 he wrote an essay on Bhils of western Rajasthan. An administrator T.H. Hadlay wrote about Bhils of Mewar. In the Journal of Royal Asiatic Society of Bengal in 1975 John Stuart studied the tribes of Marwar, their habits and behaviour. Besides, these foreign scholars, the Meenas of Jaipur and Mewar were studied by Das in the year 1866. Sarat Chandra Rai studied the customs of Bhils residing in the hills of Rajsamand area.

L.P. Tensi Toria studied ancient communities of Rajasthan from time to time. Rajputana Gazetteers which were published in several volumes in 1879-80 and several administrative reports contained rich information about the people of Rajasthan. James Todd wrote 'Annals and Antiquties of Rajasthan' which was published in two volumes in 1920 and 1950 respectively, stated about of different tribes.

G.N. Castairs, who was born in Rajasthan, studied Bhils of Rajasthan and stated those factors which acted as obstacles in change.

A Buttelin on Bhils was published by Tribal Research Institute, Udaipur in the year 1965. The Garasias were studied by P.C. Dave in the year 1960, in which the economic hardships of Garasias were highlighted and it was tried to explain as to how far, these people have been trying gradually to integrate themselves to wider (larger) national society. Satya Pal Rouhela and several other scholars studied Gadulia lohars. Gadulia lohars are the first nomadic tribes of Rajasthan who first of all attracted the attention of social workers and social anthropologists. The efforts to rehabilitate them at one place has not met with success. N.N. Vyas studied Banjara tribes of Rajasthan in the year 1967. Similarly, S.P. Malhotra and A.B. Bose also studied Banjara tribes of western Rajasthan in the year 1963. Kathodi tribe who are also known as Katkari is another nomadic tribe of Rajasthan. 'Funch' has treated them as a sub branch of Bhils where as Farera (1962) considers them as the consequence of intermixture of several tribes. This tribe was also studied by Tribal Research Institute, Udaipur in 1967. Prior to rèhabilitation Kathodias were leading primitive economic life, were totally dependent on forest produce. Now they are settled agriculturists and do agricultural work at one place on a permanent basis. Govt provided them cultivable land for agricultural purposes and provided them all the necessary implements. But in the absence of water resources some of them have abandoned agricultural work. These people have been benefited by the schemes of forest cooperative societies. Bhils consider these people as inferior in status.

With a view to protect the cultural history of tribals, B.R. Chauhan developed the concept of tribalisation and said that before the advent of Rajputs, the tribal people had effective control in different parts of the states. Thus, in all, we reach this conclusion that there is still,' need for intensive study regarding the tribes of Rajasthan.

Main Tribes of Rajasthan

Meena Tribe: they constitute about half of the states total tribal population. These region can be divided into 2 parts–

(a) The first region is Eastern region of the state which includes Chittorgarh, Dungarpur, Banswara and Udaipur.

(b) The second region includes Bharatpur, Jaipur and sawai madhopur.

Educational and social situation: Economically Meenas are better off than the other tribes of the state. They have come in maximum contact with the so called civilized (non-tribals) people. They have adopted their manners and customs. They seem fully inclined to come within caste fold. However, the tag of reservation forces them to maintain their tribal identity and not to merge themselves into the Hindu caste hierarchy.

Garasia : Garasias are third important tribe of the state. According to1971 census, their total population was 62,509 which was 2.70 percent of the state's total tribal population. Garasias are spread over Udaipur, Dungarpur, Sirohi and Pali district. But mostly Garasias reside in abu road and pindwara tehsil of sirohi district. Their gotras (clans) resemble that of Rajputs. These people are engaged in agriculture. In comparison to other tribes the position of women among garasias is relatively better. They practise widow remarriage. Similarly, they give priority to levirate. According to their customs, the widow does not inherit her husband's property. They are very cheerful, men keep long hair and wear silver ornaments. Inspite of the fact that they are economically backward, they associate themselves with people having status and prestige.

Damor : Their population in the state according to 1971 census was 14,534 which was 0.62 percent of the state's total tribal population. Maximum number of Damors were found in Simalwara Panchayat area of the Dungapur district. In Dungarpur they were 78.4 percent of their total population. Besides they were found in Churu, Gangangar, Kota, Udaipur and Alwar. In the past they were known as Damaria. These people are divided into 2 categories

(a) Higher, and

(b) Lower

The people of first category who consider themselves as superior, do not consider the second category of Damors as their community members. They have certain typical customs. For example, the elder brother after marriage, lives with the parental family till the time when a younger brother is married. After that he lives in a separate hut made for him. This process continues till the last son in the family is married. The youngest son continues to live with the father even after marriage. Father is the head of the family. Women do not touch the plough which according to them causes pollution. The family is of patriarchal type. After the death of husband, the wife marries the deceased person's younger brother. If a widow marries some one other than her brother in law, then her children continue to stay on in the family but according to their social rules only an issueless widow can marry outside the family fold. If a widow with children marries outside the family (other than her brother-in-law ie deceased husband's younger brother) in that case she looses her rights over the children as per their social custom. They used to have purda system also. For example, the daughter-in-law used to keep purdah from her father law. Similarly, the mother-in-law used to keep purdah from son-in-law. There are separate gotras among the two categories of Damorids. The Damors of Rajasthan closely resemble the Damors of Gujarat. The Damors prefer to be called as Rajputs and do not like to be called as tribal people.

Saharia : According to 1971 census data, their total population in the state was 23299 i.e., 0.99 percent of the state's total tribal population. They are found in maximum number in Sahaebad and Kishangang tehsil of Kota distt. Elsewhere they are also found in Jhalawar, Udaipur, Jaipur, Bharatpur, Churu and in some other parts of Kota district. The commissioner of scheduled tribes has put Saharia people in the category of most under-developed tribe. They have strong faith in Hindu religion. The literacy rate among these people is very low.

Saharias consider 'Gotra' from the point of view of marriage. A man and woman can not marry within their own gotra. Besides, the following gotras are avoided at the time of marriage.

(a) Mother's gotra

(b) Father's Mother's gotra

The Gotras of Saharias are either by the name of the village or as known the Gotras of Rajputs. They prefer regular marriage even though the custom of Nata is prevalent among them. According to the custom, a man after the consent of a woman (whom he wants to marry) runs away with her. Such a woman should not be from the above two gotras. Later on, the panchayat is called and after some payment of compensation in the form of money to her husband or the family, the Nata is regularized as proper marriage. The decision of panchayat is binding to both the parties.

The villages of Saharias are of 2 types

(a) Compact village, and

(b) Scattered one

In Compact village there is an umbrella type house which they call as 'Bangla. Here they have all recreational activities. Women are generally prohibited to enter this house. They have village level panchayats having few members. Among its members the most influencial one is known as Kotwal. Generally, the rank of Kotwal is hereditary but if he is inefficient or involved in any major crime, then he can be removed also and new kotwal can be appointed. Before independence the status of kotwal in the village was that of a govt official. The kotal used to collect revenue or assisted the patwari in the collection of revenue. After independence, such powers have ceased to exist yet the kotwal provides leadership in the performance of various social and cultural activities in the village.

Bhils : The Bhils are an important tribe, not only in the state of Rajasthan but in the whole country. From historical, social and cultural point of view they have a special place. Col. Tod, ojha and several other historians have proved this fact that Bhils were the original people of southern and south western Rajasthan . Rajputs defeated them in battle and established their own rule. For example, the kushala Bhil of Kushalgarh was defeated by Rathores who established their own rule. Dungarpur was associated with Dungaria Bhil. Banswara state was once ruled by Bansia Bhil. They were all displaced by Rajputs and compelled to take shelter and make their abode in the unapproachable places of Arawali hills. As they were good fighters and very much conversant with the topography, routes and geographical conditions in the region they became headache for Rajputs. The Rajput rulers also thought it as farsightedness to exten the hand of friendship to Bhil sardars and gave them respectable status and position in their courts. Rajputs gave Bhils higher status than that of untouchables. Rather, they never treated them as untouchables.

During the Mughal period the Bhils and Rajputs came much closer to each other. The Bhils always stood behind the Rajput rulers and left no stone unturned to protect the honour of the mother land and showed their full loyalty.

There has been a tradition which existed among Rajput rulers for a long time that whenever a new king sat on the throne, he was considered as the legal ruler when acknowledged by Bhil sardar. Among the kings of Sisodia dynasty there was a tradition that whenever a king sat on a throne, his Rajtilak was performed by Bhil sardar. Thus, it was clear that the Rajput rulers showed great farsightedness in seeking the cooperation of Bhils.

Dialects: These people use several dialects. Because they are scattered in large area, the local places have also affected their dialects. The Bhils of Gujrat, Maharashtra and Rajasthan have been respectively affected by Gujrati, Marathi and Rajasthani dialects. Specially, Rajasthani and Gujrati language/dialects have greatly affected their language. Some scholars believe that Bhils are very ancient inhabitants of the country. They had come from North Western region several hundred years before, BC. Col. Todd does not agree with this view that they have come from far off places. He considers them as sons of the forest. R.B. Russel in Gazetters of Banswara state (1908) wrote that they are most ancient inhabitants of the country. They are dark complexioned and small in stature.

Origin of the term Bhil

The word 'Bhil' is derived from the Dravid word 'veel' or 'veelu' which means bow. It is said that these people were experts in archery. Till recently, they used to roam in the forests fearlessly armed with their bow and arrow. Some people associate the origin of the term Bhil to 'bhillow" word of Greek language which means bow. Several ancient epics (writings) have mentioned Bhils. Epics like Ramayana, Mahabharata and Jain stories cite, several examples regarding Bhils.

Russel and Heralal stated that earlier there was a practise of keeping Bhils as watch men (chaukidar) of the village. They were conversant with all the routes and were experts in trekking.

Herbert Riseley, after studying Bhils of Rajasthan, put them in the category of Dravidian race. Gupta studied Bhils of Rajasthan and found similarity between these people and Chenchus of south India on the basis of race. In 1944 Stephen Fuch studied the Bhils of Rajasthan and considered them as one the most original inhabitants of the country. Mythological stories and great epics like Ramayana and Mahabharata 'testify the fact that they were natives of this country before Aryans. But keeping in view their cultural practices, beliefs and superstitions it will not be wrong to say that they were neither Arya nor Dravida. Because even Dravidian were at a higher cultural stage. Rather, they had come to India much before these two.

Social organization: In the social organization of Bhil Tribe certain peculiarities can be noticed. A brief account of their social institutions has been stated as below:

(a) Family: Bhils have two types of families.

(a) Nuclear (b) Joint

(a) Nuclear family consists of husband, wife and their unmarried children.

(b) Joint family, besides the members of nuclear family may include unmarried brother or sister or widowed mother. Among Bhils, such joint, families in which 3 generations live together, are rarely found. According to the social custom, a son lives separately after marriage and he has no economic connection with his parental family. Neither father nor the sons are responsible to each other, though there are instances of economic cooperation between two brothers.

Bhil family is patriarchal, patrilocal and patrilineal. Family is the smallest unit of social organisation. Though father and son live separately, their dwellings are closer to each other, within the same khera or phala (block). The eldest son has special rights. After father's death, he performs the death rites and is considered as the head of the family. He undertakes the responsibility of unmarried brothers and sisters. But in case of any differences between him and the widowed mother, the later undertakes the whole responsibility and becomes incharge of the family property. Girls have no right in family property. Among Bhils, the social position of women is better in comparison to the Hindu society. The person keeping more than one wife is supposed to have higher status and position in Bhil society. The unmarried girls specially enjoy greater freedom. She can marry against the wishes of her father and the custom supports her. The youngest son has right to the house of his father after father's death.

Gotra (clan) system prevails among Bhils. Marriage within the same (gotra) clan is prohibited. They marry outside the gotra. They have different notions regarding the origin of gotra. Clan has no separate social and political organization. Its significance is confined merely to the determination of marriage. Generally, the people of the same Gotra reside had one phal (a barrack or a block).

Marriage: Usually Bhils follow the rules of monogamy. Only chief or economically rich Bhils keep more than one wife yet there are exceptions. For example, S.L. Doshi studied Ghatali village. In that village, out of 110 families, 63 had more than one wife. Some of these people had between 2 and 5 wives. Mann believed that where there are more wives, women play more important role in economic activities than the men. Having more wives in the family also elevates husband's status in Bhil society. Bhils prefer to marry at a place where they have some prior acquaintances. The following types of marriages are prevalent among Bhils

(a) Levirate

(b) Exchange marriages

(c) Marriage by elopement

(d) Marriage by purchase

(e) Marriage by service, and

(f) Marriage by capture

The details regarding these types have already been discussed in a separate chapter on marriage. Widow remarriage and divorce are also common among these people. Both, husband and wife enjoy, the right to divorce. If a woman divorces her husband, then in that case she or her parental family has to return the bride price.

The impact of Hindu society, especially the untouchability and hierarchal nature of caste system has brought the notion of superior and inferior (high or low) among these people. For example, a Kabir panthi Bhil will not accept a shambhu Dayal Bhil girl in marriage because the former (kabirpanthi) considers himself as superior.

Bhil Villages are usually of three types—

(a) Multi caste villages: In these villages, besides Bhils people of other castes also reside. From settlement point of view in such villages the dwellings of Bhils are located at one corner. Usually, such villages are found both in plains and hill regions also. Such villages are usually very few in number.

(b) Compact villages: Such villages are located in the plains. The houses are compact and situated in small areas.

(c) Scattered villages: The village is spread in a wider area. There is more distance between 2 houses. Several houses (dwellings) make a pal (khera) and several kheras make a village. In Dungarpur a pal is known as village. The head of the pal is called 'Gameti', sometimes he is also known as 'patel'.

The first type of villages are not very well organized. The Bhils have one or two of their representatives in the panchayat. Like that every caste/ tribe has their representative in Panchayat. In second type (compact) of villages there is no intermediary between village head and the family head. The Bhil villages are well organized.

Economic organization: At present the main occupation of Bhils is agriculture. But it is not a means of livelihood due to scarcity of land and poor means of irrigation. Animal keeping is another important subsidiary means of livelihood. These people have a custom of giving animals in dowry on the occasion of marriage of the daughter. They also collect medicinal herbs from forests. The control over the forests by the govt has adversely affected their economy. These people also work as labourers in road construction, employed by the contractors. They also collect forest produce to make their living. They move to the non-tribal villages and to the nearly towns in search of work. At the initial stage outside contact has not been very fruitful as they were exploited by the outsiders. They have mostly suffered from indebtedness.

Developmental plans, especially schemes meant for the development of tribal areas have helped these people to ameliorate their economic life.

Bhils have been greatly influenced by Hindu religion. They believe in Hindu Gods and Goddesses.

They believe in human spirits also. They have faith in evil spirits. The use of magic is very much common and it is used to get rid off the evils. In magical practices women are also active participants. Thus, these people are very superstitious.

However, outside contact and spread of education in tribal areas has somehow brought changes in their attitude. Some Bhils have embraced Christianity though their number is not very significant.

There have been several social movements in which Bhil have activity participated. First of all Surmal Das in 19th century tried to bring reforms among these people. He taught them to take bath everyday before eating their meals. He advised them to worship Gods and follow the path of non violence. He also advised them to wear sacred thread.

Another great social reformer was a Banjara, Govind Singh, who was later on known as Govind Giri. He started Bhagat movement, about which we have already discussed in a separate chapter on social movement. This movement divided Bhils into 2 divisions-Bhagats and non-Bhagats.

Sub castes among Bhils : Bhils are divided into various sub castes viz Bhilala, Barela, Mankar, Nihal, Patlya, Rathia etc and there is a notion of high and low among these people. At present after their contact with Hindus Bhilala and Barela treated themselves separate from Bhils. Bhilalas consider themselves superior and trace their origin from Rajputs. They are further sub divided into hierarchical order. Economically they are better off. Barela also trace their origin from Rajputs. They are less progressive than Bhilala. They are also divided into various gotras.

Their Gotras bear the namas of trees, animals, birds etc. The marriage by capture, marriage by elopement were once popular among them.

Patlya : They also associate themselves with Rajputs. Their gotras resemble that of Rajputs. In the past they used to practise marriage by capture and widow remarriage. They have too much faith in magic and superstitions. They also invite Brahmin priests and believe in Hindu Gods and Goddesses and worship them.

Rathia: Usually they work as labourers. They are socially and economically quite backward compared with the above category of Bhils.

Mankar: They consider themselves as Rajputs. They are further subdivided into 2 categories

(a) Chaukaria, and

(b) Tarvi

Chaukarias are sub divided into several gotras. Where as Tarvi's marry within their own caste. Tarvi's are sub divided into 2 main sub castes.

(a) Rathavi Tarvi and

(b) Dohand Tarvi

Among Tarvi's, women enjoy enough freedom before marriage, widow remarriage and divorce are recognized. Some people believe that Tarvis had embraced Islam but they believe in Hindu Gods and Goddesses also.

Position of Women among Bhils : Traditionally men's place is higher than that of women. Yet by and large women's position is better off compared to other tribes of Rajasthan. They follow the practice of divorce and widow remarriage. Though their society is patriarchal and there are cases of battering of women, such cases are very rare. The position of widows is not like that of Hindu society. They (widow) are respected in the family and in the community.

Ornaments are the weakness of Bhil women. Large part of their body is covered with ornaments. Women play significant role in family economy.

Thus, Bhil tribe is known for its social, economic and cultural characteristics not only in Rajasthan, India but in the whole of the tribal world. Their typical customs, their loyalty and their participation in social movements, their expertise in archery etc all these are now things of the past. Now these people have by and large adopted the Hindu religion amd culture.

Meena Tribe

Meenas are an important tribe of Rajasthan numerically they are the largest in number in the state. These people are basically agriculturists. In the past they had the best agricultural land in their possession. But owing to certain reasons they were displaced from their fertile land and forced to move to the less fertile regions.

The origin of the term 'meena' is from the word 'meen' which means 'fish'. These people believe that the 'meen desh' their home land consisted of Rajasthan, Haryana and Uttar Pradesh.

Like Bhils, Meenas were also rulers of many parts of the state of the present state of Rajasthan and like Bhils, the Meenas also fought the Muslim and Rajput rulers and eventually lost their kingdom. They continued guerrilla warfare but could not succeed in regaining their lost territories.

There are several legends regarding the origin of the meenas as the descendents of the ruling clan but the British historians in India disowned this fact. Meena people blame the British Rulers in India to associate themselves with the criminal tribes.

Meenas are divided into two categories:

(a) Chaukiar Meenas, and

(b) Zamindar Meenas

The later were engaged in agricultural activities where as the former used to collect revenue from the people.

Some Meenas were affected by Religious reform movements and became vegetarian who were later known as 'Ujle Meena: (pure Meena) where as those who continued their old tribal customs and practices were named as impure Meenas (maile Meenas). The descendents of Meenas who established their marital Relations with Rajputs were known as Parihar and Rawat Meena. These people are mostly found in Tonk, Bhilwara, Bundi and Ajmer.

Cultural Life: These people are basically agriculturists and reside in villages. Generally Meenas of one gotra reside in one village but now the situation is changing. Now there are villages where Meenas of several gotras reside. These people are the first among tribals in Rajasthan who came in close contact with the non tribals. They reside in villages along with non tribals ie Hindus and Muslims.

Meenas are patriarchal and pratrelineal. The impact of non tribals is very strong among these people. It is reflected in their social institutions. For example, child marriage is very much common among these people. The girls are married at a very tender age, some times below 8 or 10 years but she goes to her husband's home only after the performance of 'Gauna' ceremony (ie when the girl becomes young and attains puberty).

The position of women is quite pitiable among Meenas. She has traditionally no right over family property. Though widow remarriage in permissible, it is by and large confined to the system of levirate ie a widow is married to her deceased husband's younger brother.

Though traditionally Meena tribe permits women for remarriage, but in this custom the new husband has to pay back the fixed amount to her former husband as decided by the panchayat.

The impact of education has been very strong among boys of Meena tribe however, in this sphere the girls have lagged far behind.

The Meena boys who were already married at an early age (before attaining higher education and subsequent employment in the city) seem to be unhappy with their marriage and many a times remarry according to their own choice, thereby deserting their previous wife. However, now Meena girls have also started getting higher education and have become conscious about their rights. Yet child marriage and dowry is still very much common in Meena community.

Nata: It is a sort of divorce in which if any Meena woman decides to leave her husband and children and wants to marry another man, she is by custom permitted to do so after giving certain amount of money to her previous husband (whom she decides to leave). This amount is generally paid by the person who marries her. If the woman is deserted or a widow then in that case the amount is paid to the male guardian who so ever he is either from parent's side or from in laws side. Thus, the 'nata' is purely based upon the wishes of the women, which has empowered Meena women to leave the husband and marry some one else if the need be.

Occupational Mobility: Due to education and subsequent occupation, large number of Meenas have moved from their native places to the urban ward areas. After education and benefits of reservation Meenas have been able to attain maximum number of employment meant for scheduled castes in the state under the reservation quota. The other tribes of the state viz Bhils, Saharia and Damore etc are lagging far behind.

Meenas are, by and large completely acculturised. They have started several Hindu caste customs in all the social and religious spheres. They call Brahmin priests at their house on important religious and ceremonial occasions.

Tribal chief (chief of the village) among these people is known as 'Panch Patel' who is a respected person in the village. 'Panch patel's status is hereditary. That is the eldest son of the 'panch patel' will be entitled to occupy his father's position after his death. Besides, there used to be panchayats also which in the past were very powerful.

Clan System : Meenas are sub divided in various clans (gotras). Alone in Rajasthan there are about 1200 gotras of Meenas. Marriage is prohibited among the gotras of father, mother and father's mother.

Economic Position : Compared to other tribes of Rajasthan, the social and economic position of Meena tribe is much superior. As they originally occupied fertile lands and had closer contacts with the neighbouring non-tribals they became conscious regarding the education of their children much before the other tribal groups in the state. They occupied most of the employment positions reserved for tribes in the state under reservation quota. The subsequent generation of such persons among Meena community has been put in a much better position to compete for the job due to their better education. However, occupational mobility has caused occupational inequality also among these people. Those who obtained jobs, have been placed in higher socio-economic positions. Such families have saved their village land from fragmentation, introduced tractors, pump sets etc in their agriculture where as the poor people in the village are still following the traditional methods of cultivation. Thus, among these people, the rich Meenas are becoming richer. Every year several persons compete for highest job positions (IAS) in the country.

Thus, according to 2001 census data, the state of Rajasthan had the total population of 5.65 crores, registering the population growth of 28.41 percent during the decade 1991 and 2001. Area wise Rajasthan is the largest state in India after the formation of Chhatishgarh state from Madhya Pradesh. The tribal population according to 2001 census was 7097706 which constitutes about 12.6 percent of the state's total population. The male-female sex ratio in Rajasthan was 921 females per every 1000 males. Compared to this the sex ratio among the tribals in Rajasthan was relatively more favourable to women. It was 944

females per 1000 males. Of course, there were sharp regional variations also. For example, the number of women per 1000 men in Dhaulpur distt. was 834 (which was lowest) and it was 1028 in Dungarpur.

References

1. ICSSR, *A Survey of Research in Sociology and Social Anthropology* (1972).
2. Doshi S.L., *Bhils Between Selfawareness and Culture Synthesis* (1971).
3. Mann and Vyas, *Indian Tribes in Transition* (1980).
4. Verma A.C., *The Bhils* (1978).
5. Vyas N.N., *Bondage and Tribal Exploitation in India.*
6. Shashi S.S., *The Tribal Women of India* (1978).
7. Sharma Rajiv Lochan, *Janjatiya Jeevan Aur Sanskriti* (1967).
8. Gupta Moti Lal and Sharma D.D., *Satmajik Manavshastra* (1980).
9. Doshi S.L., *Social change in a Bhil Village* (1981).
10. Rajasthan Government *Tribal Area Sub Plan* (A Report).

❑❑❑

19

Tribal Development Programme in Rajasthan

In the Fifth schedule of Indian constitution different programmes were launched from time to time to improve the condition of tribes in the state. Under these programmes the main focus was to improve their economic condition, abolish the bonded labour and to remove their indebtedness etc.

The planned development in tribal region started along with the first five year plan. First tribal development block was started in 1956 in Kusalgarh. In 1955 modifications were made under Rajasthan land act with a view to protect the rights of the tribal people on the land. According to the modification the transfer of tribal land to the non-tribal people was banned.

Under Second Five Year Plan, there was provision of Rs. 249.83 lacs for the welfare and development of tribal areas, out of which Rs. 206.93 lacs was actually spent on tribal development. In the Third Five year plan period 14 tribal development blocks were established in the state. In 1967-68 four more tribal development blocks were established. These tribal development blocks included the population of 698 thousand persons which was about 22.93 percent of the state's total tribal population. Under Fifth Five Year Plan (1972-77), like in other states, in Rajasthan also such areas were identified where tribal population was in majority and intensive efforts were made for the development of such areas.

Tribal Sub-plan

Tribal sub plan was started in the year 1974-75. Its aim was to improve the economic position of tribal people, so that these people might get social justice. They had been exploited and suffered from centuries. Central assistance was provided under special assistance programme. Besides, tribal development deptt also provided the economic assistance under this programme, Irrigation, electricity, agricultural research, community irrigation by diesal pumps, distribution of seeds and fertilizer etc were started. Efforts were made to provide occupational training to the tribal people. Provision was made to provide scholarship to the tribal students.

Modified Area Development Approach

This scheme was started in 1978-79. Under this scheme 2939 villages from 13 districts were undertaken for tribal development programme. These districts were Alwar, Dhaulpur, Bhilwara, Bundi, Chittorgarh, Jaipur, Udaipur, Jhalawar, Kota, Pali, Sawai Madhopur, Sirohi and Tonk.

Saharia Development Programme

Saharias are the most backward tribe in Rajasthan. They are mostly concentrated in Shabad and Kishangang Tehsil of Baran district. These people were primarily agriculturists and also depended on forest produce for their economic needs. In 1971 Saharia population in the state was 22069 which in 1981 increased to 33978. The financial help for this programme came from central assistance and state tribal development programme. Money was spent on agriculture, animal keeping, cottage industry, forestry education, rural housing, drinking water etc.

Development Programme for Tribals in the State

Tribal Area Development Plan was started in the state for 14.3 lakhs tribes of the state. Provisions for education, health, residence, hostels for tribal students (both boys and girls, free education, scholarship and training centres etc were established. Thus, effects for the development of tribal people in the state were made through various schemes and programmes. But tribal people mostly had unirrigated, poor quality of agricultural land. They suffered from unemployment, economic exploitation, poverty, illiteracy, malnutrition, superstition and several other social vices for long time. They had depended on the forests for their livelihood. But owing to restrictions by government on the forests, these people had economic setback.

For the solution of these problems certain developmental programme were inevitable.

After independence the following objectives were laid down for the development programmes for the tribals in the state.

1. Enactment and implementation of protective law to give protection to the tribals from exploitation in the state.
2. Formation of a spiral agency to organise the tribal development programme.
3. Formation of such schemes for the development of tribals, which may treat tribal families as a unit and concentrate on them.
4. Formation of internal structure for tribal area development.
5. Development of human resources in tribal areas through education and training.
6. Arrangement of education, medical treatment, drinking water, employment, transport, means of communication with a view to make qualitative improvement in tribal life.
7. Eradication of poverty by making family centred development programmes.
8. Protection to the poor in case of continuous drought.
9. To provide nutritious food to the child and mother of poor families.
10. To provide them loan and market facility through cooperatives.

Thus, the government of Rajasthan had undertaken various efforts to remove poverty and unemployment among the tribals. Efforts were made to bring about qualitative improvement among the tribal people through minimum need based programmes. All these activities countinued till Seventh Five Year Plan. During Seventh Five Year Plan (1985-90), the following objectives were laid down for the development of the tribals-

(a) Eradication of poverty through family control schemes.

(b) Removing basic structural constraints in tribal areas.

(c) Protection of the tribals from exploitation .

For attaining the above objectives the government of Rajasthan took the following objectives in five year plan:

1. First of all, to improve the economic situation of the tribal people efforts were made to generate the additional resources of income. Efforts were made to grow food crops, flowers and vegetables.

Besides this, poultry development seri, fisheries culture and improved methods of agriculture and irrigation etc were also given special emphasis.

2. Different legislation for protecting the tribes from exploitation and Tribal Land Owernship Act (1995), Rajasthan Land Revenue Act (1970) laws relating to indebetedness, bonded labour and minimum wages etc, were implemented seriously so that the interest of the tribals are protected.

Rules Relating to Appointment

There was provision of the research for the tribal people in government jobs and to keep the seats vacant if the suitable candidate of reserved category were not available. There is relaxation in age limit i.e. up to 33 years, and relaxation in fees for application forms etc.

Relaxation on forests: For constructing house, agricultural tools the tribals were given some relaxation, provided wood from the forest, besides they were provided firewood from the forests, were permitted to use forest grass lands for animals and some relaxation in the use of forest produce.

Human Resource Development Among Tribals

For this work special emphasis was given in Seventh Five Year plan, For example, in the sphere of education students were provided uniforms, books, stationary.

2. Provisions for hostels etc. after education the training faciltieis were provided for getting employment for example STC, B.Ed., training for stockman, ANM, Ayurved compounder, RAS , IAS, Bank, Rly recruitment board, IIT, fisheries, handicraft etc were started.

4. Under the tribal development programme so far there have been changes in the nature of education, medicine and nature of means of transportation.

5. Efforts have been made to rehabilitate the refugee families in the tribal areas. As women had not benefitted from the earlier schemes, efforts were made in this sphere also regarding their nutrition, training in cottage industries etc.

6. Because of the loss of the forests the environment had been adversely affected. There had been scarcity of water which ultimately affected the agriculture also. Thus, the problems of tribal people increased with the loss of forests. In this direction following efforts were made –

(a) Small nurseries with utility plants were developed at different places.

(b) Schemes were launched to plant trees on the vacant land in tribal areas.

(c) Under friend of tree programme the tribal people were made the guardians of the tree so that environmental balance could be restored.

Under Poverty Eradication Programme

Efforts were made to provide economic assistance to 3 lakh poor tribal families so that these could come up above the poverty line.

Under Seventh Five Year Plan, multi dimensional efforts were made to improve the position of the tribals. The poorest tribal families were given special emphasis. To implement the welfare schemes in tribal areas, development of human resources was given special importance.

Eighth Five Year Plan (1992-1997) and Tribal Development Programme

In the context of Eighth Five Year Plan it was realized that the basic priorities areas should be the same which were in seventh five year plan but special efforts were made to provide education and training to the tribal people, so that they could develop their self confidence. In the seventh plan development was primarily individual or family centred but in the eighth five year plan, development process was group (community) oriented. Tribals were made collectively oriented for various economic activities, like animal keeping, poultry farming, vegetable growing, raising of sheeps, fishery development etc Thus, the cooperative movement was popularized in tribal areas.

In Eighth plan education was given special importance. In 1989-90 an institute was opened for tribal students (scheduled tribe) to prepare them for competitive examinations.

During the course of five year plan it was realized that before starting any economic activity for the tribal people it was necessary for them to have the contact with the regular market and to understand its complexities. Before we start producing anything, we need to know regarding the supply of raw material, availability of financial resources, the production progress and later on its sale in the market. The tribal people would need to get acquainted with this whole process then only they could become able to take full advantage of it.

Regions where the tribal groups are not concentrated, the individual welfare schemes would be launched for them. Thus, at various levels schemes will be started to eradicate the poverty. For example, under Eighth Five Year Plan the following annual programme for 1993-94 was stated –

(a) Encouragement (incentive) to particular crops: Keeping in view the local resources and the Environment the crops of 'Arandi' and 'Soya' were given priority. Because these crops would yield better economic results and improve the economic condition of the tribal farmers.

(b) Development of horticulture : Efforts were made to popularise horticulture among tribal people. At several places nurseries were established and plantation work was undertaken keeping in view the climatic conditions.

(c) Development of seri culture: First of all this was started in Udaipur region in the year 1983. It showed good results, later on, it was started at Chittorgarh. Efforts were made to develop seri culture as subsidiary occupation along with agriculture.

(d) Animal husbandry: Tribals were acquainted with the refined techniques of animal keeping. For example, opening of dispensaries for the treatment of animals, improvement of breed, to keep animals who yield more milk etc. Under this plan there was provision of distributing better variety of sheep to 1200 tribal families.

(e) Fisheries: To popularise fisheries among tribals 306 tribal fisherman were acquainted with the latest technique and training for fishing. They were given boats and nets at concessional rates. Provision was made for the insurance of 2800 fishermen. For fisheries at least one cooperative society was started each at the Udaipur, Dungarpur, and Banswara region.

(f) Forestry: The growth of forest is essential for maintaining the environmental balance. The tribal economy, initially has been forest based. These people used these forests for a very long time, and consumed the forests produce, did not play any role in the increase of forests. Because primitive economy, initially was basically consumption economy, the increase in tribal population resulted into the decline of forests at a faster pace.

Tribal areas had enough vacant land where plantation work could be started. The plants could be grown keeping in view the nature and type of natural conditions. For example in certain are as

Bamboo forests could be grown which would later on provide raw material for cottage industry. Thus, efforts were made in this direction.

(g) Cooperative institutions: In 7 th and 8th Five year plan also active efforts were made to check the exploitation and growing poverty among the tribal people. For this purpose cooperative movement was made more and more effective. A programme was launched to make available the essential goods in villages, collection of forest produce through tribal people and in return pay them the appropriate amount. Under 8th five year plan it was planned to encourage the tribal handicraft through exhibitions at different places, provide tribal people loan to start the work, encourage the tribal people to start the small cottage industries, and the traditional work in which they were engaged since long time e.g. basketry mat making, wooden work, iron smith etc. these people could raise their income through these activities. It was found during the period 1993-94 that about 7.50 lacks tribal people were benefitted through cooperative societies. Through these societies the tribals were encouraged to start dairy, bidi making, computer learning etc and there was provisions to get loan also.

(g) Irrigation: Under tribal sub plan elaborate schemes were prepared for irrigation in tribal area. Most of the tribal people depend on agriculture for their living. As there are immense possibilities of the development of irrigation facilities in tribal region, therefore 148.49 lakh rupees was made available during the year 1993-94.

Under these schemes efforts were made to repair the dry wells and make water available. Efforts were also made to make water available at higher altitudes. Loans were given to farmers for lift irrigation scheme etc.

Similarly efforts were made to produce more electricity in the tribal areas. Roads were constructed in the tribal areas so that the region could be well linked with the non-tribal areas also.

(h) Education: Educationally the tribal region has been far behind. In the year 1981 the general average of education was 24.34 percent where as it was only 10.28 percent among the tribal people. Thus, under 8th five year plan multidimensional efforts were made in this sphere e.g hostel and scholarship/freeship facilities for poor students, the facility of books in the schools through book banks etc. under this plan special efforts were made for the education of girls.

(10) In the sphere of medical and health, provision of mobile units was made for remote and unapproachable areas.

(11) Efforts in the plan were to provide professional training to the unemployed tribal youth. They were given training in allopathy and ayurvedic training of teachers, Bed CT etc., industrial training (ITI) and also training in small scale industries etc. Thus, through various five year plans efforts were made to eradicate poverty, illiteracy and indebtedness and to improve the social and economic status of the tribal people.

Inspite of all these efforts, the tribals are still lagging behind than non-tribals in various socio-economic and educational spheres. Among the tribals, there is a section of people, whom we can term as creamy layer, who have really been benefitted by the various schemes launched by the government. This no doubt has given rise to class inequality among these people, which was unknown to the tribal world in the past. The benefits of reservation have not reached those who deserved the most. The poor have became poorer. Yet there has been one advantage of all these things ie it has brought awareness and awakening among the tribal people. The mobility has increased over the years and there is increase in occupational mobility, from rural based agricultural occupations to city based occupations. Reservation has placed these people in every sphere of life.

References

1. Danda A. K., *Tribal Economy and their Transformation* (1973).
2. Tribal Development Plans (1977).
3. Sahai B.N., *Pragmatism in Development* (1969).
4. Verma, M.K. *Dynamics of Development: An International Perspective* (1978).
5. Sharma Brahma Dev, *Adivasi, Vikasd* (1994).
6. Mathur H.S., *Development Administration in Tribal Areas* (1976).
7. Raijada Ajit, *Tribal Development in Madhya Pradesh* (1984).
8. NCRT, *Tribal Education in India* (1967).
9. Rao D.V. Ramanu, *Tribal Development* (1992).
10. Vyas, N.N. *Bondage and Tribal Exploitation in India* (1980).
11. Sadashiv S. N., *Reservation for Social Justice* (1986).
12. Singh Parmanand, *Inequality Reservation and Discrimination in India* (1982).
13. Srinivas M.N., *Nation Building in Independent India* (1976).

❑❑❑

20

Reservation Policy

As we have stated that the tribal people are socially and culturally very backward, therefore, it was thought to provide them with certain facilities so that they could be brought at par with the rest of the society.

As a matter of fact in every social system there is some amount of inequality which is reflected in the form of stratification. Stratification basically reflects the inequal distribution of wealth, prestige and power. That means, in the social hierarchy people with more power, status, wealth and prestige are better off and are placed on the higher ladder in the social hierarchy. On the other hand, people with less wealth (resources), power and prestige, could be placed at the lower ladder. Tirbals in Indian society, by and large, fall in the second category. Though among tribals also there is some amount of inequality within the groups or communities, it is insignificant, keeping in view the non-tribal societies. In any society the meaning of democratization process is to get rid off those obstacles (hurdles) which make it difficult for some people to attain (achieve) the opportunity. For example, Indian society has/had debarred people of some groups/community in several social spheres like religion, education, occupation etc. Our caste system has been the best example, which for centuries debarred lower castes/utouchables from certain social, economic and cultural spheres, which were meant for higher castes. Thus, people born in a particular caste/ community could not be given certain opportunities irrespective of individual/personal capabilities. This has been an inherent defect in our social system, though it did not exist in the ancient past when man's personal capability and merit was the criterion of his social status and position in the society.

There has been an usual tendency among human beings to take advantage of their power and position in the society. In other words, people attain position, power and wealth, by exploiting those who are in the lower categories in the social hierarchy. Such a situation makes a section of the society poor and socially and culturally deprived. If we dwelve into ancient past ie pre-vedic or even vedic period we find that ancient Indian culture was based on the ideals of social equality and fraternity. There was varna system based an specialization of work. It was unlike the caste system where status was ascriptive. In those times every person irrespective of birth, had an opportunity to develop one's skill and ability. Later on, the rigidity of the caste system closed the doors for certain sections of the people, based at lower caste hierarchy and they were supposed to serve (work) the so called higher castes (savarnas). Thus, among non-tribal Indian society, a significant number of people who are at the lower ladders, remained socially, culturally and economically deprived for a long period. Individuals born within these categories had no opportunity in socio-cultural and other spheres and they were supposed to act like their ancestors. Thus, these people remained deprived for generations. But this was not the case so far as tribal people are concerned. Most of them were already deprived in socio-eco sphere. Though they had their own distinct culture, in the process of cultural contact they lost even the good qualities of their culture. Some of the tribal groups in India like Gonds, Bhils and Meenas, who were once rulers, had been thrown out, made to run to the forests and other deserted places in search of shelter and safety. Thus tribals, have been by and large the poorest people in our country. Therefore, after independence, our government thought of doing something to ameliorate their lot and to elevate them socially culturally and economically.

Independent India adopted democratic system and provided doors for every section of the society, in social culture and economic sphere. It wanted to bring social equality ie every person should be given equal amount of opportunity for development. In social context the meaning of social equality is that in society every person should be given opportunity. For depressed and backward sections of the society the meaning of social equality means that appropriate opportunities of development should be made available to them. Traditionally, these people have been devoid of such opportunities. This was only possible through the policy of reservation. Historically, lower castes and tribals were included in the category of depressed classes. Though problems of scheduled tribes have been partly different because historically, tribal people have not been the part of the basic Hindu social organization. They used to live in remote and unapproachable areas away from the non-tribals and had their own distinct social organization and culture. With exceptions apart, there had not been much change in the position of tribals in terms of their separate territorial areas. But the Britishers in India encroached upon their territory. There was development in the means of transport and communication. The tribals in India were also not free from the British domination.

During British period in 1919 some efforts for reservation for depressed sections were made. During that time Dr. Ambedkar was also drawing the attention of the people toward the hardships of depressed classes. The British government in 1923 passed a proposal which stated that no educational institution should be given a government grant if it did not admit the children of the depressed classes. In 1928 the government of Bombay state formed a committee to collect information regarding the backward castes. This committee in its report in 1930 divided backward castes in 3 categories:

(1) Depressed Castes

(2) Tribals, and

(3) Backward Castes

The third round table conference, while condemning the idea of communal reservation, emphasised on the need of reservation for depressed classes. It gave several arguments in its support.

The British Prime Minister was impressed by the arguments put forth by Ambedkar and in 1932 he declared communal award under which provision for separate representation for depressed classes was made. But Gandhiji did not agree with this proposal. He believed that separate electorate system will keep depressed classes away from Hindus and will divide the two.

Owing to the increasing pressure of social circumstances the depressed classes were accepted as scheduled castes. Thus, the Act of 1935 replaced term depressed classes by scheduled castes. For improving the position of scheduled castes and scheduled tribes the issue of Reservation was taken seriously. At last on 25th May 1949 the constituent Assembly decided for the reservation of jobs for scheduled castes and scheduled tribes. Thus, there was consensus among constituents on this issue that the basis of backwardness would be social, economic and educational in which backward castes, scheduled castes and scheduled tribes would be included.

Scheduled Tribes and the Constitution

The Constitution of India provides various safeguards in favour of scheduled tribes. These are

(a) Protection and (b) Development

The Protective Provisions are contained in articles 15 (4), 16 (4), 19 (5), 23,29,46, 330, 334, 335, 338, 339(1), 371(A), 371(B) and 371(C) of the constitution.

Provisions relating to the development of scheduled tribes are mainly related to the articles 275(1) and 339(1).

Article 15(4) states about the promotion of social, educational and economic interests. For example, reservation of seats in educational institutions, relaxation in qualification for admission and providing housing accommodation.

Article 16(4) deals with reservation for backward classes who are, in the opinion of the state, not adequately represented in the services of the state.

Similarly, article 29 provides protection to ST communities to conserve their language, dialect and culture. And article 46 provides for promotion of educational and economic interest of SC and ST and other weaker sections.

Articles 330, 332 and 334 deal with the reservation of seats in the house of people and in the legislative assembly of every state.

Provisions relating to the economic development of scheduled tribes were made through articles 275(1) and 339(2). Like wise there are several other provisions made in the constitution to ameliorate the lot of scheduled tribes.

In the year 1990 a national commission for scheduled castes and scheduled tribes was established through constitutional amendment and it was expected that

(a) The commission shall see it that the government shall properly implement the laws made from time to time for S.C. and S.T.

(b) It will examine the specific complaints of SC and ST people.

(c) Shall participate in the planning process for the social and economic development of scheduled castes and scheduled tribes and shall evaluate the progress made under central and state governments.

(d) Shall submit annual report about measures taken to prevent discrimination.

(e) In its report it shall state regarding those efforts to be made by central and state governments for the welfare, security and social and economic development of the scheduled castes and scheduled tribes.

(f) The commission shall undertake those tasks/activities which the president of India desired for the welfare, development and progress of scheduled castes and scheduled tribes.

Thus, apart from providing reservation the government has also given numerous concessions to schedules castes and scheduled tribes in direct recruitment as well as promotion. Infrastructure has also been built up, with certain procedural and institutional safeguards which are as follows:

(a) Age Relaxation: There is upper age relaxation of 5 years for the persons of scheduled castes and scheduled tribes.

(b) Fee concession: The members of SC and ST category will give only one fourth of the fees for admission to any examination for selection on service or post.

(c) Travelling allowances for interview. For positions in class III and class IV category of the government advertised posts- to and fro second class train fare is given (for interview or written exams), for class I and class II category of posts, the UPSC gives allowances at the prescribed rates to all candidates including those of SC and ST.

(d) Reservation in confirmation: All posts, filled by direct recruitment, reservation applies also at the stage of confirmation.

(e) Reservation for scheduled castes and scheduled tribes candidates in work charge (establishment) duty related staff. This has to be done in accordance with the percentage.

(f) Representation of scheduled castes and scheduled tribes in the appointment of posts filled by transfer or deputation.

In this case a fair portion of appointment have to be made/posts have to be filled by employees of SC and ST category.

Relaxation of Standards and other Steps taken for Filling Reserved Vasancies

(1) Relaxation of standards of suitability.

(2) Relaxation of experience and qualification.

(3) Requisitions for reserved vacancies.

(4) Procedure for advertising of reserved vacancies.

(5) Anouncement of reserved vacancies on all India Radio and Notifications to the directors of state social welfare/Harijan and Janjati welfare.

(6) Separate Interviews for SC and ST candidates

(7) Carrying forward of reservations and exchange of reservations between scheduled castes and scheduled tribes.

(8) Carrying forward and reservations of a single vacancy arising in a single recruitment year.

(9) Further relaxation of standards in non-technical and quasi-technical class III and class IV Posts.

(10) Scientific and technical posts Prior to 1975 were exempted out of the purview of reservation, meant for SC and ST. In 1975, however, these posts were also covered under reservation scheme.

Other Concessions in Posts Filled by Promotion

These are

(a) Relaxation of standards in departmental examination

(b) Age relaxation in promotion post

(c) Safeguards against suppression of SC and ST candidates in promotion

Procedural safeguards

(a) Model Rosters for reservation

(b) Liaison officer and special cells

(c) Annual statements

(d) Prior approval for dereservation.

Institutional safeguards

The Institutional safeguards are as follows-

(a) High Power Committee

(b) Commissioner for SC and ST

(c) Committee of Parliament on welfare of SC and ST.

The High Power committee headed by Prime Minister was formed in 1968 to review the matter in terms of recruitment and to issue necessary policy directions. The commissioner of scheduled castes and scheduled tribes was appointed under article 338 of the constitution to look after the matters regarding appointment, promotion etc of central government employees.

The committee of parliament on welfare of scheduled castes and scheduled tribes examines the position regarding representation of SC and ST in services under various ministries and other government organizations and make suitable recommendations for bringing about improvement there in. This was a sort of welfare committee.

Thus, various concessions like relaxation in upper age limit, unlimited number of chances available with the relaxed age limit for appearing in competitive examination, full exemption from payment of examination fees, relaxation in standard of suitability etc were the benefits given for the proper representation of SC and ST candidates in various government services. In this way the policy of reservation was aimed to uplift the ST candidates in socio-economic and cultural spheres and to bring them at par with the rest of the society.

Special Recruitment Drive for SC and ST

Special recruitment drive was carried out in 1989 to fill up the backlog of reseved vacancies. The drive covered ministries/deptts, public sector undertakings, public sector banks and insurance corporations.

A second drive was launched in 1990 to fill up the backlog of reserved vacancies as on 31.3.90 including the vacancies left unfilled in the previous drive.

A Third drive was launched in the year 1991 to fill up the backlog of reserval vacancies as on 31.3.91 including the backlog of reserved vacancies unfulfilled in the previous drives.

Another recruitment drive was also launched to fill up the backlog of reserved vacancies as on 31.3.93.

State governments also prescribed reservation keeping in view the tribal population in their states.

Besides, reservations in parliament and state legislatures also took place under the articles 330, 332 and 334 of the constitution.

Benefits of Reservation

No, doubt, the reservation policy has definitely helped the members of scheduled tribes to elevate their socio-economic position in the society. Some of these have attained high positions in service sector and won elections of Central and State legislatures. But the general perception has been that the success of reservation has not been to the desirable extent. Within scheduled tribes all people especially the poor and resourceless persons have not been benefitted. Only the rich among the tribals have been benefitted. Thus, there has emerged a creamy layer. In the creamy layer the coming generation has better opportunity to attain the benefits of reservation more easily. If the parents are in higher job positions, the children have an opportunity for better schooling which would make the attainment of goal easier. Thus, the benefits of reservations which are not unlimited in number, are being availed by a few families or a group of families within a tribe. These benefits were beyond the reach of the poor sector in the tribal society.

This issue has been raised several times as how to make the poorest among tribal the beneficiary of reservations. Can the benefits reach the poorest persons. Some people talked about one time reservation. Even the constitution initially had put the time limit of 10 years. But the policy is effective till date and no change is expected in near future. The reason is, it has become a very sensitive issue. It is easy to suggest that the creamy layer should be kept apart from further benefits of reservation, that the one time reservation policy should be adopted, etc but in practice it is very difficult to bring about such changes as the whole issue might take political colouring. Therefore, the political parties irrespective of their ideology, are scared of touching this issue.

There has been anti-reservation movement in the past, launched by the savarna youths but it did not receive open support of any political party. As it is a sensitive issue, therefore political parties, keeping in view their own vested interests do not dare to make any drastic structural changes. Yet some efforts could easily be made from within so that benefits of reservations would reach the poorest sections of the tribal society.

Thus, during freedom movement it was realized that whatever the policy framed for changing to the inequality in the society, Tribals along with scheduled castes shall be included in that.

In the early decades of this century during the freedom movement this logic was taken as the basis of reservation for almost all the higher positions the members of the higher castes had the monopoly and they considered depressed castes as inferiors.

Under the constitution several welfare schemes were prepared for the benefit of scheduled tribes. For scheduled tribes the arrangement of reservation has been made in educational institutions, public positions and political institutions.

For bringing improvement in the position of scheduled castes and scheduled tribes, a National commission was formed. The tribal people, after culture contact and along with the benefits of reservation seem to have improved their social, economic and cultural life to a great extent. Education was the first sphere toward which maximum people from all over the country get attracted, except those tribes which resided in isolated and remote areas and avoided any interaction with the outside groups or those tribal groups which were involved in deviant sort of activities like committing theft etc, most of the tribals started sending their children to the schools. Like non-tribals the tribals also, initially sent their male children to school. In the beginning they did not give any importance to the education of the girls but now they have started sending their daughters also to the schools and colleges.

After education, the tribal youth has developed craze for non-traditional occupations and the reservation has by and large helped them to some extent in this regard. In this way we find that most of the tribes in India have come very close to the so called civilized society in socio-economic and culture spheres while abandoning their tribal rituals, customs and practices. But some of the positive aspects of tribal culture have disappeared under the process of social change.

At last it can be said that the policy of reservation, irrespective of its criticism from certain quarters, has helped the tribals in their vertical mobility and in bringing them at par with the rest of the Indian society.

References

1. Colamen J.S., *Inequality of Educational Opportunity* (1966).
2. Jha, Dayadhar, *State Legislation in India* (1977).
3. Patel *M. L. Changing Problems of Tribal India* (1974).
4. Padhi and Mahapatra, *Reservation Policy in India* (1988).

5. Prasad Anirudha, *Reservation Policy in India* (1991).
6. Bose, S.C. *The Indian Struggle* (1967).
7. Mathur, H.S. (Ed., *Development Administration in Tribal Areas.*
8. Verma G.P., *Caste Reservation in Indian Law and Constitution* (1980).
9. Sharma, B.A.P. and K. Mudhusudan Reddy (Ed.) *Reservation Policy in India* (1987).
10. Sadashiv, S.N. *Reservation for Social Justice* (1986).
11. Singh, Parmanand, *Inequality, Reservation and Discrimination in India* (1982).
12. Hasnain Nadeem, *Tribal India Today* (1983).
13. Shrinivas M.N., *Nation Buinding in Independent India* (1976).
14. Vyas, N.N. *Bondage and Tribal Exploitation in India* (1980).

❑❑❑

21

Socio-Cultural Similarities Between Indian and North American Tribes : A Case of Cultural Parallels

Man is a unique creature. This uniqueness is due to his physical and mental capabilities which gave rise to culture. Culture gave man a unique position which no other living being could ever attain. Thus, man is the creature of culture and in the absence of which he would have been just like an animal. Though universal yet every society has its sown particular cultural characteristics. Broadly speaking culture is a way of life which varies from place to place and from most primitive to the most advanced society.

Man is also a mobile creature. Before the advent of science and technology the natural barriers like oceans, rivers and mountains had restricted human mobility. Though since time immemorial man was a mobile creature, this mobility had been restricted to short distances. Individual mobility was almost negligible. People moved in groups and families in search of food, shelter and security. Early man had not developed even the skill of planting a tree. In economic sense it was a stage of consumption economy. Human beings were totally dependent on nature. Productive economy had not yet come into existence. Even at that time man had developed a sort of social structure, though it was in a loose form. Social structure here has been defined in terms of social institutions ie family, marriage, religion and clan etc. With the passage of time the institutional behaviour became more and more regulated and these basic institutions became very powerful force in the society and their rigidity still persists in traditional societies especially in tribal societies all over the world. Thus, every where in human society, the people developed particular characteristics through its social institutions viz family, marriage, religion and political organization etc and so on.

Broadly speaking, man developed a way of life having similar cultural characteristics or elements at a particular point of time, in a different society (at the same) which can be termed as cultural parallel. In other words, cultural parallel means existence of similar cultural traits and elements at the same point of time, independent of each other at two or more places. People who develop these cultural traits are ignorant of each other or never come in contact with each other, yet they have certain similar cultural traits or practices. This is true about the tribals of India and north America. This can be cited as an example of cultural parallel.

India and north America are thousands of miles apart and until a few centuries ago its people were completely ignorant about the existence of each other. Both the places have large number of tribal population, who claim to be the original inhabitants of these countries and there is no doubt about this fact. In both the places there are certain tribal communities who are in a state of extinction due to one reasons or the other.

In India, there are more than 500 tribal communities, spread over all the parts of the country with large concentration in central and eastern part. After independence the Constitution of India had listed about 550 tribals groups for the benefits of reservation. By and large, number of tribals in India have lived in a peaceful atmosphere and the neighbouring civilized communities with whom they first came in contact, always had a sympathetic attitude toward these people. As the tribals were very poor people, their neighbouring non-tribal communities became a source of their livelihood, excepting those tribes who lived at unapproachable places or those who were displaced away by the outsiders due to one reason or the other. Their main problem was poverty and limited economic resources. Inter-tribal hostility was also minimum. India has second largest concentration of tribal population in the world.

The continent of North America consists of Canada, United States of America and Mexico. The continent has several hundred tribal communities. Before Europeans came to this continent, the tribals were its original inhabitants. History also testifies to this fact. Canada was a British colony for a long time. Mexico was ruled by Spanish people and became free in the year 1820. The United States of America has a long history of struggles and wars between the

European settlers on the one hand and tribals on the other. However, it became an independent nation in the year 1776 with 13 states in its federation. Later on, other states also joined the federation. However, till 1850 the state of Alaska was ruled by Russia. In the year 1850, the U.S.A. purchased the state of Alaska from the Zar of Russia on payment of 1.5 million dollars. At present there are 263 tribal groups or bands living in United States who speak between 50 and 100 languages, but as recently as 200 years ago it was estimated that there were at least 600 tribal groups, speaking fewer than 300 languages. If we dwelve into the past, we find that most of the north American tribals had been economically better off. But they faced problems after 14th century, when Europeans came to this country, initially as adventurers, traders and later as settlers and rulers. These people displaced the tribals from their original homeland and forced them to move to the interior. On the contrary tribals in India did not face such problems. Rather the tribal communities in India who came in contact with the non-tribal communities, were benefitted economically, socially and culturally.

The tribals residing in India and North America have some of the similar cultural traits and cultural practices. These can be noticed in the sphere of marriage, family, clan organization, religion and various social practices, rituals, taboos and totems etc.

Institution of Marriage

Marriage is an important event in the life of the tribal people. In these societies where economic life is very hard, marriage had significance from economic point of view also. Most of the tribals both in North America and India are very rigid in their attitude towards selection of marital partner. While in case of a few tribals some element of flexibility is also discernible. Some tribals societies give ample liberty to the marriageable persons in the selection of their spouse. In the case of former i.e. where there was rigidity, the selection of marital partner was purely a parental or family affair. For example, in India among Bhotia of middle Himalayan region and Maria and Muria tribes of Bastar region there were dormitories (night clubs) where boys and girls used to invite the boys and girls from other villages, gave ample liberty to their children. In such cases the parents gave ample liberty to their children.

At both the places the tribals used to marry at a late age i.e. girls after attaining the puberty and boys after attaining the youth i.e. when they become economically productive but in India there was reduction in the age of marriage, especially after the contact of the tribals with the neighbouring non-tribals in the villages. Even child marriages became common among some of the tribals. For example Meenas and Santhals etc. married their children at an early age. Such a situation did not arise in case of North American tribals so far as the age at marriage is concerned.

Some of the similarities in the marital practices can be noticed in the selection of marital partner, forms and types of marriages at both the places i.e. India and North America.

At both the places the tribal people adopt various ways of acquiring mates. As we have stated earlier that among the tribals, who are more rigid in their attitude and outlook, the marriage is purely a family affair. It is an affair between the two families. Of course, the clan rules are strictly followed. Close relatives and other kin members also play important role. Similarly, among the Cheyenne and Arapacha tribes in North America marriage was an affair between families and close relatives.

Status compatibility: Some of the tribals both in India and North America, who enjoyed superior status position within their tribal community, always preferred to establish marital alliance in the family, enjoying similar social status. For example, in India Bhil Sardars, Gond Raja and rich Santhals etc. were particularly conscious regarding the marital alliance in the status family. Among some of the North American tribal communities e.g. the Tlingit parents were always concerned that their children should marry within their own class and having similar social status.

All the tribals at both the places follow rules relating to clan/subclan, fratry and moiety into consideration. Usually a tribe is sub-divided into various clans and sub clans etc. Certain subclans or fratry and moiety is avoided for marital selection. The Tlingit tribe in North America strictly avoided marriage with a tribal group having similar mythical ancestor yet there are instances of violation of these strict rules, specially in case of inter-tribal or intra-tribal conflicts. That is, when a tribal group was defeated by another tribal group and winner tribal group captured their women and later on, married them.

Similarity is found among some of the tribal groups in the selection of marital partner, the criterion what is termed as forced marriage and the marriage by elopement.

In forced marriage the girl was forcibly taken away without her consent. For example, if a boy liked a particular girl he with the help of his friends would forcibly take her away whenever he found an opportunity at a lonely place i.e. in a fair, farm or in the forest and started living with her. In elopement the boy and girl liked each other but the parents did not agree to their marriage. Therefore, they would also run away from the home and started living as husband and wife. Later on, the parents of boy and girl were made to agree for marriage by the elderly members of both the parties and marriage was soleminised. In India, Bhotias had the custom of forced marriage and marriage by elopement. Though forced marriages were rare occurance, the marriage by elopment were quite common. Among North American tribals also there were instances of marriages by elopement. The boy and girl wishing to marry each other, secretly left the camp to live together. If such relations did not have the approval of the parents for arranged marriage but later on, if they proved stable they were generally accepted and enjoyed all the benefits of the regular marriage. There were also instances of forced marriages among the warrier tribes of North America where looting and raides were quite common. Inter-tribal or intra-tribal conflicts used to arise and in such cases the winner party used to take away the women and of the defeated group and later on married them, but now such instances have became a thing of the past.

Marriage by trial and marriage by service were also the ways of acquiring a mate among the tribals, both in India as well as in North America. Among the Bhil tribe in India there was the custom of 'GOLEGADHERO'. The Bhils of Gujrat state used to perform this ceremony on the occasion of 'Holi Festival'. It was the test of a Bhil boy and his physical power was tested which would prove his capacity to provide security to his wife. Similarly, among Angamy Nagas in India head hunting was quite popular in the past, which was a sign of bravery.

Marriage by service was practiced by Gonds, Baigas and Birhor tribes in central India. Among Khasas of Uttaranchal and Gujars of Himachal Pradesh. The popularity of bride price also gave rise to this custom. The poor people of the above communities if they were unable to pay the bride price to the parents of the girl, the eligible boy who intended to marry the girl, would go to the house of the girls' Father and lived there for a prior fixed duration and work in his farm, collect the fuel from the forest and looked after his animals. It was only after the satisfactory completion of the specified period that the marriage ceremony used to take place, otherwise the duration of the profixed period could be extended also.

Likewise among some the North American tribes an alternative to marriage by service and marriage by trial was practiced. For example, a 'commanche' man (an American tribe) had to prove himself as hunter and a warrior before he could marry. However, the instances of marriage by service were also rarely seen.

The custom of levirate and sororate also existed among the tribals at both the places both in India as well as in North America. In levirate a widow woman was married to her deceased husband's younger brother; in sororate a person used to marry his wife's younger sister. If he marries his sister-in-law when his wife is also alive, this is called contemporary sororate. However, both levirate and sororate have been popular among the tribals at both the places.

Thus, in several marital practices there is similarity between the tribals of North America and India.

Family: Family is one of the most important and basic social institution in human society. It is as old as human race. Among the people in simple (tribal) societies also the family ties were extremely important who generally identified with their extended families. Tribals in India usually have patriarchal type of family system excepting in case of Khasi, Garo of North east and the Nayars of south India who practiced matriarchy, whereas, in North America a very substantial number of tribal groups are of matriarchal type. Among Tlingits, Haida and Tsimshians on the north coast society there was matriarchal system where the children inherited through the mother. While their own children depended on the authority of the wife's relatives, such as wife's brother. This closely resembles with the custom prevalent among Khasis and Garos in India. At both the places descent is inherited through mother and father has secondary position in the family.

Thus, while in tribal societies at both the places (India and North America) marriage and family ties were extended to the last but divorce was not difficult. The couples could divorce simply if they wanted to.

Religion: Like all other human beings tribal also have been following religious practices from the very beginning. They too have their own deities, believe in spirits, and ancestral worship etc. In Indian and in North American tribal societies the role played by priest and shamon is very important. The ceremonies are usually conducted by shamon. Among North American tribals the shamons used to perform all the secret ceremonies in a similar fashion as it was performed among the Indian tribes. He also played role in curing the illness. At both the places the tribals believed that the evil spirits were responsible for causing illness. But where as among tribes in North America women priests were very common and like male priests they also played role in curing illness, ancestral worship and ceremonies for having good crops and avoiding natural calamities, the women priests among Indian tribes were very rare and they did not play the role of a shamon. At both the places the shamon acted as a medicine man also who cured illness of all sorts through spell and other rituals. The tribal people associated the cause of illness as a curse of ancestral deities or due to evil spirits, whom they propitiate through shamons. Iroquois, an American tribe believed that illness was caused by evil spirits and the spirits of human beings.

The tribal people of both the distant regions are very superstitious and believed in totems and taboos. A totem was a sacred bird or a plant or an animal or any other natural object which was worshipped.

Taboo means avoidance or keeping one self away from the object or a thing or a living being. These vary from society to society. There are taboos associated with regard to women, marital practices or with a natural object etc.

In traditional societies many practices relating to women were considered as taboo. For example there were taboos relating to menstruation, pregnancy, child birth and worship of certain deities or spirits etc. In some tribal societies women are supposed to keep themselves away from religious worship and the institution of priesthood.

Interestingly, there are similarities regarding certain taboos. Among Siox tribe in North America a mensturating woman is considered as polluted and one could not eat or drink from the dishes or pots used by her. She could not touch any weapon, shield or medicine bundle. These mensturating women on each month had to observe the rules. Similarly, during the child birth they had to live in a separate hut or a tents. Likewise, among the Khas tribe in India a woman had to remain in exclusion for 4 days, during the mensturating period. She could not enter the kitchen, cook meals or even touch the family drinking water. Whenever, any other person touched her, he or she had to purify herself or himself by touching cow urine or sacred gold water.

Among he Khas of Jaunsar Bhawar in Uttaranchal in India the taboos associated with a pregnant wife are applicable in case of her husband also. These toboos are : not entering the kitchen, avoiding crossing river, carrying heavy head load, use of axe etc This also indicates husband's sympathetic attitude toward his wife and bond of love and affection; what is also termed as couvade relationship.

In the selection of marital partner the tribals follow certain rules everywhere. At both the places the tribals follow incest taboo in the selection of marital partner. Similarly, in the selection of marital partner the tribals avoid certain clans, sub clans, fratry and moiety etc. This is just like rules relating to endogamy and exogamy i.e. marrying within certain clans and sub clans after avoiding certain others both in India and North America.

Death and Taboo: There were taboos among certain tribes of North America associated with death. For example, a person of Navajo tribe whose wife had died, could not become involved in an emotional relationship for one year after the death of his wife. Only after one year, as per social custom he was allowed to marry. Such a custom resembled the people of Kumaon valley in Uttaranchal region in India where upper caste Hindu men did not marry for one year of his wife's death. It was only after the performance of annual ritual he could purify himself and could marry if he wanted to.

Taboos Relating to other Natural Objects

In North America people in Apache tribe believed that if a person leaned against a tree that had been struck by lightening, he or she would fall ill. Among the Pima tribe if a person made fun of a person with mental disability, he risked having he same fate, befall his own child or relative. Similarly, among Khas tribe of Kumaon Himalayas, a person did not cut tree which had been struck by thunder lightening. These people did not imitiate a deaf or a mutle person for fear of being cursed and meeting the similar fate. Nomadic Bhotias of Kumaon and Garhwal Himalayas who are traders, moved from one place to another and camped near the road side on open ground, leave their belongings inside the tent and move from village to village to sell their goods. No trespasser could ever dare to touch or steal any of his belongings for the fear of magic and other calamities that might befall him.

The tribals of both the places in India and North America have rituals which are symbolic acts or gestures that follow set patterns and determine how a ceremony will be conducted. Thus, in the sphere of totem and taboo, there is some similarity among tribes of these two distant places.

Nomadism : Until today there were a few tribes both in India and North America who were leading nomadic life either wholly or partly. The nomads move from one place to another due to economic reasons. They do not have permanent homes at one place. The Bhotias of middle Himalayas were transhumane and moved from their winter to summer resorts. They were traders and animal keepers who moved from one place to another for trading purposes. In America, the Apache tribe partly lived a nomadic life. Similarly, in several parts of North America the tribals engaged in trading etc either partly or fully used to led a nomadic life and moved from one place to another.

In India, the Gadulia lohars of Rajasthan till today are nomads who move from one place to another in a group or cluster of families and prepare agricultural implements and make their living possible. Other nomadic tribes viz Aherias who are in Rajasthan and Delhi who prepare mats, move from one village to another—Bahelias are bird catchers. Saharias (Rajasthan) used to collect forest produce. Bajigars are acrobats and Mirariss are entertainers who moved from one village to another to entertain the villagers through their artistic skill. Kalanders of Uttar Pradesh are also acrobats. Thoris of Gujarat prepare mats from the forest produce and sell them to the villagers. Thus, Nomadism is also a way of life found among some of the tribals both in India as well as in North America.

Tribal Art: Cultural similarity can be seen in tribal art also. Some of the tribals are experts in handicraft, in the preparation of garments, in colour combination, body painting and in the utilization of forest produce i.e. preparation of mats, wooden utensils etc. some other tribals have developed rare skill in this sphere. For example, in the Ipiutak tribe of North America the people express their artistic sense not only in Ivory Carvings, but also in the delicate shape and ornamentation of implements used in their daily life. Tribals in central India and several tribes in North America do body painting, specially on festive and religious occasions to look better and attractive.

The Head dress is given special significance by these people at both the places. For example, Nagas and Bishon Horn Marias wear special headdress on festive occasions. Similarly, the members of Bear, Buffalo and Night societies wear special headdress while dancing around the scared stone on special religious occasions. Bhotia and Manipuri women are expert in the preparation of wollen garments.

Thus, in various socio-cultural spheres, there are similarities between Indian tribes and the tribes of North America. The above stated similar cultural practices state the existence of cultural parallels.

References

1 Ross Thomas E. and Moore Tyrel G. (Ed.), *Cultural Geography of American Indians,* Westview Press, Inc, Boulber (USA) 1987.

2. Moulton Candy, *Every Day Life of American Indians,* Writers Digest Book, Cincinati, 2001.

3. Taylor Colin F., The *American Indians,* Courage Book Philadelphia, 2002.

4. Curtis Edward S. *The North American Indians,* Johnson Printing Corporation, New York, 1930.

5. Driver, Harold E, *Indians of North America.*

6. Manchip white John, *Everyday life of North American Indian,* Holmes and Meier Publishers, Inc, New York, 1979.

7. Nichols Roger L. and Adams George R., *The American Indians: Past and Present,* Xerox College Publishing, Waltham, Messachusetts, 1971.

8. Wissler Clark, *Indians of United States,* Double Day and Company Inc Garden city, New York, 1966.

9. Sol Tax (Ed) Indian tribes of Aboriginal America, the University of Chicago Press, Chicago, Illinosis, 1951.

10. Wilber C. Keith, *The Wood land Indians,* the Ghola Pequot Press, Oldsay Book, Cannecticut, 1955.

11. Native Americans, Vol I to IX Grolier Educational shrmon tumpike, Danbury, 2000.

12. Alwin M. Josephe, Jr., 500 N*ations : an Illustrated History of North American Indians,* Gramercy books, New York, 1915.

13. Moulton Candy, *Every day life among the American Indians* Writers Digest Books, Cincinati, Ohigo, 2001.

❑❑❑

Appendix-I
Nature & Subject Matter of Anthropology

Anthropology

Anthropology is a way of studying human beings. Anthropology is a way or rather a collection of many ways of studying human beings and their closest primitive relations.

Kroeber defined Anthropology as the science of man. In more precise words, according to him Anthropology is 'the science of man and his works and behaviour. The subject of Anthropology is concerned with men in groups with races and peoples and their actions and deeds. According to Haddon, Anthropology studies the nature of man. Herskovits stated that Anthropology is the study of man and his works. Hoebel defined Anthropology as the study of man and of all his works. It studies about the races of man and customs of people. Anthropology is an exciting discipline as it encompasses all of the human experience right from its inception.

Jacobs and Stern stated that Anthropology is the scientific study of physical, social and cultural development and behaviour of human beings since their appearance on earth. According to Boas, Anthropology studies man as a social being. Penniman stated that in one aspect Anthropology is a branch of natural history. In other words, Anthropology is the science of history.

The Encyclopaedia Britannica maintained that Anthropology is a branch of natural history which studies human races. In the words of Lucy Mair Anthropology means 'talking about man, as psychology means 'talking about mind'.

Thus, Anthropology studies varied aspects of man and his works. Right from the origin of man on the earth, it studies various aspects of its physiological, mental, social and cultural development and behaviour.

As we will state later on, Anthropology has several branches or sub divisions. Anthropology in its totality, is to be thought of as one of the most highly specialized branch of the science and at the same time one of the broadest.

Origin of Anthropology : Various Anthropologists have given an account of the origin and development of Anthropology. Most of them are scholars like Haddon (1934), Penniman (1935), and R.H. Lowie (1937). Here we shall mention Penniman's classification of four phases of the development of word Anthropology. He has discussed these phases in time perspective. The four phases are:

1. Formulative period (before 1835)
2. Convergent period (from 1835 to 1859)
3. Constructive period (from 1859 to 1900), and
4. Critical period (from 1901 to 1935)

Formulative Period: This is the stage of the origin of Anthropology as a discipline. The pioneering thinkers and scholars of this period were the greek scholars. Prominent among these are: Herodotus (484-425 BC), Democritus (460-370 BC), Potagoras (480-410 BC), Socrates, (470-399 BC), Plato (427-347 BC) and Aristotle (348-322 BC) etc. Herodotus who is known as the father of history in ancient literature, travelled widely and came in contact with people with different language and culture. He discussed languages, material culture and social customs etc. He was the first person to talk about a custom which is known as convade (the detailed description of covade relationship has been given in the chapter of kinship). Herodotus also talked about different types of marriages prevalent among different groups of people which he had met during the course of his journey. Thus, he paved ground for the subject matter of Anthropology by way of its origin. His contribution to the subject took place in the early part of formulative period

Herodotus paved way for other Greek thinkers towards study of society and evolution of culture.

Democritus analysed prevailing human customs. He also discussed evolution of human society. According to him society came into existence out of man's own necessity. As man alone was unable to protect and defend himself in the midst of nature, therefore, he formed society. Man learnt several things from birds and animals. For example, he learnt weaving from spiders and singing from swans etc.

Potagoras (480-410) stated that man was the center of everything. Early society was homogeneous, unified and undifferentiated and some of the social inventions like language, family, justice and morality etc were made in the early stages of human evolution.

According to Socrates (470-399 BC) every society in guided by certain universal values which transcend various social customs. He mainly put forward the philosophical aspect of social thinking. After Socrates, his disciple Plato (427-347 BC) became very popular. He talked about the ideal society. From evolutionary point of view Plato depicted the development of human society in a unilateral form. His notion of limited population and selective breeding was probably the first comprehensive scheme put forward by any thinker.

Among Greek thinkers and philosophers Aristotle occupies very important place. He was the first to use the term 'Anthropologist' who talks about himself. He said that the social traits which depict the past must be studied. Existence of city in his opinion is an indication of man's better life. He argued that man by nature is a social being and his social potential was deeply rooted in language, habits, customs and rational thinking. Thus, Aristotle was full of Anthropological insight but culture is acquired by learning. Thus, Aristotles' views on social and cultural aspects of human society are quite significant.

Expicurus (341-270 BC) put forward his views on the importance of man and society which is now a central theme of Anthropological study. The western thinkers were dominated for several centuries by the views of the Augustine. He believed that God created the universe. He concluded that social behaviour was to be judged not by man but almighty alone. He, thus, opposed any form of independent scientific enquiry about man and society. Therefore, his critics opposed him as anti Anthropological.

Missionaries, travellers and diplomats gave good deal of information about people of Asia. In 13th century, the ruling Pope sent Carpini to Mongol court to establish diplomatic relations with the Mongolian empire. After his return he wrote history of Mongol in which he gave a good account of Anthroplogical information viz people's physical appearance, manners of living, habits etc. William Rubruquis (1215-1270 A.D.) travelled in Asia and gave an account of the items of material culture, food habits, duties of women, manners of burials etc.

Macro Polo (1254-1313 AD) in his work, The Book of Diversities, gave factual information regarding trade relationship, market system, money values, housing types, division of labour, marriage practices, religion and burial rites etc.

Vasco de Gama (1397-1499 AD), a widely travelled person described the troubles of journey. He also wrote about the appearance, dresses, ornaments, languages, trade items of people who came in his contact.

In 1942 Columbus, with his famous fleet of ships, sailed out to discover the diversities of the world, gave the first information about Indians by stating that they walked around naked, although some women used coverings of leaves, they had no iron weapons and these people were timid, simple and extremely liberal.

French writer Michel de Montaigne (1533-1592) wrote about cannibals prevalent at that time among the south American Indians who now cease to exist.

Seventeenth century onwards the discipline of Anthropology was more theorised and formulated by the writings of philosophers, social thinkers and such other academicians.

Francis Bacon (1561-1626) classified all existing sciences and carefully pointed out their merits and demerits.

Thomas Hobbes (1588-1679) formulated his theories for the study of society. He was of the view that society was formed by the social contact and therefore he did not speculate on the evolution of society, and he felt that nature had made men equal in body and mind.

Herbert of Cherberry (1583-1648) studied primitive religions in detail and he was among the first of his period of recognize, 'Paganism' as a legitimate form of religion. Viewing religion as a cultural phenomena Herbert felt that it must constitute an inherent form of religion. Yet religious systems and forms of worship differ greatly from society to society. He mentioned five common forms of religion. These are as follows:

1. All believed in supernatural power.
2. All worshipped it
3. All demanded virtue and pity.
4. All committed sins, and
5. All are meted out punishment in life as well as after death.

On the basis of all these and several other comparative studies, the concept of 'culture' as we now conceive in Anthropological perspective, began to emerge. Grotius argued that natural law was the basis of social life.

The contributions of Van Leuwenhock were very important for the development of physical Anthropology. To lock the basic elements of all social phenomena was the human mind itself. According to him human mind was by nature rational.

Some scholars of the 18th century felt that while the physical laws of the universe appeared stable but societies were constant in a state of flux. Italian scholar G. Vico (1688-1744) pointed out that change itself was a regular phenomena, therefore, it must be governed by law. He wrote about non-literate societies and their social traditions.

Montesquieu in his famous book—The Spirit of Laws (1748) attempted to discover the universal properties like the 'spirit' of all laws and also made enquiries for the corresponding similarities and diversities. The nature of laws, according to him was determined by their own socio-cultural frameworks, which interacted with all internal and external elements that falling within culture. He pointed out that nature and climate influenced more strongly the savage society than technologically developed countries. He was of the opinion that even polygamy, cannibalism, idol worship, slavery and such other prevailing customs had their functions within the cultural framework in which they appeared. That is why some of his critics and commentators on his works had considered him as an early functionalist, who stressed the functional inter-relationships among social institution.

After Montesquieu, other scholars of 18 th and 19th centuries who talked about the different aspects of savage societies and their cultural components were Voltaire (1694-1778), Turgot (1727-1781), David Hume (1711-1776), Immanual Kant (1724-1804), Fredrich Hegel (1770-1831), Karl Marx (1818-1883), Fredrict Engles (1820-1895), Saint Simon, and August Comte (1798-1857) etc. attracted the attention of Anthropologists. Simon and Comte also exerted their wide influence. Hume wrote on religion. In his book, The Natural History of Religion, he expressed religion as human thinking and rise to social phenomena.

August Comte and Emile Duikheim expressed the importance of society over individual. Christoph Meiners (1747-1810) highlighted the importance of studying culture empirically. He studied primitive social institutions, their customs and habits. Hegel believed in the evolutionary scheme of the culture, but emphasised biological analogy.

August Comte (1798-1883) is one of the founding fathers of sociology. Positive and philosophy is his important work. According to him all forms of society should be studied objectively, for value judgement simply had no place in science.

Thus, all the scholars believed in the existence of some sort of society and social order since very beginning. Various social institutions were in existence irrespective of the changing nature of society from simple to complex.

Convergent Period (1835-1859) : During this period the scholars from different countries expressed views regarding the biological and social aspects of the origin of human beings. Most of them had expressed their diverse views that ultimately led to the formation of the theories of culture. Prominent among these scholars were Karl Marx, Charles Lyell, William Smith etc. Marx talked of the dialectical process as the moving power of history which was marked by conflict. A French archeologist Perthes came across stone axes near a river bed. Charles Lyell, the British Archeologist also confirmed that. This paved way for the Archeological origin of culture.

Darwin's theory of evolution, which appeared in his book, Origin of Species (1959), gave an account of the physical evolution of man. He talked about the struggle of existence, natural selection and survival of the fittest, which threw light on the position of man. This established the physical evolution of man. But religious priests and missionary men criticised Darwin for neglecting supernatural power (i.e. God) which according to them was the only creator of universe, man and culture. Thus, during this period, there were diverse and conflicting views regarding origin of man and society.

Constructive Period (1859-1900) : After convergent period constructive period started. During this period, Anthropology grew as independent discipline in the form of teaching as well research in several universities in U.K. Eminent scholars like Tylor, James Frazer, Henry Maine, Mc Lennan and Morgan etc enriched the discipline by their contributions. It is during this period that several branches of the discipline of Anthropology came into existence. In Europe, U.K. and USA, Anthropology as a subject started gaining popularity. Even in France Emile Durkheim and his associates like Paul Rivet, Marcel Maus, Levy-Bruhl etc. recognized the importance of studying primitive societies which ultimately helped Anthropology to flourish. During this period reversal important journals like American Journal of Folk—lore, Bulletin of Royal Anthropological Society of Britain and Ireland (now known as Man) etc. were started. Besides, scholars and social scientists, the contributions made by colonial administrators were also very significant. This all enriched Anthropological knowledge. Specially the contribution made by British administrators in India, paved way for opening the discipline of Anthropology at the university level.

Critical Period (1900 onwards)

In his book entitled Hundred Years of Anthropology in 1935, Penniman used the word 'critical for the period ranging from 1900 till 1935. During this period, some developments took place which were of critical nature, that is why this period was known as the critical period. For example, in 1908, University of Liver Pool (London) offered first chair of Anthropology to Sir James Frazer. During this period reversal Anthropology concepts came into existence, which led to the development of many schools of thought in Anthropology viz structural, functional, school of diffusion, culture and personality etc. During this period, Malinowaski flourished in Anthropological arena. Radcliffe-brown was another known anthropologist of this period. His theory of social structure is quite well known. American Anthropologist AL Krocher, Ruth Benedict, Margaret Mead, Rohert Red Field and Clark Wissler etc. added their contributions to the Anthropological thought and Anthropological concepts developed during this period.

Thus, the above periods throw light on the origin, and development of Anthropological ideas, giving the discipline a shape which brought Anthropology at par with other social sciences.

Nature of Anthropology

Various scholars have described the scientific nature of Anthropology. Hoebel stated that the first characteristics of Anthropology is that along with natural science it embodies the characteristics of both biological as well as social sciences. As a social science, Anthropology studies man's social and cultural development and it also studies different aspects of man's behaviour in comparative and analytical manner. Man is not only just other living being, he also embodies cultural historical and other social qualities. Penniman called Anthropology as a branch of natural history.

Some Anthropologists viz Radcliffe-Brown, Malinowski believed that Anthropology could be meaningful only as a science. They did not approve of the association between history and Anthropology and stated that Anthropologists should study those societies which can only be directly observed. Contrary to this some Anthropologists believed that Anthropology is mere history and its total study should be based on historical events and facts. But Anthropology is indeed related to both. None of them can be ignored. Without understanding the past, it is difficult to understand and analyse the present. Society exists in process. Past events lay their lasting impact on the present. Therefore, in Anthropology man's past as well as present, both are studied in a scientific manner.

Thus, there is no doubt that Anthropology is a science. In Anthropology data are observed, collected, classified and analysed. On the basis of the existing facts, future is anticipated and what will happen is indicated on the basis of what is.

There has been good deal of controversy on this issue that whether Anthropology is a social science or a natural science. Famous Anthropologists Fortes and Nadel etc termed Anthropology as a natural science and stated that human societies can be studied by the methods adopted in natural sciences. The real task of Anthropology is comparative study of evolution, development and change regarding human societies and ascertain social laws like natural laws, social law can also be ascertained.

That is the real task of Anthropology that like natural laws, social laws could be found.

Expressing their opinion against the above views Kroeber, Bidney and Radcliffe-Brown stated that human life has not only natural or physical or mental level, it has social level as well. While expressing their opinion, those scholars further stated that human society like solar system is only a natural system, rather it is a system of social and human relationship. Anthropology, studies man and culture. Broadly anthropologists can be divided into two parts.

(1) Physical Anthropology

(2) Cultural Anthropology

Physical Anthropology studies origin of man, physical structure, evolution and diversity etc and its method of study is just like that of natural sciences where as cultural Anthropology deals with man and his culture. Moreover, its method of study is like that of social sciences because it is closer to social sciences. In this way Anthropology is both a natural as well as social science.

In the words of Jacob and Stern Anthropology describes the facts related to man and culture. It classifies and analyses facts and events and drawn general conclusions. It determines the process, causes and direction of change and indicates change that would later place in future.

Scope and Subject Matter of Anthropology

Almost all the Anthropologist are unnious on this point that as a science Anthropology is a systematic study of man. There are several types of characteristics and diversities found in human societies. These diversities are both of physical (physiological) and cultural in nature and exist in society since the origin of man and continue to exist till now. Human society is divided into various racial types on the basis of certain physiological and biological characteristics. These are physiological appearance, colour of the skin, blood group, texture of hair and other physiological characteristics etc. On the basis of these physiological characteristics, human societies exist on various parts of the earth. The geographical and climatic conditions determine the racial characteristics. For example, human society is broadly subdivided in 3 racial types. These are

1. Caucasoid
2. Mongoloid and
3. Negroloid

The above three races are further subdivided into several types. This is a well known fact that variations (differentitions) in various physiological characteristics i.e. colour of the body, texture of hair, colour of eyelids etc which are on account of different geographical and climatic conditions, have given rise to racial problems or racism. Thus, racism came into existence. The problem of 'racism' came after the culture contact i.e. when the people of different racial groups came in contact with each other and would continue to exist in society to a lesser or greater extent irrespective of its attainment of cultural levels and civilisational standards. Even the most advanced and prosperous countries on earth are not free from this stigma. Thus, racism is a stigma in our present society. Similarly, there are cultural variations. Various human groups and sub groups have their own distinctive culture. The environmental factors have laid their impact on the culture everywhere. That is, in the beginning the cultural growth was in accordance with the environment. But after reaching a certain stage of development man was able to win over the environment and the cultural growth/development took place according to the environment which was by and large dominated or in accordance with the man.

The unique characteristics, (both mental and physiological) which man had, gave rise to culture, which made him quite distinct in comparison with other living beings. This uniqueness which was initially embelled in him by nature (by birth) made him a distinct creature.

The scope of Anthropology can be divided into following parts—

(a) Anthropology studies man : Most of the Anthropologists admitted this fact that Anthropology is the scientific study of man. It systematically studies various aspects regarding man in a scientific manner. The various aspects, which are included in the scope of Anthropology are stated below:

(b) Origin and growth of man : Anthropology studies man from its origin till now. It studies those unique characteristics which separate man from other living beings.

(c) Study of human races : Anthropology classifies human races on the basis of physical characteristics. It also makes comparative analysis of different races. On the basis of physiological characteristics, it classifies human groups, the growth of man's physiological characteristics from the beginning—all this constitutes the subject matter of Anthropology.

(d) Study of culture and works of Man : Anthropology is the study of man and all of his works. Culture is man made part of the environment. Man is the creator of culture. Man is responsible for the origin and growth of culture. Besides this, the scope of Anthropology is quite wide in which all aspects of man made acquired things are included. Thus, whereas on one hand, the origin of man (physical structure) and growth constitutes the subject matter of Anthropology, on the other hand culture and man's works make the scope of Anthropology. Because its area is quite developed and wide therefore, it can be further subdivided into various sub-branches. For example, one branch is social Anthropology in which social institutions, social system, social organizations are particularly studied.

Thus, the subject matter and scope of Anthropology incorporates all the subjects related to the origin of man, physical structure, society and culture, its study area is not confined to particular period or society, rather it includes both past as well as present.

Different Branches of Anthropology

As has been mentioned earlier Anthropology scientifically studies man's biological, cultural and social evolution and development, its scope is quite wide and therefore it would not be justified to study all these aspects under one subject. Therefore, it seems quite reasonable to divide it into different independent branches. Every branch has developed its independent method of study. Broadly speaking Anthropology may be divided into two branches. These are

(a) Physical Anthropology, and

(b) Cultural Anthropology

But different scholars have sub divided Anthropology into different branches. Jacob and Stern have given the following classification

(a) Human evolution or the study of fossil man.

(b) Physical Anthropology

(c) Archeology or Pre-history

(d) Cultural Anthropology

(e) Scientific Linguists.

Ralph Piddington made the following classification

(a) Physical Anthropology

(b) Cultural Anthropology

Piddington further sub divided Cultural Anthropology into

(a) Prehistoric Anthropology and

(b) Social Anthropology

Hoebel has given the following classification of Anthropology

(1) Physical Anthropology

- (a) Human biology
- (b) Anthropology

(2) Archeology

(3) Cultural Anthropology

- (a) Ethnology
- (b) Linguistics
- (c) Social Anthropology

Ralph Linton in his book, the study of man sub divided Anthropology into following branches

I Physical Anthropology

- (a) Human a Paleontology
- (b) Somatology

II Cultural Anthropology

- (a) Archeology

(b) Ethnology

(c) Linguistics

E.A. Hoebel in his study, Man in the primitive world made mention of the following branches of Anthropology

(I) Physical Anthropology

(a) Anthropometry

(b) Human biology

II Archeology

III Cultural Anthropology

(a) Ethnology

(b) Linguistics

(c) Social Anthropology

Thus, various branches and sub branches of Anthropology as given by Hoebel may be presented in the following chart

Anthropology (Branches and Sub-branches)

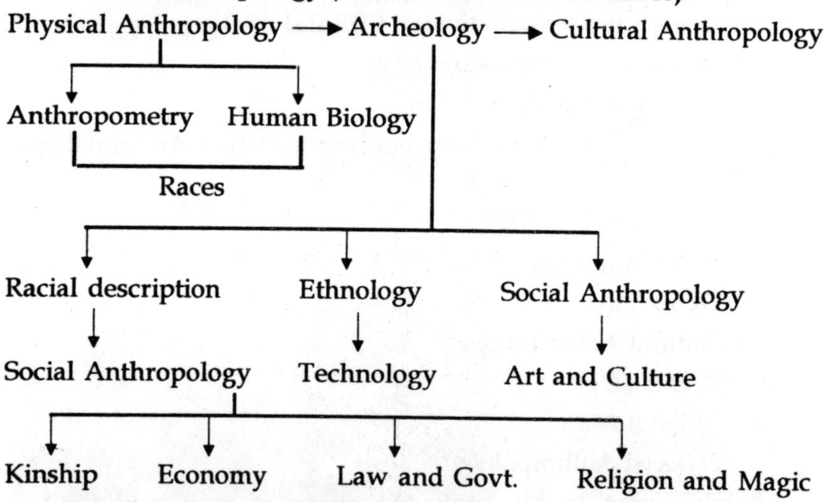

Physical Anthropology: This includes structure of human body, nature and variations. All these aspects are studied scientifically. It also studies evolution of human society, difference between man and other living beings, inheritance and mutation etc. In addition to that the impact of environment on human mind, intermixture between various races etc. in Physical Anthropology. As Hoebel said Physical Anthropology is the study of physical characteristics of hominoids. Its main branches are: Human genetics, Human paleontology and

Anthropology. Human paleontology studies human skeltons, its remnants, human structure, difference in human structure, process of evolution and differentiation etc. In Anthropometry the characteristics of human body are measured.

(2) Cultural Anthropology: As we have stated earlier, man is the creator of culture. Rather man is the only living creature who possesses culture. The unique characteristics which human body possesses has helped him in giving rise, growth and development of culture which has put man apart from other living beings and has put man on a different plane. Man has made both material and non material aspects of culture which have proved beneficial to him. In the beginning man was nearer the animal world and was more and more dependent on nature. The development of culture, especially the development of material culture has made him conquer nature and dominated over it. This is also well known that culture is transmitted from one generation to another. The elements of culture which do not have any utilitarian value, cease to exist.

According to Beals and Hoiser the Cultural Anthropology studies origin, history, evolution and growth of culture. Its studies structure of culture and effectivity at every place. Thus, the scope of cultural Anthropology is quite wide. Therefore, it is divided into following parts

(a) Archeology
(b) Ethnology
(c) Linguistics
(d) Social Anthropology
(e) Applied Anthropology

References

1. Spencer R.F. (Ed), *Method and Perspective in Anthropology* (1954).
2. David Bidney, *Theoretical Anthropology* (1953).
3. Haddon, A.C. *A History of Anthropology* (1910).
4. Herskovits, *Man and His Works* (1955).
5. Hoebel E.A, *Man in the Primitive World* (1949).
6. Kroeber A.R., *Anthropology* (1948).
7. Pocock D.F., *Social Anthropology* (1961).
8. Radfield Robert, *Peasant Society and Culture. An Anthropological Approach to Civilization* (1956).
9. Penniman T.K., *Hundred Years of Anthropology* (1965).
10. Friend John, *Cultural Anthropology* (1976).

❑❑❑

Appendix-II
Some Anthropological Concepts

Age Class

A social group wherein all members are precisely or roughly of the same age.

Age of Consent- The youngest age at which a female can agree to have sexual relationship which if it occurs, is not potentially definable as rape so far as the behaviour of the involved male is concerned the specific age of the involved female varying in accordance with the cultural values and legal statutes prevailing in a given place and time, by loose extension The lowest age at which a person can meaningfully agree to be married.

Accephalous- The term accephalous is used in relation to societies to describe those that are stateless. In such societies positions of authorities within kinship or domestic group provide a means of control together with institutionalized behaviour relating to lineages, tribes and tribal segments.

Avoidance- In many societies persons or groups who stand in particular relationship, avoid each other. As a mode of behaviour avoidance always expresses respect. For example, there is a relationship of avoidance between a person and his younger brothers wife. The extent of avoidance varies from society to society and may include such prohibitions as not eating, touching, seeing each other's face etc.

The Incest Taboo

Every society has certain rules regarding marriage but every society, by and large avoids sexual interaction with some close relatives like parents and sibblings.

Incest taboo means avoiding sex relationship between certain individual as determined by social rules of that particular society. For example, in Indian society, besides certain relatives from both father and mother's side, the norms of incest taboo are followed within caste/Gotra and in certain cases a village also. Among tribes, it is applicable in case of clan, moiety and fratry.

The commonly accepted sociological explanation for the universality of incest taboo is that it avoids social conflicts that would destroy family and kinship group.

Ambilineal Descent

The reckoning of descent group membership through either mother's or father's line at the individual's option.

Anthropometry

The Physical Anthropology specially concerned with measuring the function and size of the human body and its parts.

Anticipatory Socialization

The tendency of some people, particularly the upwardly mobile, to internalize the values and/or conform to the norms of a group to which they do not belong but with which they wish to be associated.

Anticipatory socialization is functional for the individual only within a relatively open social structure improvising for mobility (R.Merton, *Social Theory and Social Structure* F.265).

Associational Society- The large scale industrialized society characterized by urbanization, a finely wrought division of labour, specialization of role and diversity of status, predominance of secondary group relationship and by rapid change and an associated general disregard for tradition which do not appear to have utilitarian value.

Avunclulate- The term is used in the context of matrimonial societies. It is used as authority of mother's brother over his sister's children in a matrilined society and sometimes to describe the indulgent relationship that exists between maternal uncle and nephew in many societies and which includes, for example privileged joking.

Thus, in this custom, as the norm in some societies specifies that a man should play the role of father or the special authority and associated rights and responsibilities that men of some societies have relation to their sisters' children and, occasionally, relative to other aspects of family life of their sisters.

Avunculocal- Pertains to the norms and/or to the related practices, that a newly married couple should establish their residence with one of the grooms' maternal uncle, contrasted with matriclocal, neolocal and patrilocal.

Amitate- The term is used in two related senses :

(a) The special social relationship existing in some societies between a female and her father's sisters, or

(b) The special authority, and associated rights and responsibilities, which the women of some societies have in relation to their brother's children.

Age-Set

Age Set may be taken to mean the youths who have been initiated during a single period, whether this is marked by a single proclamation or continues for a fixed number of years. Those who actually went through the ceremonies together will then be called a subset.

Acculturation

The Process where by an Individual or a group acquires the cultural characteristics of another group through direct contact and interaction. From an individual point of view this is a process of social learning, similar to that of socialization in which linguistic communication plays an important role. From a social point of view acculturation implies diffusion of particular values, techniques and institutions and their modification under different conditions.

Assimilation- The complete merging of groups of individuals with separate cultures and identification into one group with common culture and identity. In most sociological usage, assimilation may refer to both the one way absorption or blending of divergent cultures. Assimilation is similar to acculturation, in which a culture is modified through contacts with one or more than one cultures, but assimilation involves complete change or elimination of cultural differences and differentiating group identification.

Enculturation- Herskovitas was the first to use the term 'Enculturation' which denotes the process whereby the individuals are taught to adopt the values and to manifest the behaviour that are approved in their society. In other words, it is the process of acquiring the cultural traditions of a society.

Culture Trait- It is a smallest indivisible element of a culture. It is one of the smallest identifiable unit in a culture-sometimes termed as culture element. As culture is material and non material, the culture traits are of both the types. Among material culture; its examples are watch, radio, pen, knife, cycle, table, hankerchief etc while non material elements are a word, an idea, any custom etc. In the words of Hoebel, a culture element is a pattern of behaviour (or material product of such behaviour) that may be treated as the smallest unit of its order.

Culture Complex

A functionally interrelated set of culture traits which may be considered as a unit set apart from other comparable set. Thus, culture complex is whole set of culture traits that cluster together in a meaningful interrelationship. Its examples are marriage, language, war, etc.

Culture Pattern-In any given society, a specific and enduring organization of culture traits and culture complexes of very similar to and often used synomymously with both cultural configuration and ethos. The culture pattern is grouping of traits complexes, into a sort of generalized picture of the culture as a whole. It is the organization of culture complexes constituting the entire cultural configuration of a society.

Culture Area- In the study of any culture, its physical aspect cannot be ignored. The culture area has gradually come to involve a segment of land as well as a type of culture having certain linear and temporal dimensions.

Cultural alternative- In the life of the members of a given society, a tolerated variation in attitude, belief or behaviour-especially, a behaviour (including the use of particular physical objects) which is acceptable, but not required, on the part of the individual or group in a given social situation or in situation where given societal participants have or more acceptable means the drinking of tea and of coffee are alternatives in our culture.

Cultural Drift- It denotes that type of cultural change which is made up of an accumulation of small unplanned alternatives, any one of which would be unnoticed in itself but which together can have a significant impact over the years.

Couvade

Greek social thinker Herodotus was the first to report about the prevalence of couvade. It is a custom in which the husband observes by way of imitation, labour pains and other taboos which are to be practiced by his wife as per the norms of the community.

Tylor collected information from 282 societies. He cited the example of couvade, a peculiar custom in which men imitate the habits of women, specially during pregnancy and labour pains. According to him it was not being practiced in matriarchal societies where the position of women was better. According to him 20 societies in the intermediate patrimatri lineality stage adopted the custom of couvade and others had already dropped this because it had lost its functions and utility.

Among Indian tribes the Khasas of Himachal Pradesh (Jaunsar Bhavar) used to follow this practice in which the husband was supposed to imitate and follow certain norms, preprescribed for his wife. For example, when the wife is pregnant, she will not enter the kitchen, shall not cross the river, will not use axe for cutting wood, shall not carry heavy load on her head etc. like wise the husband shall also not take up the tasks forbidden for his wife during this period.

Anthropologists state that this practice (customs) increases love and affection between husband and wife.

Cultural Islands

Immigrants often start their life in a new land as members of segregated groups. They flock together because they feel more at home with their own people. Moreover, the native group often encourage the segregation. Newcomers are hard to understand : suspicious are aroused of. These little segregated group are known as cultural islands.

Culture Shock : For many young people, even in our own society today, the transition from farms and small towns to great cities involves what sociologists call culture shock. The ways of new secondary groups are so different. The more isolated the community from which youth comes, the more likely is the transitional shock to be great.

Explicit of Culture and Implicit of Culture

First used by Clyde Kluckhohn in 1949, explicit is the outer and facial aspect of culture, where intrinsic elements, core etc. of culture are not discussed. Just contrary to the explicit, implicit of culture deals with the integral aspect of culture. Here an inside view of the culture is presented.

Culture Construct (Ralph Linton (1945) was of the opinion that when we see something from our own eyes and if that is culture, then whatever we write about the inside aspect of culture, that should be called culture construct.

Autonomous Culture Robert Redfield (1956) was of the opinion that there are some primitive tribes in the world, which are self sufficient and require nothing from the outside would and hence their culture is also autonomous. In the past there have been certain tribes which did not come in contact with the outside world and were self-sufficient, while the culture of the peasant society, which shares many things from the outside world is 'half-culture'.

Ethos and Eidos

According to Kroeber eidos is the formal appearance of culture derived from its constituents. Constrasted with the aggregates of constituents is the ethos.

Covert and Overt Culture

Covert refers to those aspects of a groups' culture which are not amenable to direct observation by the ethnographer. It includes values, beliefs, dreams, fears etc.

The term overt refers to actions and artifacts of the people, which can be directly perceived by the ethnopgrapher such as house types, clothing, gestures, speeches, etc.

Cultural Relativism

We can understand the action of other group if we interpret their behaviour in the light of their motives and wishes.

Thus, the function and meaning of a trait are relative to its cultural setting. A trait is neither good or bad in itself. It is good or bad only with reference to the culture in which it is to function.

The concept of cultural relativism does not mean that all customs are equally valuable nor does it imply that no customs is harmful. Some patterns of behaviour may be injurious in any milieu, but even such patterns serve some purpose in the culture and the society, will suffer unless a substitute is provided. The central point in cultural relativism is that in a particular cultural setting, certain traits are right because they work well in that setting, while other traits are wrong because they would clash painfully with parts of that culture.

Thus, cultural relativism holds that the customs of one culture can not objectively or validly be judged superior to those of another.

Cultural Pluralism

It is form of accommodation in which ethnic groups retain their distinct cultural differences and traditions, while cooperating, peacefully and relatively equally in political, economic and social life.

Thus, culturally diverse groups can live in harmony, without coming in conflict with each other. It is believed that culturaly diverse group can live in harmony and that mutual understanding rather than assimilation is the goal.

Cultural Revitalisation

The term refers to the process through which a society in decline reinterprets symbols from its cultural repertoise and revives its members' will to survive. The new identity is a combination of old and new elements.

Cultural Lag

The concept of cultural lag was propounded by WF ogburn in his book entitled **Social Change.** He made a distinction between material culture and non-material culture. When changes occur in material culture, these changes in turn bring changes in non-material culture also or in other words both material culture and non material culture run side by side, parallel to each other. But material culture runs faster than the non-material culture non-material culture lags behind. For example, changes in Technological spheres take place rapidly, but it takes longer time in the sphere of habits, attitudes and customs etc. thus, the situation of 'lag' arises. People imitate things from utiliterian point of view. Because the adoption of culture traits of material things, brings immediate benefits. For example, a tribe in Australia adopted steel axes in place of stone axes after the arrival of Europeans in their home land but all people did not do so because the tribe had associated religious and sacramental values with the stone axes. The result was slow changes in the attitude and out look of the tribe. They could not associate their rituals and customs or the sacredness with the steel axes which were more beneficial to their economy. Thus, it is a case of culture lag. The Hypothesis of culture lag holds in particular that in modern societies there has been a tendency for changes in the political, educational, family and religious institutions to fall behind technological changes.

Compulsive Deviance

It is the deviance that the individual himself cannot control. The individual is compelled to continue or resume his deviant behaviour despite the severe social penalties but result from it and despite his attempts to reform. Alcoholism and Drug addiction are special forms of compulsive deviance.

Primitive Communism

A form of communism found in certain non-literate societies, in which all the major economic resources (e.g. land, Boats etc) are owned by the community as a whole rather than by individuals, families, kin or other groups.

Companionate Marriage

A type of trial marriage arrangement in which the couple agrees not to have children until they are certain that their marriage is going to be successful. If marital relationship does not prove to be harmonious, the marriage is dissolved by mutual consent. When children result from the marriage the union is considered binding. This forms of marriage has been proposed in the past as a type that might be legalized. The main proponent of this idea was Judge Ben B. Lindsey.

Cultural Universals

The ideas, habits and conditioned emotional responses which are common to all sane, adult members of the society....this terminology applies only to the context of a particular culture. An element classed as a universal in one culture may be completely lacking in another.

Ralph Linton cites as examples the use of a particular language, particular patterns of costume and the ideal patterns for social relationship.

Technological Lag

The concept of Technological Lag was given by Mac Iver and page in their book 'Society'. This term is appropriate where any one of the interdependent functions within a technological process fails to achieve or gain the degree of efficiency requisite for the harmonious cooperation with the rest, so that the productivity of the whole process is impaired or blocked at this point. An obvious example is 'industrial bottleneck'.

In other words, situation of Technological lag arises where changes take place rapidly in one sphere of Technology, where as the other sphere fails to comply with these changes. For example, there is increase in the number of motor cars in the city. This requires that the roads should be widened. But because of big buildings on both sides of the road, the road could not be widened to cope with the heavy traffic. One would like to buy a car but would not like to damage his building. An example within the more inclusive system of Technology is offered by Ogburn. We exploit efficiently the products of the forest but fail to apply equal efficiency to the maintenance of the forest itself. The criterion of Technological lag depends on availability to measure the relative efficiency of the various interfunctioning factors and thus to show the failure of a particular factor to keep instep.

Culture Construct

Ralph Linton used the term culture construct in 1945. He studied the cultural behaviour among different societies and talked of three types of cultures.

(1) Real Culture

(2) Ideal Culture and

(3) Culture Construct

According to him culture construct consists of sum total of the behaviours of a society's members so far as these behaviours are learned and shared. A real culture Pattern represents a limited range of behaviour within which the response of a society's members to a particular situation will normally form. Thus, various individuals can behave differently but still in accordance with as real culture pattern In addition to these two types of pattern or culture, it also includes a certain number of traits which may be called an ideal pattern. In addition to these two types of Pattern or culture, it also includes a certain number of traits what may be called an ideal Pattern. Linton was of the opinion that the way of life of People is one thing and what we study and write about is another dimension of culture. The former is reality, the latter is our understanding of the same. If the former is to the called culture, then the latter may be called culture construct.

Culture of Poverty

The culture of Poverty thesis is the oldest one and originated in the religious writings and institutions of theology. Many researchers noted that the life style of the poor differs in certain respects from other members of the society. Poverty and life style share common characteristics.

Oscular Lewis, the American Anthropologist introduced the idea of culture of Poverty in 1950. He stated that poor people develop a culture of their own or rather a sub culture which is not part of the behaviour pattern of the value system of the society in which they live. some of the important features of the culture of poverty stated by him are as follows-

(a) Lack of effective participation and integration of the poor in major social instiutions of the larger society.

(b) Low wages, cronic unemployment and underemployment leading to low income, lack of property ownership and absence of savings etc.

(c) People with culture of Poverty produce very little in return.

(d) People with culture of Poverty are aware of the middle class values.

(e) Poor housing conditions, crowding, gregariousness and above all a minimum organization, there may be a sense of community in urban slums and urban neighbourhoods.

(f) Inspite of generally low level of organization there may be a sense of community in urban slums and urban neighborhoods.

(g) On the family level, the major traits of culture of Poverty are absence of childhood as a socially prolonged and protected stage in life cycle. These are high rate of divorce and desertion by male family head—a relatively high incidence in the abandonment of mother and children, a trend towards mother centered families (female headed households) and a much greater knowledge of maternal relatives.

(h) On the level of individual, the major characteristics are strong feelings of marginality, of helplessness, of dependency and inferiority. Thus, culture of poverty is seen as a response by the poor to their position in the society. As Lewis states : It is a reaction of the poor to their marginal position to a stratified and highly and individualistic society.

(i) Other traits include high incidence of maternal deprivation, of morality and weak age structure, confusion of sexual identification, lack of impulse control, strong present time orientation with little ability to defer gratification and to plan for future, sense of resignation and fatalism, widespread belief in male superiority and high tolerance for psychological pathology of all sorts, exclusive concern with immediate gratification and frequent endorsement of delinquent behaviour.

Mass Culture

Some social scientists believed that urbanization, industrialization, bureaurcatisation and geographical mobility have undermined the importance of Primary groups or close relationships among people. As a consequence society tends to be a mass of automised, undifferentiated and shapeless individuals. Thus, mass society generates mass culture. In other words, the elements of culture that develop in a large, heterogenous society as a result of common exposure to and experience of the mass media, such as popular, songs and dances. The emergence of mass culture is a part of the power of common unifying cultural values and attitudes in a new and vast populations of modern national social units.

Counter Culture

Groups' ways of thinking and acting which are in opposition to the prevailing norms and values of the society. It is also known as the specific form of youth culture, prevailing in several industrial Western societies.

Cultural Imperative

A Cultural form essential for the survival of any society. Cultural imperative would include methods of providing food and shelter, of caring for the young, of transmitting knowledge, of limiting internal conflict, and so forth. Cultural imperatives are based on the physiological and social needs of men in all the societies. Frequently they are referred to as the functional requisites of any society.

Cross Cultural Method

The gathering of comparable data from different cultures in order to test hypothesis concerning individual and group behaviour. The cross cultural method is a way of learning which theoretical generalization or concepts have applicability only within certain cultures, and a method of developing more universal generalizations.

Cultural Monism

A doctrine that advocates assimilation of ethnic minorities into the dominant culture of a society to attain cultural uniformity within the society, and thus eliminate the possibility of internal conflict between ethnic groups.

Cultural Drifts

Gradual, broad, sweeping changes in values or behaviour are constantly taking place in all the present day so called civilized societies. Such changes are called cultural drifts. The concept was given by Herskovits (1949) who described it as a process where minor alterations slowly change the character and form of a way of life, but where the continuity of the event is apparent.

In the course of a cultural drift most of the people develop new ideas of what society should he like and how society should treat them.

Each cultural drift arises through the interaction of many causative factors. Cultural drift provides an opportunity for social movements to hasten developments already underway.

Cultural Specialities

Cultural specialities are parts of a culture which all people need not learn. They are acquainted only by certain individuals and groups e.g. lawyers, doctors, teachers, farmers etc learn special parts of the culture.

Cultural Alternatives

Two or more forms of behaviour that in a particular society are acceptable in a given situation. These alternatives represent different reactions to the same situations or different techniques for achieving the same ends. In simple cultures the same range of cultural alternatives is more likely to be familiar to and agreed upon by all members of society than in a complex culture. In a complex culture the range of acceptable norms of behavior often varies from one subgroup to another. Members of one subgroup may reject the legitimacy of certain alternatives accepted by members of other sub groups. In other words in the way of life of the members of a given society, a tolerated variation in attitude, belief or behaviour which is acceptable, but not required, on the part of any individual a group in a given social situation or the situations where given social participants have two or more acceptable means by which particular groups can be achieved. The drinking of tea and of coffee at family meals are alternatives in our culture. Growing of moustache is an alternative for men.

Sub Culture

Every society is stratified and this is more true of modern industrial society with enormous amount of complexities. The simple (Primitive) societies were more and more of egaliteran nature.

In a stratified society there is a tendency for members of each stratum to develop their own sub culture, ie certain norms, attitudes and values which are distinctive to them as a social group. When some members of society experience similar circumstances and problems which are not common to the members, a sub culture tends to develop. For example, the members of lower structure have lesser opportunities in the society and poor chances of improving their social status, therefore, they develop fatalistic attitude towards life. This attitude becomes part of their sub culture. Members of a social group who share similar circumstances and a common sub culture will be likely to develop a group identity. They tend to have a consciousness of kind, a feeling of kindship with other group members.

Cognitive Culture

Ideas, attitudes, values and beliefs constitute the cognitive culture of a cultural system. These cognitive elements of culture provide members of a society with a frame work for viewing the world, a means of constructing and understanding reality, and consist of the thoughts that shape their existence. Normative culture consists of the rules for behaviour, but it is cognitive culture that is the source of these rules.

The cognitive elements of culture cover all aspects of human life, from simple to complex.

Implicit Culture

Those aspects of culture of which the members of the society are only partially or not at all aware. It consists of assumptions and premises underlying behaviour and thought, but not usually verbalized or recognized by a person from different culture, because those who share the culture many so thoroughly accepts certain assumptions that they are not at all aware of them. Implicit culture is sometimes referred to as covert culture.

Cultural Monism

A doctrine that advocates the assimilation of ethnic minorities into dominant culture of a society to attain cultural uniformity within the society and thus eliminate the possibility of internal conflict between ethnic groups.

Cultural Survival

A culture trait that is maintained even though it no longer performs its original functions. Often a trait originally fulfilled a utiliterain purpose, but in time, due to technological or other changes has ceased to be of utilitarian importance, is maintained because it is traditional or decorative.

Examples of cultural survivals that are readily observable include men's coat-sleeve buttons, the use of fire places in houses with central heating and the use of candles where there are electric lighters cultural survivals are sometimes referred to as cultural residues.

Cultural Deprivation

The sub culture of low income groups is deprived or deficient in certain important respects and this accounts for the low educational attainment of these groups. This is because of neglect of education of the child, his family, neighbourhood and the sub culture of his groups. The so called culturally deprived child is deficient or lacks important skills, attitudes, and values which are essential for high educational attainment. His environment is not only poverty stricken in economic terms but also in cultural terms.

Cultural Imperative

A Cultural form is essential for the survival of any society. Cultural imperatives would include methods of providing food and shelter, of caring for the young, of transmitting knowledge, of limiting internal conflict and so forth. Cultural imperatives are based on the physiological and social needs of men in all societies. Frequently they are referred to as the functional requisities of any society.

Contra Culture

A sub culture that stands in opposition to important aspects of the dominant culture of the society. The term was introduced by J.Milton Yinger to designate a particular type of sub culture in which certain values and social norms of the dominant culture are specifically rejected and contrary values and norms are deliberately accepted.

Delinquency and drug eddiction often have a contra culturala aspect, but some what less closely political and religious movements among disprivileged groups may also invert the values of the influential but inrecesible dominant groups.

Cultural Convergence

The development of similar culture traits in two or more cultures either through diffusion or parallelisms i.e. either through contact between cultures or independently.

Sensate Culture

Used by Pitrium A Sorokin in which materialistic and empirical values predominate. In such a culture, ultimate reality is seen as comprising only natural phenomena, subject to empirical investigation: no reality exists beyond what can be revealed in sense perception.

Ideational Culture

A type of culture proposal by Sorokin in which the highest values are non-material, tansandental (transcendental) and supernatural. Ultimate reality is spiritual and non ulitarian. Rather than stressing the manipulation of the empirical world to improve the quality of life, as to the sensate cultures, the ideational culture emphasized adjustment to the existing world.

Idealistic Culture

Proposed by Sorokin it is a synthesis of ideational and sensate values. These two types of cultural elements are integrated so that spiritual and material values are important, although spiritual values tend to predominate.

Double Descent

A system of descent in which every individual belongs to two groups of kindred, one through his father and the one through his mother, both of which are based on unilateral descent.

Cake of Custom

The term suggested by Bagehot to denote the fact that, so far as institutionalized processes and associations are concerned, there is strong resistance to change.

De-tribalisation

It is a recent phenomena through which culture change could be studied. When we idealized the traditional Advasi Culture, we may identify the genius of the tribal style of life with simplicity, self-reliance homogeneity, cooperation, distinctiveness, honesty etc, but when one notes that these values of tribal culture are being replaced fastly by complexity, heterogeneity, competition, conflict, frustration etc, one feels ethically disturbed and calls this patterns of change negatively as de-tribalisation.

Descent

The Process or the result of originating from a given ancestor or a given group. When identity with a certain family gives one membership in a wider group, the process is called descent.

Double Unilineal Descent

In Kinship terminology, denotes a descent system where in any given individual belongs equally to both matrilineal and patrilineal kinship groups; sometimes termed double descent or dual descent.

Succession (In Anthropology) rules governing the transmission of privilege, office, or authority. In (Political science), the process involved in the transference of office or of sovereignity from one social unit to another.

In Sociologically oriented human ecology, the situation prevailing when, following invasion, a particular area is covered to some new use.

Dual Divisions

Some societies are divided into two complimentary halves. The name given to these divisions is moieties which simply means halves. Several tribes in North America, Australia, and India or else were, are divided into exogamous moieties. That is, every member of the tribe belongs by birth to one of two halves, and must marry a member of the other. But moiety divisions are not always exogamous and even when they are, their principal significance is commonly in the field of religion rather than in marriage relationships. The two divisions cooperate in important rituals, each having its appropriate tasks and both being indispensable to the success of the ceremony.

Local Descent Group

The members of a lineage who actually do live in close, every day contact have been called by Leach the local descent group.

De-Brahminisation

VKRV Rao puts forward the idea of De-Brahminisation which

stands for a process of social change in which the Brahmin derives his own high position in the traditional social system and moves towards acquiring for himself high education, and well paid prestigeous jobs in the bureaucracy. The Brahmin also leads in the modern professions, social reforms and industrial entrepreneurship. While the Brahmin is busy westersing the traditionally lower castes and getting sanskritised though not neglecting to acquire the symbols of secular status to the extent they are able. 'De Brahminisation is not identical with disanskritisation'. Though related to it.

Ethnic Group

Traditionally, a group characterized by unity of both race and culture, now often denots any social group, which as part of the larger socio-cultural system, is perceived as being some what distinctive because its members adhere to a religion that is more or less unique to them, because of some special national origin or language or because they are racially different from the majority etc. The four main indicators of ethnicity are

(a) Race

(b) Region

(c) Religion and

(d) Language

Ethnogenesis

This term refers to creation of a new group or tribal identity. The development of a new tribe with its own distinctive culture and language generally involves splitting of one society. In course of time the scattered groups of refugees from several tribes or group may form a distinctively new society.

Vertical Group

A group made up of people who are not equal in social status, a group with a membership made up of people from two or more social classes or castes.

Ethnic group-are vertical since they are of course made up of individuals in various social classes.

Horizontal Group

A group made up of people who are essentially equal in social status contrated with vertical groups.

Opler's Concept of Unity and Extensions

Moris Opler, an American Anthropologist studied an Indian village in 1948 and 1952 and analysed various aspects of the village life. He developed the concept of 'unity and extensions' in his paper, extensions of an Indian village published in the **Journal of Asian Studies** (1956). He suggested that a village in India, irrespective of caste complexes and economic disparity, provides a homogenous cultural unity, which is extended beyond the political boundary of a village through network of matrimonial relations, kinship ties, economic transactions, intervillage fairs and festivals. Thus, the concept of unity and extensions as depicted through the study of an Indian village, throws light on the indigeneous character of Indian civilization.

Gould's Concept of Centripetal and Centrifugal

Gould argues that when a village in India is conceived as a self-contained entity to some extent, it may be called centripetal. However, when the activities of the village extend to outside the village especially to towns and markets then it may be explained as centrifugal dimensions of an Indian village.

Family of Orientation

The nuclear family into which a person is born or in which his social organization occurs, contrasted with family of procreation which is the nuclear family of which a person is spouse.

Family of Procreation

The nuclear family in which a person is spouse contrasted with family of orientation which is the nuclear family into which a person is born or in which his social organization occurs.

Folk Society

As described by R. Redfield, a small, isolated society which is highly integrated and which is further characterized by informal social control and by the predominance of the sacred over secular and traditional over innovative and by primary group relationship.

In folk society the moral order is great and the technical order is small.

Vertical Extended Family

A family in which parents, their married children and their grand children share a residence and constitute a functioning social unit.

Horizontal Extended Family

A household and cooperating unit of two siblings and their respective spouses and children.

Matricentric Family

A family that is headed by a woman, often serially married to a number of men.

Foraging Society

A society with an economy based solely on the collection of wild plant foods, hunting of animals, and or fishing.

Formal Group

A social group whose structure and activities have been rationally organized and standardized with definitely prescribed group rules, goals and leaders. Formal groups tend to be either large or part of a larger organization. An army or a labour union could be examples of formal groups.

Informal Groups

A group without formally stated group rules, goals or leader. It is typically small and often casually and spontaneously formed. Interaction is based on common interests and intimate contact. Informal groups may or may not have strong group norms, and adherence to group norms rests on personal loyalty rather than on explicit group rules. Children's play groups and gangs as well as chiques are examples of informal groups. Though the term Informal group and Primary group are at times used synonymously there is, difference also. A primary group may be highly structured by traditional roles or by bureaucratic or traditional organization or by bureaurcratic or organizational definitions. Such a group is not properly an informal group.

An Informal group does not have standardized or internalized group goals, and especially not goals imposed from the outside.

Unibonded Groups

A group whose members are united by only one common interest or purpose only small part of each member's life and personality is involved in the group and relations among members are characterized by specificity, or a limited range of right and obligations.

Group Identification

A process in which an individual incorporates within himself the expectations, standards, values and goals of a group, and utilizes them in the organization, reorganization and stabilization of his social self. It is not necessary to be a formal member of a group in order to identify with it.

Group Dynamics

The study of small groups, of the patterns of interaction within a group, and of interrelationships within a group and its environments, including other groups.

Hypergamy

A custom forbidding the women in a particular social structure to marry into a lower stratum, they are permitted to marry in their own social structure. However, the term is also often used to refer to the practice of women of lower standing marrying men of higher standing. For example, in India if a higher caste young man marriages a lower caste girl i.e. marriage between a boy of higher caste with a lower caste girl.

Hypogamy

Marriage of a woman with man of lower social structure i.e. a lower caste young man marrying a higher caste girl.

Tribe Caste Continuum

The term 'continuum' was first used by Robert Redfield (1941) in his book, The Folk Culture of Yukatan (1941). In Indian Anthropology tribes caste continuum had attracted the attention of Indian ethnographers and census people since the last decade of the 19th Century. Many census commissioners of India forced difficulty in deciding where the category of tribe ended and caste began. Risley found it quite difficult. Bailey argued that where as tribe is typically organized on the basis of segmentary solidarity, caste is based on organice solidarity. Risley pointed out that it was difficult to draw a demarcating line between tribe and caste where as Bailey presented a more interactional mode for considering the position of the tribe vis-a vis caste as a two ideal poles in a linear continuum.

Universalization and Parochialisation

First defined by Mckim Marriott in his study of a U.P. village

(Kishangarhi) in 1995. According to Marriott the concept of universalisation refers to the carrying forward of materials which are already present in little tradition, which it encompasses. The opposite process, that of Parochialisation, is defined by him as the downward devolution of great traditional element and their integration with little traditional elements.

Rural Cosmopolisation

Oscar Lewis developed the concept of Rural Cosmopolisation in his study of Rampur village near Delhi, which was published in 1958. Earlier he had studied villagers in Maxico, Cuba and Spain. He intended to analyse peasant life in India on account of the development and action programmes which tried to raise the standard of living of the villages. A rounded description of Indian village life, including inter-caste relations, jajmani system, kinship, economic life, factors, politics and leadership etc. formed the comparative analysis of Indian and Mexican village. It appeared, that Lewis attempted to examine peasantry, rather than a single village and sharing its inter-relationship with the Indian civilization. Thus, Lewis takes a very wide canvas to make a comparison between peasant life style of an Indian and Mexican village and refers to the widespread inter-village connections as rural cosmopolitanism.

Ethnocentrism (Ethnocentricism)

Sumner (1906) using the term stated that 'Ethnocentrism is a habit of every group of taking for granted the superiority of its cultures' Ethnocentrism makes one's own culture a yard stick to measure all other cultures which are good or bad, higher or lower.

Thus, Ethnocentrism is a tendency to use the norms and values of one's own culture or sub culture as a habit of judging others. All known societies are ethnocentric, the backward primitive people have a similar feeling of superiority over the so called civilized people. Several studies have proved this fact that ethnocentricism is a universal reaction, found in all societies, in all groups and in practically all individuals.

Although ethnocentrism is partially a matter of habit, it is also a product of both deliberate and unconscious cultivation. We are trained to be ethnocentric to such a degree that it is doubtful whether any one can avoid being ethnocentric. Our culture complex of nationalistic Patriotism is perhaps the greatest source of deliberately cultivated ethnocentrism.

Looking-Glass Self

The term was suggested by C. Cooley. It denotes three stage process whereby an individual develops an idea of what type of person he is. The three stage processes are (a) Imagination of how he appears to others; (b) Imagination of the others judgement about his appearance, and (c) resulting feelings about his own judgement.

Thus, looking glass self is a person's perception of himself as determined by the way he imagines he appears to others. It is the conception of the self that is formed as a consequence of the attitudes other people have toward him.

Matrifocal Family

A family form in which the mother, sometimes assisted by other women of the household is the most influential socializing agent and is central in terms of cultural values, family finances, patterns of decision making and effective ties.

Marginal Group

A culture group that has relinquished some of its traditions and separate identity and partially accepted the values and ways of life of a culture it is in the process of adopting.

Marginal Area

Territory at the periphery of a culture area where two or more cultures meet, and where the culture traits of neighbouring cultures are to be found. Marginal areas are the farthest areas one can possibily include within a particular culture area.

The Marginal Man

The Marginal Man is one who straddles between two cultures, having one foot in each. The immigrant is potentially such a man.

The young person from an isolated rural community moving to the large city is a marginal man who often suffers intensely from the strain of making transition.

Nativism

A revitalization movement initiated by members of a society to eliminate foreign persons, customs and objects in order to improve their own way of life.

Privileged Familiarity

A Cultural Practice of allowing or even prescribing a high frequency of interaction and special forms of familiarity (for example joking) between people of certain statuses.

Patriclan- is the largest group of agnates between whom marriage is forbidden and sexual intercourse is regarded as incestuous.

Proselytism is practice of conversion to another faith.

Ritual Language is a symbolic ritual code consisting of estoric word (mantra), gesture (mudra), Sound (dhvani) and everyday language of interaction (vyaherika).

Preimogeniture- A system of inheritance in which the first born son inherits the entire property of the father, with none of the inheritance going to the other children. This was practiced by the upper class in western Europe in middle ages where it kept the large estate intact.

The Kula

One of the most famous gift exchange institutions is the Kula, which was first described in detail by Malinowski. According to him among the Trobriand islanders every person who can, forms partnership for the exchange of small ornaments with other men in his own or in other islands. These ornaments are of 2 kinds; neckless of red shell and armlets of white shell. The exchange is not a single transaction in which both partners give and receive. When they meet, the one whose turn it is makes a gift, the return gift is made at the next meeting. If the partners are neighbours the two meetings may follows close on each others' heels. But the spectacular part of the exchange takes place when people travel by canoe to visit their partners in other islands. Exchanges are not made in all directions, but in a fixed order like a grand chain in a dance. Each man's overseas partners are in the island on the either side of his own and each man receives necklaces from the partners on the one side and armlets from those on the other. The most highly prized of these objects are named. No one may retain possession of Kula object for long. For a little time he has it to boast of and wear on ceremonial occasion. Then it must go to one of his partners.

Those who went on Kula voyage did not take their gifts with them, they arrived empty handed, offering only by their presence that a debt of honour was due to them.

The Kula partner buys glory, he also buys friendship. His partner in distant islands are allies to whom he can look for protection in what would otherwise be hostile country.

Potlatch

Potlatch means give and the principle that a gift deserves a counter gift was important in this institutions as in the Kula. But it had a significance beyond that of linking of pairs of individuals in a relation of friendship. A potlatch was a public distribution of goods, made both to establish certain claims of the giver and to recognize the claims of the receipients. The kwakuths had an elaborate ranking system which placed every man in order according to his degree of closeness in descent to the remotest remember ancestor. The line of eldest sons was senior and provided the chiefs of different descent groups. Chiefs had special ritual privileges, titles and two right to use songs and dances, carved marks, and so forth. But in order to demonstrate his claims to be a chief a man had to give a Potlatch which he recalled his famous Potlatches and other deeds of his ancestors, and made the distribution to his guests in strict order of ranks. Thus, among the tribal inhabiting in North Western Coast of America potlatch is a cereomony in which an individual supported his claim to a selected new status by lavishly distributing material goods to the guests, such ritual gift given demanding eventual reciprocity by the guests.

Patronymic

Patronymic denotes (a) A surname derived from a patrilineal relative such as father, or (b) the type of society in which child resumes the surname of his father or of his father's sib.

Quasi Group

An unstructured and unorganized collection of people, such as an aggregate social category crowd or public whose members have a potential for group formation, although they may not be necessarily fully aware of it or prepared to join or form a group.

Racism

Robert Knox, Arthur De Gobineau and Josiah Nott in 1860s formulated racist doctrine. The word 'racism' was introduced in the 1930s to refer to doctrines of racial superiority, particularly to the thesis that race determines culture, it continued to be used in this sense until the 1960s when it was given a wider connotation. Before we understand the term racism, it is necessary to understand the word race. A race is a group of persons connected with common origin. More clearly the term was understood in terms of common physical/ biological characteristics i.e. colour of the skin, height, texture of heir, colour of eye lids, blood groups etc. Broadly speaking, the colour was given utmost importance and people while belonging to (fair colour) colour were considered superior to those with black, brown or yellow. As the people and countries belonging to white racial groups were socially and economically superior/more harmful to the people of other categories, they exploited and dominated the other groups and categories of people for a few centuries. Even the bureaucrats and anthropologists at the times, supported the false notions of racism. The term race is alright as it distinguishes a particular group of people on the basis of certain physical/biological characteristics. But the term 'Racism' which offers an explanation of inequalities within as well as between races is detrimental to the unity of the society at large. Racial conflicts in South Africa and America have been the consequence of such thinking and attitude.

After 1960 the strong notions regarding race and racism started fading down and the anthropologists of the period also proved that the racism is a myth and there is nothing like superiority or inferiority associated with a particular race.

Sanskritization

The concept of Sanskritization was developed by an eminent sociologist and social Anthropologist M.N. Srinivas in his book on 'Religion and society among the coorgs in south India'. It is a process where by members of the lower caste start adopting the culture, traditions, habits manners, rituals, beliefs, ideology, style of life and diacritical marks of the higher castes and there by try to improve their position in the caste hierarchy. According to Srinivas sanskritization represents actual or aspired cultural mobility within the framework of the established 'great tradition' and stratification system of caste.

The lower castes try to improve their position in the local caste hierarchy through the processes of sanskritization. Initially, the term raised much controversy among the social scientists.

Dominant Caste

The concept was also developed by M.N. Srinivas which attracted the attention of Indian sociologists and social Anthropologists. The

concept of dominant caste has been found to be useful in the understanding of Indian Rural Society, as certain castes play dominant role in the social life of villages.

The leaders of the locally dominant caste may arbitrate in village disputes, in disputes between two castes or in the family disputes. They may decide the rewards and punishment to be awarded to disputants in the cases which go before them and determine the civic and economic privileges of various caste groups. Another important function of dominant caste has been to set norms for social life in rural areas.

As a major power holder in the village the dominant caste has traditionally supplied the village elite.

M.N. Srivinas systematically examined the role of dominant caste in the following words.

'A Caste may be said to be dominant when it preponderates numerically over other castes and when it also wields preponderate economic and political power. A large and powerful group can be more easily dominant of its position in the local caste hierarchy is not too low. When a caste enjoys all the elements of dominance it may be said to be dominant in a decisive way. The factors which help a caste group to become dominant, were numerical preponderance, economic power, ritual status or a high level of education or occupation.

Self-fulfilling Prophecy

As suggested by R.Merton, a prediction which is false as stated but which evokes behaviour such that the original statement finally becomes true-for example, if enough depositors believe the rumour that a highly solvent bank is about to close, the resulting sum on the bank may actually cause to fail, contrasted with self-defeating prophecy.

Self-Defeating Prophecy

A prediction which is true as stated, but which evokes behaviour that conditions change and the original statement no longer holds for example, a study indicates that marriages between certain types of people have very great chance of failing, information which, as a part of the engagement process, results in a weeding out of all but the most determined of such people, thus lowering the predicted failure rate; sometimes termed suicidal prophecy or self-destroying prophecy.

Sanctions

Sanctions are rewards or punishments used to establish social control i.e. to enforce the norms in a society. Sanctions may be applied in various ways, ranging from use of physical force to symbolic means, such as flattery sanctions are used to force or persuade an individual or group to conform to social expectations.

The basic purposes of sanctions are to bring about conformity, solidarity and continuity of a particular group, community or larger society.

Sub Urbanisation

The recent move termed what Fava called 'sub urbanization' as a way of life presents an intervening sociological picture of people trying to cling to some of the values of rural living while participating in an urban social structure. Suburbs are characterized by availability of open space, thus allowing single family dwellings and a relatively lower population density than cities.

Non Conforming Behaviour and Aberrant Behaviour

Departures of behaviour from social norms can be caught up in the single concept and associated term deviant behaviour. Both non-conforming and aberrant behaviour are deviant behaviour, yet there is a difference between the two.

The non conformer announces his dissent publicly, unlike the aberrant, he does not try to hide his departure from social norms. The aberrant criminal seeks to avoid the lime light of public security. The non conformer challenges the legitimacy of the social norms he rejects or atleast challenges their applicability to certain kinds of situations. In contrast, the aberrant acknowledges the legitimacy of the norms he violates. He may try to justify his own behaviour but he does not argue that theft is right and murder is virtuous.

The non conformer aims to change the norm he is denying in practice. He wants to replace what he believes to be morally suspect norms with ones' having a sound moral basis. Where as the aberrant tries primarily to escape the sanctioning face of existing norms without proposing substitutes for them.

Suburb, Suburbia

As city development has taken the form of an outward movement of population to the surrounding areas to form new settlements, often taking the form of housing estates both publicly and privately financed, so the term suburb has grown in rise and the kind of life lived by the inhabitants (sub urbanites) has given rise to the term suburbia.

Between 1950 and 1960 there was a particular interest in the phenomenon, not connected with the problems of urban redevelopment following the war in Europe.

Inner Directed Society

An abstract or ideal type formulated by David Reisman and collaborators which develops in its typical members a social character whose conformity is ensured by their tendency to acquire early in life an intermilized set of goals.

In common practice concept of inner directed was often applied to an ideal type of individual and termed inner directed man.

Open Class Ideology

A system of beliefs centered on the idea that any person can rise to any position and social class in society by hard work and ability, regardless of his class origin and his present condition or status.

Open-class System

A social class system in which there is freedom of vertical mobility, that is, one in which an individual can readily increase or decrease his social class position. No legal or traditional restrictions are placed on upward or downward mobility, and rising to a higher social class is positively valued in the society.

Other-directed Society

A generalized or ideal type of society formulated by David Riesman and his collaborators which develops in its typical members a social character whose conformity is by their tendency to be sensitized to the expectations and preferences of the other. According to Riesman, other-directed was the characteristic of modern urban, industrial and bureaucratic society, were getting along with others in a mobile and impersonal world demands sensitively to the norms of the immediate social situation.

In common practice the concept of other directedness is often applied to an ideal type of individual and termed other-directed man.

Stem Family

A family in which, in each generation, the ancestral home has attached to it one married child as the family head, while rest of the married children are owened and given their independence as the ideal type of such a family being made up of members who, if their presence is needed at ancestral home, are ever ready to give up whatever independence they may have achieved.

Tribe

The word 'Tribe' is a social group usually with a definite area, dialect, cultural homogeneity and unifying social organization. It can include several sub groups, such as clans or sibs. A tribe ordinarily has an ancestor and a patron deity. The families or groups comprising the larger tribal units are linked through 'blood ties', as the term is commonly used, and through religion, social and economic functions.

❑❑❑